The New York Times

FINALLY SUNDAY CROSSWORDS
75 Puzzles from the Pages of *The New York Times*

Edited by Will Shortz

ST. MARTIN'S GRIFFIN   NEW YORK

The New York Times

SMART PUZZLES

PRESENTED WITH STYLE

Available at your local bookstore or online at www.nytimes.com/nytstore

St. Martin's Griffin

MNOP

ACROSS

1 Wind source
7 Escalates
13 Watercolor technique
20 Annual event held at the Kodak Theater, with "the"
21 Hero known for his nose
22 Intertwined
23 Give Axl and Pete a break?
25 Like the Twenties
26 Language that gave us "pajamas"
27 Saroyan's "My Name Is ___"
28 Elton John/Tim Rice musical
30 A bit more than never
31 ___ Palace
33 Tripping over a threshold, perhaps?
37 Bubbly place?
38 Carries, e.g.
39 BlackBerry and others, for short
40 Footwear that's hard to run in
43 Art school subj.
45 Pea farmers?
51 Summer apartment with no air-conditioning?
54 Home of the Blues: Abbr.
55 Powerful engine
56 Barkin of "Sea of Love"
57 English author Blyton
59 Co. bigwigs
62 "___ true?"
63 Solar ___
64 Swindler
67 Went long
69 Floral Technicolor dreamcoat?

73 Madrid newspaper
76 This-and-that preparation
77 Island near Naxos
80 Certain grains
81 Sets (on)
84 Fourier series function
85 Lively sonata movement
87 Pauline Kael's "___ It at the Movies"
89 Blow away
91 Strutting bird on an ice floe?
94 Residents at a Manhattan A.S.P.C.A.?
98 Yours, in Giverny
99 Nemeses
100 Actor Ventimiglia of "Heroes"
101 DC Comics superheroine
103 Genetic molecules
105 Move a movie camera around a community?
110 Some casino staff
113 Little or Short
114 Greenish-blue
115 Interlaken's river
117 Emmy-winning co-star of "Chicago Hope"
119 "Symphonie Fantastique" composer
122 Explanation for an interception?
125 One of the Andrews Sisters
126 Early anesthetics
127 Like some Swift writing
128 Electra's brother
129 Twos
130 ___ Falls, N.Y.

DOWN

1 "Yipe!"
2 Jellied dish
3 Extended operatic solo
4 Quarter back
5 Onetime HBO sitcom
6 Prime meridian std.
7 Deliverers of the unreturnable
8 Hess who was a dame
9 Cue
10 Airline to Stockholm
11 Digs up
12 Propose
13 Mustachioed TV muckraker
14 Plastic ___ Band
15 Suffix with form
16 Perennial N.L. leader of old
17 Sharing a memo with
18 For this reason
19 Lawn gadget
24 1980s street artist Keith
29 Spot
32 ___ impasse
34 Dobbin's nibble
35 "Dear old" guy
36 ___ mgr.
38 Batting coach's concern
40 One with a handle
41 "Damn Yankees" vamp
42 Too suave
44 Without ___ (quietly)
46 Series finale?
47 What a bee produces
48 "Superman II" villainess
49 Some
50 Favor cloyingly, with "on"

52 Just for laughs
53 Many a New Year's resolution
58 Pulls
60 1977 thriller co-starring Bo Derek
61 "The Odd Couple" director
65 Some legal scholars, for short
66 "The Time Machine" race
68 Co-founder of the Nonaligned Movement
69 Fastidious
70 Lane in Metropolis
71 Postrevolutionary councils
72 Language akin to Yupik
73 A Walton
74 Singer Lovett
75 "What's New Pussycat?" response?
77 Poop
78 Comics canine
79 End of some firm names
82 2005 Hoffman title role
83 Winter Olympics powerhouse: Abbr.
86 Summer at a ski resort, e.g.
88 Taj Mahal, e.g.
90 Bleach
92 One of the original Mouseketeers
93 ___ cloth (lingerie fabric)
95 1983 Duran Duran hit
96 China shop personae non gratae
97 Orlando-to-Ft. Myers dir.
102 Shortly

by Tony Orbach and Amy Reynaldo

2 LINKS TO THE PAST

Note: When this puzzle is done, interpret the answers to the seven starred clues literally, in order from top to bottom.

ACROSS

1 Figure in "Lost Horizon"
5 Intelligent, creative sort, supposedly
10 Fancy wheels
14 Pet protector, for short
19 Monthly bill: Abbr.
20 "___ Gold"
21 ___ Sea, 2,000-square-mile saltwater lake
22 Singer Collins and others
23 *Boondocks
26 Former presidential candidate in the Forbes 400
27 Standing by
28 Symbol of modesty
29 Away with an O.K.
31 PBS funder
32 Mobile-to-Birmingham dir.
34 *Ambulance destination
37 Group of genetically related organisms
40 "Buy ___ regular price, get . . ."
41 Directional suffix
42 It's within your grasp
44 With 51-Down, cry of sorrow
45 Specter in the Senate
48 Emulates AZ or T.I.
50 *Imam or priest
54 1986 Indy winner Bobby
57 Vacation itinerary
58 Literary heroine whose best friend is a goatherd
59 Copy
61 Looney Tunes nickname
62 San ___, Calif.
65 Straighten out
68 G or R issuer: Abbr.
69 *When the heavens and earth were created
72 Car driven by James Bond in "Octopussy," for short
75 Forward
76 "Sweet" stream in a Burns poem
77 Roadie's armful
80 Noisy but comfy chair
82 Wallop
84 First name in skin care
86 Material with a distinctive diagonal weave
87 *Deputy
92 Serving in the navy
94 Tweets, e.g.
95 Grandfathers of III's
96 Unpaid debt, e.g.
97 Let go
99 Strait-laced
101 Field for a fault-finder?
103 *Week after Christmas
108 G, musically
109 Lead-in to calculus
112 1, to a trucker
113 Love sign
115 Dog-___
117 Actor Jannings and others
118 *Lights out in New York City
122 Bathroom fixture
123 "Yeah, right!"
124 Children
125 Part of a French opera
126 Open stars?
127 Tops
128 Like mesh
129 Bartlett, e.g.

DOWN

1 A mechanic might see it a lot
2 Flared dress
3 Publicity push
4 Group with the 22x platinum album "Back in Black"
5 Saturn offering
6 P.S. in a Beatles song
7 Mortgage adjustment, for short
8 Subject of some modern maps
9 "___ Mio"
10 "Chicago Hope" actress
11 Choler
12 Nick, say
13 World Cup shout
14 Small, fruity dessert
15 Luster
16 Worrisome sight on the Spanish Main
17 Bee's target
18 Back on board
24 O'Brien's predecessor
25 Get together
30 Birthplace of James K. Polk and Andrew Johnson: Abbr.
33 Abbr. on a cereal box
35 Like most dorms nowadays
36 ___ Page, woman in "The Merry Wives of Windsor"
38 1950s Hungarian premier ___ Nagy
39 Birds with showy mates
42 "Hey there!"
43 Pacific capital
45 Foreman foe
46 Pleonastic
47 "The Divided Self" author R. D. ___
49 Former Swedish P.M. Olof ___
51 See 44-Across
52 Director Sergio
53 Bonnie in the Rock and Roll Hall of Fame
55 Wanted poster letters
56 Field of green
60 Sister of Erato
63 Indian tourist locale
64 Cover girl Cheryl
66 Cousin of a raccoon
67 Something to play
69 Forehead coverer
70 Desk tray
71 Memory: Prefix
72 They may be crunched
73 Wrangler rival
74 All over
77 No matter the cost
78 ___ items
79 Those hoofing it
81 Events that are barrels of fun?
83 '60s radical grp.
85 Eye irritant
88 Suffix with diet
89 Relinquish
90 Kind of saw
91 Peace Prize city
93 Verdi's "Celeste ___"
97 A-listers
98 Breakdown of social norms
100 Playful rodent
101 Payola, e.g.
102 Promise, for one
104 Gave the once-over
105 Exams for future docs
106 Uncooperative
107 Field Marshal Rommel
110 ___-car

by Alan Arbesfeld

111 Lawn tool
114 Method: Abbr.
116 "Hurry!"
119 Result of bringing
    someone home,
    for short
120 Etymologist's ref.
121 Science writer
    Willy

3   YOU ARE THERE

ACROSS

1 Where to spot a king or queen
5 ___-approved
9 Ridicule
13 Part of a college application
18 Socialite with a self-named perfume
20 Versatile body builders
22 Two-door
23 Lord's home
24 Corrupt financier's command?
26 Grocery store lineup
28 Trading post buys
29 Frequent figure in Renaissance art
30 Mama Bear at the stove?
32 Part of 5-Across: Abbr.
33 U.R.L. start
37 Starfish feature
38 "Catch-22" bomber pilot
39 Crowning point
42 View ruiner
44 Disputed
47 Pets with dewlaps
49 Like Larry King, repeatedly
50 Coaches
51 Word with beauty or pizza
52 Dumber than dumb
53 Heat
54 Alpo or Purina One?
56 Sanctioning assn. for pugilists
57 Like many a 21-Down
58 Percussion instrument in Off Broadway's "Stomp"

59 Topic in transcendentalism
60 Members of la familia
61 Familiar flight pattern
62 Painter Andrea ___ Sarto
63 Critical
64 Toxic spray
65 Give ___ shot
66 Droopy
67 In high esteem
69 U.S.S. Enterprise title: Abbr.
70 Certain power
71 Post-O.R. location
72 Greeting from Smokey the Bear?
74 Happy shouts
77 Good points
79 Pair of opposite electric charges
80 Best Actress nominee for "Indochine"
81 Singer John with the album "Bruised Orange"
82 Bacchus, notably
83 Agitated
84 "The Bald Soprano" dramatist
86 Schnauzer sounds
87 Poet Hughes
88 Cursor attachment?
89 Some food additives
90 Integral subj.
92 Pumpkin grower's cry of surprise?
95 "No problem!"
97 Something made in the still of the night?
100 Above: Lat.
101 Scheduled activity at a Vegas chapel?
106 Like "Have a nice day!"
108 Greek moralizer

109 What drives you to get better?
110 Fills to the gills
111 Waxes
112 Exam with 125 questions: Abbr.
113 Bygone depilatory
114 Douglas ___, first president of Ireland

DOWN

1 Unfavorable
2 Clears
3 Songbird at an eye drops factory?
4 Popular brand of bouillon
5 Kind of port for a PC
6 Daze
7 ___ Walcott, 1992 Literature Nobelist
8 ___ nitrite
9 Gets set
10 Unfavorable
11 Indifferent
12 Hatches, say
13 Capital subj.
14 From Polynesia and environs
15 Globe : Boston :: ___ : Baltimore
16 Inclined
17 Happy shout
19 Bohemian
21 Cool sort
25 Part of 85-Down
27 Searches high and low
30 Curator's selection
31 Some have a silver lining
32 Mean
34 Sodom or Gomorrah?
35 Snake with "lightning bolts" on its back
36 Baseball's Martinez and others
39 Culture medium

40 Triumphant spicy meal for the Three Little Pigs?
41 Affliction
43 Relatives of kites
45 Movie star with the most Oscar nominations (16)
46 Starter, perhaps
47 "___ a Spell on You" (classic 1956 Screamin' Jay Hawkins song)
48 King Minos' daughter who aided Theseus
52 Sch. or hosp.
54 Disagree strongly
55 Pioneer automaker
58 Fried rice ingredients
60 Some church income
61 Christopher Columbus, in the Indies
62 TiVo's, e.g.
63 Big-enough catch
66 Clear
68 First commercially successful computer
69 Sometime
70 Darling family pet
72 Early Coloradans
73 Draft picks
74 "Quality Is Our Recipe" franchise
75 Not as good as claimed
76 Worked on a shift, maybe
78 Held for later disbursement, as funds
80 Ngo Dinh ___, South Vietnam's first president
82 Plan of action

by Lynn Lempel

85 School inits. in Harlem since 1907
87 From that point on
91 Earthy mixtures
92 Radiation reducer
93 Kishkes
94 Big name in daytime TV
96 Liechtenstein's locale
97 Very dry
98 Biggest export of 99-Down
99 See 98-Down
101 Witch
102 "Give ___ the play": "Hamlet"
103 Show presenter, for short
104 "More later," on a sched.
105 Still
107 Legal conclusion?

4 STORY CIRCLE

ACROSS

1 Do well in the Olympics
6 Choose to take part
11 Modern storage sites
16 Sky Chief company
17 Satisfactory
21 Low soccer score
23 Place in trust
24 Stabilizing track
25 Weaver's supply
26 Word with mail or letter
27 Actor Edward James ___
28 2001 headline maker
30 It's worth its weight in gold
31 PC linkup
32 Tweaks
33 Michael of "Juno" and "Superbad"
34 "Ixnay"
35 Bygone leaders
38 Fathers
40 Norse pantheon
41 Another name for 72-Across
45 Center
46 A Marx brother
48 Thither
50 Longtime Susan Lucci role
52 ___-Caps (candy)
53 Tulsa sch.
54 Largest moon of Saturn
55 Subject of a tipster's tip
56 Joe Montana or Jerry Rice, informally
57 Windsor's home: Abbr.
58 Additions to a musical staff
60 ___ but when
62 Blissful
64 Crackerjack
65 Expressed a welcome
68 Org. with spring playoffs

69 Dried seaweed popular in Japanese cuisine
72 Part of Canis Major
73 Boot camp affirmative
75 Fanatic
79 Be more than a dream
80 Lite
82 Clip, e.g.
83 Bring up, perhaps
84 Suffix with magnet
85 7'6" Ming
87 Green-eyed
89 ___ in Charlie
91 Wall-E's love in "Wall-E"
92 One side of an exchange
93 It may be bid
95 Big band instrument
96 It comes in volumes: Abbr.
98 Cartoon pooch
99 Slugger's stat
100 Tandoor flatbreads
101 Popular
103 Prefix with sphere
104 Galley figure
105 Bones may be found in it
107 Cousin of a clog
109 Oscar winner Patricia and others
111 It's found near the tongue
113 Achilles and Hector
115 Clothes rack abbr.
116 Gridiron scores: Abbr.
117 Scientologist ___ Hubbard
118 Crown covering
120 "Did you start without me?"
124 Rachmaninoff's "___-tableaux"
127 Island where Sundanese and Madurese are spoken
128 Take too much of, briefly
131 Windbag's output
132 Gulfer Auki

135 Certain infection
136 Operatic heroine wooed by Beckmesser
137 1963 animated film with the song "Higitus Figitus," with "The"
141 ___ Gold, character on "Entourage"
142 Stanford's Big Game rival
143 1998 animated film featuring the voice of Pierce Brosnan
144 Hollywood, with "the"
145 Notwithstanding that, for short
146 ___ jure (legal term)
147 "The Canterbury Tales" traveler
148 Gun for hire
149 Loser at Gettysburg
150 Heir, perhaps
151 Org. in Clancy's "Red Storm Rising"
152 Gives birth to a kid
153 Bit of cheer
154 Road twist

DOWN

1 Work together
2 1981 film in which Helen Mirren plays a sorceress
3 Onetime MTV animated title character and others
4 With 12-Down, 1889 Twain novel
5 Weathercast figure
6 Slothful
7 Underwater families
8 Japanese market: Abbr.
9 Memo header
10 Subtlety
11 Things first on the way up?
12 See 4-Down
13 Perceived to be

14 With 76-Down, 1953 Ava Gardner film . . . as depicted elsewhere in this puzzle?
15 ___-Japanese
16 Gumshoe
17 Relative of a grapefruit
18 Does some heavy lifting
19 Red alert?
20 Bilbao bloom
22 W.W. II vessel
27 Kind of inspection
29 ___ Gordimer, Literature Nobelist
35 Aid in finding a station
36 Magical glow
37 River that flows past more than 40 castles
39 Bishop's group
40 1973 Rolling Stones #1 hit
42 Davy Jones's locker
43 Years in old Rome
44 Drilling grp.
47 One of Iago's victims
49 Words of commitment
51 Five-carbon sugar
59 Culture areas?
60 Passover month
61 Arrive by air
63 "Winnie ___ Pu"
66 Pot-___ (French stew)
67 Overhang
69 Conductor Lockhart and others
70 Rustic transport
71 2001 Anjelica Huston miniseries, with "The"
72 Some steaks
74 Hot desert winds
76 See 14-Down
77 Magic trick's climax
78 Supreme Egyptian deity
81 Soap box?
82 One of Santa's reindeer
86 Drilling grp.

by Kevin G. Der

5 GROUP FORMATION

ACROSS

1 It's open for dinner
6 High ball, in pool
12 Pond organism
16 Sedaris of "Strangers With Candy"
19 Dish that may be served on a boat
20 Three-line poems
21 Put into piles
22 Traversing
23 Contents of four answers found in this puzzle
25 It covers a lot of leg
27 Good for nothing?: Var.
28 Alexander the Great conquered it
30 Rarely counterfeited bills
31 Fictional Plaza Hotel resident
33 Alexander the Great conquered it
34 Group formed at C.C.N.Y. in 1910
36 Weapon with many warheads
37 Roof of the World natives
40 Monaco is one
45 Given an eyeful, you might say
47 Accepting bribes
48 Brazil's ___ Alegre
49 "And all too soon, I fear, the king shall ___": "Richard II"
50 1971 album dedicated to Buddy Holly
52 Picasso's ___ Period, 1901–04
53 Surname of two British P.M.'s
54 Waterford purchase
55 Empties
57 Labor leader Chávez
58 Bridal wish list
62 Like some twisted ankles
63 Sam's Club rival
64 1992 Damon Wayans comedy
65 "Old MacDonald Had a Farm" sounds
67 Womanizers, slangily
68 Nitrogen compounds
69 Weenie roast needs
70 Cars that go toward other cars
72 Subjects of pneumography
73 Fended (off)
75 Something that's been clarified
76 Tavern orders
77 Old cracker brand
78 Co-organizer of the Montgomery bus boycott, 1955
84 Ill-looking
85 Renaissance painter Uccello
87 Bavaria and others, once
88 Bout of revelry
89 By and large
91 Engine attachment
92 Claw alternative
93 Group formed at Howard University in 1911
94 Sci-fi author's creation
96 Kentucky Derby drinks
98 Fire extinguisher's output
101 Mideast hub
103 Fill a box, say
106 Jason Bourne, in the Bourne series
108 Four groups found in this puzzle
112 Bounder
113 Umpire's wear
114 Retro headgear
115 Jay Silverheels role
116 Have a bite of
117 Quelques-___ (some: Fr.)
118 2000 Olympics locale
119 Golfer who said "Never concede a putt"

DOWN

1 "No ___"
2 First word in many church names
3 Pursue violent options
4 1980 double album by Springsteen
5 Raises
6 C&W singer Wooley
7 British art museum
8 Book of Hours entry
9 ___ & Tina Turner Revue
10 Determination
11 Ruhr industrial city
12 Gets several views
13 Actress Anderson
14 Social reformer Margaret Fuller, to Buckminster Fuller
15 "I already ___"
16 Skin So Soft seller
17 Lab test subjects
18 Asian bovines
24 Sheltered side
26 Meryl Streep title role
29 Most corrugated
31 Novel on which "Clueless" is based
32 Writer O'Flaherty
33 Like final contracts
35 Mexican-style fast-food chain
37 Comfortably warm
38 Personal, as thoughts
39 Group formed at Miami University in 1839
41 Furies
42 Antihistamine brand
43 Steals the show from, say
44 Urban railways
46 Figures out intuitively
51 Legal precedents
52 No longer on vacation
53 Oscar winner for "GoodFellas"
56 Remove the suds
57 Inducements
58 Pointy-eared "Star Trek" character
59 Highly respected
60 Round percussion instruments
61 Term for a judge
63 Enigma machine, e.g.
64 Nyasaland, nowadays
66 ___-European
67 New Journalism pioneer Gay
69 Areas of expertise
71 Choir attire
73 Liveryman's command
74 Celtic priest of old
79 Group formed at Trinity College in 1895
80 Wisconsin home of Lawrence University
81 Timberland limit
82 Villainous Uriah

by Patrick Berry

83 Desires
85 Product with a circular red, white and blue logo
86 Semiterrestrial organism
87 The Who's lead singer
90 Match played at the local arena
95 Elizabethan collars
96 Dean's 1960s singing partner
97 Apartments, e.g.
98 Undisputed point
99 W.W. II general Bradley
100 Red's pal in "The Shawshank Redemption"
102 Slip (into)
103 English collar
104 French family member
105 Speak up?
107 The Mustangs of the N.C.A.A.
109 Get a total
110 J.F.K. board info
111 Ground cover

ACROSS

1 Explorer who has a monetary unit named after him
7 Nasal tones
13 "Huddled" group inscribed on the Statue of Liberty
19 Chip in
20 Notre Dame cry
21 Like an ass
22 Dirt-dishing lass who's been cut off?
25 Summery
26 "Livin' la Vida ___"
27 Danish coin
28 Star of football, to most of the world
31 Jeanne d'Arc, for one: Abbr.
32 Seasoned rice dishes
36 Wayne ___ (Gotham City abode)
38 Entertainer Béla
40 "Right away, boss!"
42 Cheese choice
44 Dad is familiar with top Broadway star?
51 Block buster?
52 Peeples of "Fame"
53 Played again
54 Constellation near Scorpius
55 More raspy
57 "Finnegans Wake" wife
58 Epic poem in dactylic hexameter
60 Lhasa ___ (dog)
63 Fourth of September?
64 N.Y.C. subway syst.
65 See 114-Down

66 Actor Joel's crime scene analysis?
73 Printing on many a name tag
74 Ballpark figs.
75 Japanese band
76 Some depictions on a pyramid wall
77 It may be blind
78 Bygone stadium
80 Brand that's universally liked?
83 Used a tuffet
84 Backyard briquettes
86 Hack
87 Red head, once?
90 One-quarter of a mourning lacrosse team?
95 Emma of "The Avengers"
96 Dennis, to Mr. Wilson
97 Comparatively right-minded
98 Ancient Jordanian city with rock carvings
101 Landlord
103 O.E.D. filler
106 Jedi Council leader
107 "___ ELO" (1976 album)
108 Blow the whistle
110 Fervent
113 Hollywood hanky-panky?
121 Bad way to be caught
122 Bone receptacle
123 Lament
124 Tomoyuki ___, creator of Godzilla
125 Just followed Nancy Reagan's advice?
126 Some blackboard writing

DOWN

1 Tote
2 "Wheel of Fortune" purchase
3 Some U.S.N.A. grads
4 Beg
5 Some votes in Québec
6 Calendar data: Abbr.
7 When tripled, a W.W. II movie
8 Self-control
9 "Entourage" agent Gold
10 "Seduction of the Minotaur" author
11 Prime meridian std.
12 Continental ___
13 Grand Marquis, e.g., for short
14 Superhero with an octopus named Topo
15 "How's it goin', man?"
16 Quash
17 First of 12 abroad
18 Dinner that includes a reading
20 Cry uncle
23 "Skedaddle!"
24 Beverage brewed from petals
28 Kaput
29 Dash
30 Mikhail Baryshnikov, by birth
33 Clouseau title: Abbr.
34 Common setting in an Indiana Jones movie
35 Corroded
37 Pro-___
39 Game played at the Mirage
41 "Encore!"
43 Accomplished

45 It's thrown from a horse
46 Carpenter of note
47 I.R.S. ID
48 Bob or weave
49 Said "Friends, Romans, countrymen . . ."
50 Waterproof boots
55 Noted rule maker
56 Briny
58 Set of hospital rms.
59 Fries order at McDonald's, maybe
60 Shocked and awed
61 Poli sci student's major, maybe
62 Do business with
64 Real-time e-notes
67 Word with milk or sauce
68 Colorado State, athletically
69 Future presenters of the past
70 In favor of
71 Summers
72 ___ Kundera, author of "The Unbearable Lightness of Being"
78 Bulb in the kitchen
79 "LOL!"
80 Do-gooder
81 One of the Baldwins
82 Goes back
84 B train?
85 ___ concern
87 Hombre's hand
88 Passed with flying colors
89 Southern staple
91 Financing fig.
92 One who loves pick-ups?
93 Something you love to play with
94 What oviparous creatures do

by Patrick Blindauer and Andrea Carla Michaels

98 Surmise
99 "Marcus Welby, M.D." actress Verdugo
100 Old TV western starring Rory Calhoun, with "The"
102 Character of a community
104 ___ Leppard
105 What traffic and dogs do
109 Greek theaters
111 "Wedding Bell Blues" singer Laura
112 Snick's partner
114 With 65-Across, like some orders
115 That, in Oaxaca
116 Hit TV show set in Las Vegas
117 Pill alternative, for short
118 Stumblers' sounds
119 One of 13 popes
120 Stop on a track: Abbr.

ACROSS

1 Added (on)
7 Schisms
12 Says "Two 19-Across," e.g.
16 One of the Big Three, for short
19 See 12-Across
20 More than is required
21 Home of Rainbow Bridge National Monument
22 "Riddle-me-___"
23 "Pardon me"
25 Late 1920s to around 1950
27 North Carolina town that's home to Appalachian State University
28 Summer comfort stat
29 "Save me"
31 Seeding org.
32 Statement of fact
35 "My best soldiers," according to Douglas MacArthur
36 In shape
37 A.A.A. recommendation: Abbr.
38 "Feed me"
40 Physicist Bohr
41 Exactly right, in British lingo
43 "The Thorn Birds" and others
44 Stops on the road
45 Kind of column or committee
48 Put the kibosh on
49 It has strong jaws
51 Modern trivia competition locale
54 "For me?"
57 Irishman who was a Time magazine Person of the Year in 2005

58 ___ ligation
61 Ones entering rehab
62 Enters gradually
64 Snorkeling sites
66 Break off
67 Plug
68 Gets no answers wrong on the test
69 1993 TV western starring Kenny Rogers and Travis Tritt
71 Invites to one's apartment, say
73 Scott Turow's first book was about them
74 Nevada city
75 "Shoot me"
78 Mo. with Natl. Grandparents' Day
79 ___ Dubos, humanist who said "Think globally, act locally"
80 Old verb suffix
81 Superlative on "Top Chef"
85 Fearsome Foursome team
87 Like some grain
89 Rough shelter
90 N.C.A.A. women's basketball powerhouse
92 "Lean on me"
96 Herd of whales
97 Pickup place for pets
98 Airline mentioned in "Back in the U.S.S.R."
99 Former Miss America host
100 Al dente
101 "Make me"
104 Actress Hagen
105 Singing Simon
106 Bartender's announcement

107 "Kiss me"
111 Friend ___ friend
112 Draft status
113 Where Jean-Claude Killy practiced
114 Theater area
115 Lighting director's choice
116 Bank bailout acronym
117 Big success
118 Child often having special responsibilities

DOWN

1 Where many commuters live, informally
2 Balloon or blimp
3 Sweet potato nutrient
4 Icelandic money
5 To be abroad
6 British mil. decoration
7 Enter quickly
8 Won't take no for an answer
9 Org. overseeing trials
10 Port pusher
11 Come across as
12 Holders of body lubricating fluids
13 Lake ___, source of the Mississippi
14 Pops in the nursery
15 Send
16 "It's on me"
17 Go off track
18 What kings rule
24 Classical rebuke
26 Choose to participate
30 Cobblers' needs
32 Like some bonds
33 Stilt, e.g.
34 Eyes and ears

38 Arcangelo ___, Italian violin master
39 Sign of hunger
40 Tonga-to-Hawaii dir.
42 Daytime talk show starting in 1987
44 "___ little silhouetto of a man" ("Bohemian Rhapsody" lyric)
46 Big word in German ads
47 Ballet set in the Rhineland
49 Word that led to the "Why a duck?" routine by the Marx brothers
50 Walk-___
52 Before
53 Cans
55 Nasty words
56 Housing arrangement
57 Congressional terms, e.g.
58 Scale weights
59 Functional
60 "Write me"
63 Child's wheels
65 Bank holdings?
67 Battle star
70 Hamper
71 Batsman
72 Mom-and-pop org.
76 Very, very tired
77 Singing brothers' surname
79 Presidential inits.
82 Wrap around
83 Hollywood hopefuls
84 Flapdoodle
86 "___ of robins . . ."
87 Ready for a drive?
88 Protest cry
90 Get moving again, in a way

by Randolph Ross

91 Wine order
92 Mechanic
93 Cap attachment
94 Obsession
95 Sweet treat
98 Safari leader
100 Unit of capacitance
102 Resident of the Land of Cakes

103 Places to unwind
105 Thing to wind
108 Hardwood source
109 One who knows one's liabilities
110 E.T.S. offering

8 · E.U. DOINGS

ACROSS
1 Shepherd
5 Logical beginning?
10 Regs.
14 Curio
19 Langston Hughes poem
20 Who said "No good movie is too long, and no bad movie is short enough"
21 House Republican V.I.P. Cantor
22 Windblown soil
23 Used a push-button toilet?
26 Difficult surface for high-heel shoes
27 The Jaguars, on scoreboards
28 "White trash," e.g.
29 Been in bed
30 Kind of school
31 Stop on ___
33 "Julius Caesar" role
36 12-time Pro Bowl player Junior
38 Super ___ (game console)
39 Neural network
40 "I can't drink beer this late"?
44 Operates
46 Flu symptom
47 Ovid's love poetry
48 Green
50 Largest city paper in the U.S.: Abbr.
51 Narrow estuary
54 Arg. neighbor
55 Dairy regulator?
61 Mil. unit
62 "Up and ___!"
63 It was destroyed by Godzilla in "Godzilla Raids Again"
64 Cans
66 "Zounds!"
68 Yeoman of the British guard
71 Sci-fi writer's creation
72 Like Rockefeller Center
73 Cantilevered window
74 "The Hallucinogenic Toreador" artist
76 Extinct relative of the emu
77 Baseball official gets revenge?
83 ___ Chinmoy (late spiritual leader)
84 Toon frame
85 Poetic dark period
86 "Concentrate!"
87 Govt.-issued securities
90 Pelé was its M.V.P. in '76
92 Shadow
93 "The bolt alone is sufficient"?
97 Stiff drink
101 Mil. address
102 Medicinal succulent
103 Native of Leipzig
104 One looking for a ticket, maybe
105 Spruce
108 Added value
110 Sons of, in Hebrew
112 Nashville-based awards org.
113 Pitcher Reynolds of the 1940s–'50s Yankees
114 Story of a small Communist barbarian?
118 Designer Geoffrey
119 Eric of "Munich"
120 Gettysburg general under Lee
121 Hammer part
122 "The East ___," song of the Chinese Cultural Revolution
123 Egyptian solar disk
124 Catch in a ring, maybe
125 Without much thought

DOWN
1 Bill collector?
2 Online brokerage
3 Sartre play set in hell
4 Fetes
5 Plastic surgeon's procedure
6 Shanghai
7 Colorful fish
8 Regal inits.
9 Native: Suffix
10 Emmy-winning Ward
11 Platitude
12 Miramax owner
13 P.T.A. meeting place: Abbr.
14 Sister in Chekhov's "Three Sisters"
15 Five-time Wimbledon champ
16 1960s sitcom title role
17 Prizes
18 Transmitter of nagana
24 Reno-to-L.A. dir.
25 News bulletin
30 Hawaiian attire
32 Basis of a Scouting badge
34 Neuters
35 Peyotes, e.g.
37 Litigators' org.
40 Chemically quiet
41 Mother ___
42 U.S. rebellion leader of 1842
43 Loyally following
45 Eye layers
48 McDonald's chicken bit
49 Affix
50 Having digits
52 "The wolf ___ the door"
53 Welcomed, as a visitor
55 Mated
56 Jazz genre
57 End-of-year numbers
58 P.M. between Netanyahu and Sharon
59 Aviator
60 Open
65 Neb. neighbor
67 Gets a C, say
69 Where Guinness originates
70 ___ pain
71 Words before may or might
75 The French state
78 Mantel pieces
79 Convenient meeting place?
80 Seed coat
81 "Put your feet up"
82 Tolkien hobbit
87 Overthrows
88 Oven option
89 Part of R.S.V.P.
91 Also, in Arles
92 Places for moles
93 Mustardy condiment
94 Cane accompanier, maybe
95 Curtis of cosmetics
96 Aristocrats
98 Fixed for all time
99 Gulliver of "Gulliver's Travels"
100 Gearshift mechanism, informally
104 Contend
106 "O.K. then"
107 Network signal

by Phil Ruzbarsky

109 ___ Bator
111 Author/poet Bates
114 TV schedule abbr.
115 10-digit no.
116 Former rival
of USAir
117 Printer
specification:
Abbr.

9 LITERALLY SO

ACROSS

1 Singer Lambert, runner-up on the 2009 "American Idol"
5 Talk to shrilly
10 Four-sided figure
15 Halloween purchase
19 "___ by me"
20 Slangy commercial suffix
21 Shelter org.
22 Scuba diver's worry
23 -IRC-MS-ANCES
26 Be a couch potato
27 Mystery writers' awards
28 Person with few possessions
29 Hymn whose second line is "Solvet saeclum in favilla"
31 Breeze
33 Pay stub?
35 Ninny
36 ANTI--VERNMENT UN--ST
45 Urge
46 Maker of Fosamax and Zocor
47 Moscow's home: Abbr.
48 Covered walkway
50 It's music to a musician's ears
52 AR--CL-
57 Size unit of an English soda bottle
58 Like 11-Down: Abbr.
59 Soon
60 "Is ___?"
61 Underground network
66 Shoe brand reputedly named after a Scottish golfer

70 P---ARY CARE PHY-ICIANS
76 Currency union since 1999
77 Together
78 PBS benefactor
79 Low clouds
82 Stranded messenger?
84 1991 Tony winner Daisy
86 FI-TH WH--L
92 Tips, e.g.
93 Heart lines: Abbr.
94 Where some people get tips: Abbr.
95 Like the Vietnamese language
97 Like some verbs: Abbr.
98 WHAT A -ANDA DOES IN -EIS-RELY FA-HION
104 Tiny tunneler
105 Tic-tac-toe loser
106 Box lightly
107 Hawaiian massage
112 Met, for one
115 Home of the N.H.L.'s Thrashers
120 Modern home of the biblical Elam
121 W--THL-SS R-AD-TER
124 Stun
125 Take out
126 8½-pound statue
127 Regarding
128 Bob in the Olympics
129 Connection
130 Fresh
131 Favorite baby sitter, maybe

DOWN

1 Brut rival
2 TV screen meas.
3 "It's Time to Cry" singer, 1959
4 Hook up
5 Us
6 Gallery event
7 Kung ___ chicken
8 Alternative to satellite
9 Kind of shell
10 Stick in one's craw
11 Pres. when the C.I.A. was created
12 Piece of a newspaper?
13 1,111
14 French river craft
15 National monument site since 1965
16 Skis, boots, masks, etc.
17 Mideast tinderbox
18 ___-Ball
24 Very
25 "___ off?"
30 Bygone flier
32 Fresh
34 Company name that becomes another company name if you move its first letter to the end
36 Mackerellike fish
37 Kind of acid
38 Effluvium
39 Principal location?: Abbr.
40 TV exec's concern
41 Some E.R. cases
42 Chou En-___
43 ___ Chandler, longtime publisher of the Los Angeles Times
44 All's opposite
45 Icy
49 Dog breeders' org.
51 Send another way

53 Dangerous buildup in a mine
54 Preface online
55 "Excalibur" star Williamson
56 Knotted up
62 Senator Hatch
63 Spanish bear
64 Bygone flier
65 Word often following yes or no
67 Agreement abroad
68 Atlas abbr.
69 Wharton deg.
71 Like the face after a good bawl
72 A.C.C. athlete
73 It typically has lots of horses
74 Isn't inert
75 Less bananas
79 Toledo-to-Columbus dir.
80 N.J. or Pa. route
81 Music in Mysore
83 Architectural pier
85 Tel ___
87 Cry at a circus
88 W.W. II arena
89 Wii alternative
90 Male delivery
91 Some receivers
92 Dependent on chance
96 Sources of fleece
99 NBC inits. since 1975
100 Pirated
101 British weights
102 Cry after the rap of a hammer
103 Man's name that's an anagram of 108-Down
107 Caps
108 Exam format
109 Something to be threaded

by Ashish Vengsarkar and Narayan Venkatasubramanyan

110 Pure
111 Kind of screen
113 Psyche's love
114 Sub ___ (confidentially)
116 Similar
117 Ship that sailed "the ocean blue"
118 Shore flier
119 On the ocean
122 The Cowboys of the Big 12 Conference
123 They may be cloned

ACROSS

1 "This answer ends in a T," e.g.
5 Site of Daniel Webster College
11 Ninnies
16 ___ Vincent, former Major League Baseball commissioner
19 Jesus, for one
20 Internal settler?
21 Postgame discussion
22 "___ Maris Stella" (Latin hymn)
23 Pub quantity
24 Some skiing stars?
27 Tell ___ story
29 Bluesy James
30 Importune, informally
31 Make waves?
32 Teen leader?
33 Sault ___ Marie
34 Schools of thought
35 Charge up
36 Word of leave-taking
38 Far out?
41 Hampshire's home
42 Neptune, e.g.
43 French town in W.W. II fighting
44 Threnody
46 Defiant challenge to an order
47 To whom Mortimer declares "They were the footprints of a gigantic hound!"
50 Stuck
54 William Tell's canton
55 "Dies ___"
57 "___ expert, but . . ."
58 Winter hrs. in Winter Haven

59 ___-lacto-vegetarian
60 "Henry & June" author
62 Jiffy
64 Start of a German goodbye
65 Slung mud at
67 One of a pair of biblical nations
69 Unadulterated truth
72 Something of great interest?
73 Bartholomew, for one
75 Reprimand to a dog
76 "Norma ___"
77 Rapper ___ Jon
78 Person in a race
79 Laugh half
80 Speck
82 Transportation option
84 "Anytown, ___"
87 Volcanoes, e.g.
89 Result in
91 Brings with great difficulty
93 Rich people
95 Reykjavik's home: Abbr.
96 "Shadowland" singer, 1988
97 The Charioteer constellation
100 Big name in escapism?
103 Fictional village visited by Major Joppolo
104 Window cover
105 Hotel supply
106 Nascar event airer
108 Hall-of-Fame outfielder Roush
109 Light shade
110 Pro Football Hall-of-Famer Long
111 Blacken
112 Cambodian money

114 Departure call from a Spanish vessel?
118 Mideast sultanate
120 Contents of a stannary mine
121 Notes
122 Leaves at the base of a flower
123 Long-tailed moth
124 High-school subj.
125 Cameron who directed "Jerry Maguire"
126 Most sardonic
127 Stat

DOWN

1 W.W. II general ___ Arnold
2 Pelvic bones
3 Word signed for a deaf toreador?
4 Educational work after school
5 "Wagon Train" network, 1957–62
6 Buenos ___
7 Fish in a firth?
8 Reach in a hurry
9 "Superman" villainess
10 "Wagon Train" network, 1962–65
11 Obvious statement
12 Lost it
13 Metrical accent
14 Base protector
15 "Alias" type
16 Unlike the cards in a draw pile
17 Opposed
18 Toadies
25 River into which the Big Sandy flows
26 High point
28 Reaching 21?
35 What an unevenly milked cow might have?
36 Dentiform : tooth :: pyriform : ___

37 Singer/actress Linda
39 "___ Have to Do Is Dream"
40 Camouflage?
41 Simple writing
42 Dallas sch.
45 Cooler in the summer
48 Sufficient, informally
49 Until now
51 Mythical twin's bird tale?
52 Incessantly
53 Goodman of "Splash" and "Grease"
56 Sling mud at
61 One of the Cyclades
63 Power seekers, maybe
66 "Just ___ thought!"
67 Google service
68 Each
70 "Must've been something ___"
71 What the N.H.L.'s Hurricanes skate on?
74 Immature stage
81 Year the mathematician Pierre de Fermat was born
83 Chase in films
85 ___-Japanese War
86 Lee who directed "Brokeback Mountain"
88 Create quickly
90 Part of Christmas when lords a-leaping are given
92 Relative of an iris
94 Demonstrate
97 Carol starter
98 The Artful Dodger, e.g.

by Robert H. Wolfe

99 Eager
101 Lazy
102 ___-friendly
105 Hearst mag
107 Brings (out)
110 Garden worker
111 Novelist Caleb
113 Actress Turner
115 Cable station owned by Showtime
116 "Charlotte's Web" author's monogram
117 Onetime boom maker
119 Time out?

Let's Play Bingo

ACROSS

1 *Mark your card!*
7 Items in an ed.'s inbox
10 Covered, in a way
14 Briefly, after "in"
19 1960s–'70s Ford muscle car
20 On one's ___
21 Companion of Artemis whom Zeus changed into a spring
22 It comes after a "long time"
23 The Pequod, e.g.
24 Giggle syllable
25 *Mark your card!*
27 Slacken (off)
28 Sign off on
31 Emperor who married his stepsister
32 Child of the '70s, in brief
33 Third year in 31-Across's reign
34 Like any channel between 30 and 300 MHz
35 Plumbing or heating
37 Endangered Everglades mammal
39 Starbucks size bigger than grande
41 Diagram used for brainstorming
43 Other side
44 Manfred ___, 1967 Chemistry Nobelist
45 Classic Disney film that includes "The Nutcracker Suite"
47 Gravy holder
50 Hulu, e.g.
52 Enter
56 Pair
59 The Equality State: Abbr.

60 *Mark your card!*
61 See 54-Down
63 Parking lot mishap
64 Lose luster
65 State with the least populous capital
70 Raison d'___
72 Thrown off course
73 *Mark your card!*
77 Genetic stuff
78 Tailors
79 What "prn" on a prescription means
80 Muscular Charles
82 Any trump
83 Worry words
89 The "it" in the 1990s slogan "Gotta have it"
93 Writer Zora ___ Hurston
97 Opposite of charge
98 Exposed sandbar, maybe
99 Prodded
101 Pigs
102 Golfer Michelle
104 Org. headquartered in Detroit
105 Cover girl Carol
106 Placed
108 Vaughn's co-star in "The Break-Up," 2006
110 "This round's ___"
111 *Mark your card!*
114 Deuce, e.g.
115 Paris couturier Pierre
117 Occasional 1960s protest
118 Prefix with directional
119 What an aurilave cleans
120 Affirm, with "to"
121 Elates
122 Horse of a different color?

123 Genetic stuff
124 *Mark your card!*

DOWN

1 *Mark your card!*
2 "Me too"
3 Writing's opposite
4 Depraved
5 Chemical suffix
6 Singer Jones
7 Jay who once hosted "Last Comic Standing"
8 Better, as an offer
9 Mock
10 Places of worship
11 "___ Wiedersehen"
12 Monopoly token
13 Statement of self-confidence
14 "Who wants to go next?"
15 With 49-Down, order at a Chinese restaurant
16 *Mark your card!*
17 "Walk Away ___" (1966 hit by the Left Banke)
18 Combine that makes combines
26 Second-most common Vietnam-ese family name, after Nguyen
29 *Mark your card!*
30 Novelist Janowitz
34 Hollywood crosser
36 Prefix with center
38 Circuit
40 Bone attachment
42 World Economic Forum host city
46 Base's opposite
48 Put away
49 See 15-Down
51 Sick
53 *Mark your card!*
54 With 61-Across, prospectors' targets

55 The 13th item in a baker's dozen
56 Banned insecticide
57 Vote for
58 Mo. when the Civil War started
62 Number of wonders of el mundo antiguo
66 Department store department
67 Roar for a toreador
68 Untested
69 Football stat.
71 Within: Prefix
72 Soap opera, e.g.
73 Undergrad degs.
74 The A.C.C.'s Seminoles
75 *Mark your card!*
76 Celebrated in style
81 ". . . blackbirds baked in ___"
84 Baseball stat.
85 Skin colorer
86 School near Windsor Castle
87 Went around
88 German mercenary
90 Spoils
91 Sailor's vision obstructer
92 *Mark your card!*
94 Popular 1940s radio show "___ Alley"
95 Get ready to fall, maybe
96 Star employee
99 Does perfectly
100 ___ Janis, star of Broadway's "Puzzles of 1925"
103 Like some pyramids
107 Try it out

by Todd Gross

BINGO

B	I	N	G	O
15	20	35	60	72
8	21	44	50	65
12	17	FREE	49	71
11	16	31	48	68
7	19	40	53	61

109 Trillion: Prefix
110 "___ put it another way . . ."
112 YouTube clip, for short
113 Bambi's aunt
116 Agcy. regulating guns

ACROSS

1 Low-I.Q.
4 Slender amount
8 Letterman airer
13 Venerable
19 Gasteyer of stage and screen
20 He's less than a gentleman
21 Broadcast element
22 Carnival sight
23 Goal of Sun-Maid's marketing department?
26 You might give this a gun
27 Conclude by
28 Shower with force
29 Go back to square one
31 Office holder, of sorts
32 Willow twigs
35 Word with interface or option
36 Part of a brake
39 Salad bar activity?
45 Hot air
48 Composer Thomas
50 Beat poet Cassady
51 Actress Lotte
52 Book on how to repair rodent damage?
58 Immigrant's course, for short
59 Dwellers on the Strait of Hormuz
60 Overseas news source, in brief
61 Pays down incrementally
64 Murphy's "48 HRS." co-star
65 Seeped
68 "Drat!"
69 Reason that nothing's growing on the farm?

75 Peculiar: Prefix
76 Rugby play
77 Units of sweat
80 Subject for 48-Across
85 Athos, to Aramis
86 Dish served ranchero-style
87 Take a powder
88 Question from a campaign committee?
92 Old Apple laptop
95 Push
96 Company founded in 1940 as Standard Games
97 Bottom line
98 Exercise for beginning yoga students?
103 Hang around
105 Push too hard, maybe
106 Was gaping
108 Aloha Tower site
112 Porous kitchen utensils
117 Throws together
118 Eight-time Canadian skating champion
119 Repay
120 Tardy illustrator's assurance?
124 Be on the brink
125 Up time
126 Broadway columnist Wilson
127 Whiz
128 Position player's stat
129 Baron Cohen who created 25-Down
130 Cart for heavy loads
131 Lead character on "Pushing Daisies"

DOWN

1 Took a chance
2 For the birds
3 Ones who'll straighten you up?
4 Formal order
5 Cloud chamber particle
6 Form of 4-Down
7 P.M. preceded and succeeded by Shamir
8 Easy gallop
9 Chum
10 Reagan cause: Abbr.
11 Pantry array
12 Science fiction author A. E. van ___
13 Against, with "to"
14 Well-bred
15 Cry before waving the hand
16 Ruler of the Aesir
17 Isolated
18 Had no play in crazy eights
24 Retailer beginning in 1867
25 Alter ego of Borat and Brüno
30 Start of a German goodbye
33 Haitian president Préval
34 In the public eye
37 Home south of the border
38 Gemstone sources
40 Zilch
41 Spare
42 Deadly 1966 hurricane
43 Closing bell place: Abbr.
44 Hoedown participants
45 Enter
46 Early Michael Jackson style

47 Petty
49 End of a ballade
53 Really engrossed
54 Something often thought of as impending
55 Lab challenges
56 Branching point
57 Diploma holder
62 Court of justice
63 Destitute
66 S.A.S.E., e.g.
67 Informal headwear
70 Actress Lollobrigida
71 Novelist Morrison
72 Sport of a rikishi
73 Sends out
74 San Francisco mayor Newsom
78 Ready, in the kitchen
79 U.S. Army E-6
80 Naval lockup
81 Bumpkin
82 ___ a secret
83 Pulitzer playwright of 1953
84 Heaps
86 Science fiction prize
89 Lots of moolah
90 Switch lines, say?
91 Mineral that crystallizes from magma
93 Town on the SE tip of Italy that's the title setting for a Horace Walpole novel
94 "M*A*S*H" corporal
99 Council members
100 One using a comb
101 Tokyo's airport
102 Meaning of the emoticon :-D
104 Whom a thane attended
107 Pushed, with "on"

by Michael Ashley

THAT IS TWO SAY

ACROSS

1 Horrify
6 Get ready to go
10 Leopard's home?
14 Club
19 Excel
20 Jai ___
21 Baby carrier
22 Sierra ___
23 Resort region near Barcelona
25 Drug distributor
27 Famous Giant
28 Country singer Gibbs
29 Vein contents
30 Surface films: Var.
31 Dental problem
33 Key sequence in a chromosome
36 Chitchat
37 Very noticeable
39 Jacob who wrote "How the Other Half Lives"
40 Praiseworthy
42 Self-satisfied
44 Hospital bill items
46 Prefix with function
47 Chianti and Beaujolais
50 Big rush
52 ___ Cube
56 Authors' aids: Abbr.
58 ___-Japanese War
59 Brown v. Board of Education city
60 Music compilation marketer
63 Pro ___
65 Of the mouth's roof
68 Envision
70 1873 adventure novel that begins and ends in London
73 Less popular, as a restaurant
74 "Fer-de-Lance" mystery novelist
75 Certain palms
76 "WKRP in Cincinnati" role
77 Driving surface
79 Crown
81 Flicka, e.g.
82 Attacked
83 Republic once known as Dahomey
84 Surname of two signers of the Declaration of Independence
85 From ___ Z
87 Stop worrying
90 Take part in
93 Dipstick housing
97 Masters piece
99 Car make of the 1930s
102 No. on a check
103 American everyman
106 Unaccented syllable
108 It's not to be touched
110 Like some humor
111 Andrea known as the liberator of Genoa
113 "Patience ___ virtue"
114 Ethan Frome portrayer, 1993
116 Jealous
118 "Sesame Street" regular
119 It might be assumed
120 Opera set in ancient Egypt
121 Courtyards
122 Baby bottle tops
123 Tag in an antique store
124 Med. dose
125 "Sailing to Byzantium" writer

DOWN

1 Dressy tie
2 Life magazine staple
3 Something to draw
4 Queen's servant, maybe
5 Baseball coverage?
6 Catherine who survived Henry VIII
7 Screamer at a crime scene
8 Pricey appetizer
9 Maker of the Optima
10 Wow
11 "Real Time With Bill ___"
12 Antismoking org.
13 Latin catchphrase sometimes seen on sundials
14 Casual farewell
15 Numerical prefix
16 Passing
17 Closes tight
18 Doesn't bother
24 Post decorations on four-posters
26 "The ___ Love" (Gershwin song)
29 Depression-era migrant
32 Recommendation
34 Prestigious London hotel
35 Fill the tank
38 Yellow poplar
41 Some pop-ups
43 Singer Washington
45 Author of the Barsetshire novels
47 San ___ (San Francisco suburb)
48 Singer who played herself in "Ocean's Eleven"
49 Barbershop sights
51 Stomach
53 Suitable for
54 Venerated image: Var.
55 Units of fineness
57 Offensive lines?
59 Like vinaigrette
60 "Married . . . With Children" actress
61 Gloomy Milne character
62 Flat dweller
64 One of the Pointer Sisters
66 Full of fear
67 How drunks drink
69 Dutch export
71 Judge
72 Guitarist Eddy
78 One end of a digression, for short?
80 Go aboard
82 Flimflam
83 Chisel face
85 Large wardrobe
86 "From Russia With Love" Bond girl Romanova
88 Rejected as unworthy
89 Mug with a mug
91 Corrode
92 Density symbol
93 Pill that's easily swallowed
94 Driver of the Cannonball Special
95 Excellent
96 Flu symptom, with "the"
98 Leaf vein
100 "Peer Gynt" princess
101 Bad connection, say
104 Carny booth prize
105 "Here Come the ___" (Abbott and Costello film set at a girls' school)

by Patrick Berry

107 Sneaker material
109 Struck down,
old-style
112 Harvest
115 The Great Lakes'
___ Locks
116 Slang for a
3-Down
117 Suffix with favor

Initial Offerings

ACROSS

1 Political comedian with the 1973 album "Sing a Song of Watergate"
9 Breakfast dishware
16 Whispered message lead-in
20 Agreements
21 Major-league manager who won World Series in both leagues
22 Stat. for 1-Down
23 Article written by an early American patriot?
25 Line formed at a barbershop?
26 Ticked (off)
27 Active military conflicts
28 "No way, no how!"
29 Farm worker
32 Record label for Bill Haley and His Comets
34 Enemy in the 1980s arcade game Arabian
35 Alfred of "The Da Vinci Code"
36 Ditty, e.g.
38 Japanese drama
39 Dental problem for a boxing promoter?
42 When repeated, gleeful student's cry
44 Chinese dynasty of 1,000 years ago
46 Obstruct
47 Desire to be more like an actress of Greek descent?
52 Shrubby expanse
56 Godzilla contemporary that was a giant flying turtle
57 One rewarded for good behavior, perhaps
58 Like gymnasts' bodies
59 Saturate
61 Company that makes Styrofoam
62 Dance club V.I.P.'s
65 Silent signal
66 Adorable child of an edgy filmmaker?
73 Link letters
74 "___ to Joy"
75 Cut (off)
76 So-called art silk
77 Gulf of ___, modern pirates' realm
79 Become a sailor
82 Hidden
86 "D'Artagnan Romances" author
88 Tent used by a Latin musician?
90 Theme
92 Literary pen name
93 Attack tactic
94 Television award given to a Surrealist?
100 Alias indication
102 List
103 Inception
104 "___ note to follow . . ."
105 Asian film genre
107 Foxlike
108 Safari weapon
109 Oyster bed diver
112 R&B singer Hendryx
114 Noirish
115 Rodent named for a 20th-century novelist?
120 Name beside a harp on euro coins
121 Getting ready for a hand
122 Car air freshener shape
123 Brothers
124 Less lenient
125 Draws

DOWN

1 Range: Abbr.
2 3,600 secondi
3 "Stand" band
4 Stretched to the limit
5 The Black Stallion, e.g.
6 Actress Quinn
7 Cause of congestion
8 Deadhead's supply
9 Red-haired PBS star
10 Intestinal opening?
11 Slowly started pleasing
12 John of "High Fidelity"
13 "Back in the ___"
14 Smokey Bear spots, for short
15 Express
16 Looney Tunes lothario
17 Like much of the Danube's territory
18 First name at Wimbledon
19 Dish setting for watching satellite programs?
24 Brainstorming cry
28 "Ob-vi-ous-ly!"
29 Copying
30 Mobile phone giant
31 Latish wake-up time
33 Animal that leaves when it's cared for?
35 "Singin' in the Rain" studio
37 Get closer
39 Clue game board space
40 "If only ___ known . . ."
41 Parliament vote
43 Begin liking
45 Like
48 Overly enthusiastic
49 Crush, e.g.
50 Southern Conference school
51 Salamandridae family member
53 "___ Got No" ("Hair" song)
54 Empath on "Star Trek: T.N.G."
55 London's ___ Park
60 A, in Armentières
62 Forensic ID
63 Bloomsday honoree
64 Skedaddles
66 Campus space
67 Asian tongue
68 Something on a table: Abbr.
69 Heaps
70 ___-Rooter
71 Member of a modern theocracy
72 Debut
78 III, IV and V, maybe
79 Shower need
80 Chop ___
81 Electric ___
83 Modern pentathlon equipment
84 Imperial
85 Wee
87 More likely to snap
88 "America" contraction
89 Turning the other cheek
91 Blast producer
94 "The Ecstatic" rapper
95 Household helper
96 Nissan S.U.V.
97 Someone offering a lift?

by Todd McClary

AUTHOR! AUTHOR!

ACROSS

1 Fish
6 Walk away with
9 ___ Wagner, player on an ultrarare baseball card
14 Fictional inspector Dalgliesh
18 Sounded soft and sweet
19 Name after "you"
20 Gulf Stater
21 Willing
22 Bret and Robert's treatise on acid reflux?
24 Nathanael and Jack's travel guide about Heathrow's environs?
26 Prove it
27 It includes the line "The True North strong and free!"
29 Maxima
30 To-do
31 Diminutive drum
32 Team on the Thames
34 Faux pas
37 Jonathan and Alice's account of a pedestrian in a hurry?
40 "___ hoppen?"
43 Prefix with metric
44 "Guys and Dolls" song
45 Old dancing duo
47 C. P. and E. B.'s essay on purity?
50 South Dakota, to Pierre
53 Admission of ineptitude
54 Apportion
55 "Come on, help me out"
57 Nightmare figure
58 ___ Treaty, establishing the 49th parallel as a U.S. border
59 Caleb and Robert B.'s novel about valet service?
62 Went undercover
63 Hunk's pride
64 Flag holder
65 Drop ___ (start to strip)
66 Small island
68 Six-footer from Australia
70 Richard and Thomas's book about a robot?
73 Golf ball feature
76 Advance
78 Very tense and excited
79 Went by Saturn, say
80 Make a commitment
82 British tax
83 Rex and Stephen's biography of Henry VIII?
85 Ally of the Cheyenne
87 Another ally of the Cheyenne
88 Ltd., in Paris
89 With 100-Across, Naples opera house Teatro di ___
90 Oscar and Isaac's profile of Little Richard?
94 Dells
96 Abbr. before a date
97 Hindu soul
98 He was born Lucius Domitius Ahenobarbus
100 See 89-Across
103 Big newspaper company, informally
105 Stuck

109 Dan and Virginia's story of a dark-colored predator?
111 Ezra and Irving's memoir of a stand-up comic?
113 Italian isle
114 ___ ligation
115 Breather
116 Plays the banjo, e.g.
117 Looking good
118 Coordinate geometry calculation
119 Sentence shortener, for short
120 Stations

DOWN

1 Berlin octet
2 Preparer for a flood
3 Colosseum spectacle
4 Freed
5 Gertrude ___, first woman to swim the English Channel
6 Declaration of 1941
7 Very quickly
8 Food brand name with an accent
9 Question to a brown cow
10 Golf champ Mark
11 Former stock regulating org.
12 Removes from a bulletin board
13 Part of R.S.V.P.
14 For whom Safire wrote the words "nattering nabobs of negativism"
15 Early vocabulary word
16 Madly
17 Department store department
19 One-piece outfit
23 Emmy-winning Arthur

25 They're on the Met schedule
28 Co. that dances at the Met
33 Go to bed
34 Gadget
35 "Fort Apache, The Bronx" actor
36 Horton and John's podiatry journal article?
38 Sweaty
39 In the future
40 Richard and Reynolds's bargain hunting manual?
41 Artist Rousseau
42 Posed
44 Keep away
46 Judge who presided over 1995's most celebrated trial
48 "And away ___!"
49 Some drivers
50 Sonnet ending
51 Typist's sound
52 Give ___ (care)
55 Holstein and Hereford
56 When repeated, a Thor Heyerdahl title
59 Browbeaten
60 Parisian walk
61 Grammy winner Bonnie
64 Javits Center architect
67 Response to "How are you?"
68 "___ Dream" from "Lohengrin"
69 Stiller and ___
71 Like a really good game for a pitcher
72 R&B and C&W: Abbr.
73 Very sweet, as Champagne
74 Big Red

by Randolph Ross

75 Noses out
77 Temporary falloff
79 Sad time
81 Former capital of the Yukon
83 Leaves with notice
84 ___ loop (skating move)
86 King Cole, e.g.

87 Brand that has "Real Facts" on its products
91 Bit of winter protection
92 Archie Bunker's plea to Edith
93 Baby-sitter's headache

94 Absorbs
95 Blew one's top
96 Stanford QB drafted #1 in 1983
99 Boundary
100 Semi conductor?
101 Janis's comics partner

102 Fleeces, perhaps
104 Detroit's ___ Center
106 Little, in La Scala
107 Cleaning up a mess, maybe
108 Mrs. Dick Tracy
110 Pkg. stats
112 A.C.C. school

ACROSS

1 *"Before the Mirror"*
6 Turned off
15 Bête ___
20 Westernmost avenue in Santa Monica, Calif.
21 Rewards of a political machine
22 Schindler of "Schindler's List"
23 With 29-Across, holder of the works named in the nine *starred* clues, celebrating its 50th anniversary on 10/21/09
26 One at risk of excommunication
27 California wind
28 Ready-go go-between
29 See 23-Across
35 Philharmonic sect.
36 45 players
39 2000s TV family
41 Many a school fund-raiser
46 "What's going ___ there?"
47 One who works on a grand scale?
49 Game in which players subtract from a starting score of 501
50 "Big" number in college athletics
51 Station
52 Year Columbus died
53 Letter-shaped construction pieces
54 New Deal inits.
55 "___ party time!"
56 Legal org.
59 Horse and buggy
60 Needing a massage, say

61 Be hung over, e.g.
62 Small island
63 Enchant
65 Miff
66 1970s TV production co.
67 Symbols like @
68 *"Green Violinist"*
69 Gazes at
72 Like a bond you can buy with security?
73 Savor, in a way
74 "Frasier" role
75 Short swim
76 V.P. during the Cuban missile crisis
77 In order (to)
79 Lo-___
80 "Today" rival, for short
81 Canadian-born hockey great
82 "Eldorado" grp.
83 Perfectly timed
85 Like some YouTube videos
87 House call?
88 Landlocked European
90 Vintage Tonka toy
94 Water swirl
95 In need of blusher, say
97 *"Composition 8"*
98 Old credit-tracking corp.
99 Clytemnestra, to Agamemnon
102 Light planes
103 *"Peasant With Hoe"*
106 Subject of the Joni Mitchell song "Amelia"
108 Jazz standard whose title is repeatedly sung after "Honey . . ."
109 "May I ___ question?"

110 "Rebel Without a Cause" actress
118 Operatic prince
119 Grand
120 Controversial form that 43-Down used for 23-/29-Across
121 Like some traffic
122 Lummoxes
123 One who gets a lot of return business?
124 Verb with "vous"

DOWN

1 Lepidopterist's study
2 Pain in the neck
3 Poetic contraction
4 Enters leisurely
5 Gov't investments
6 Part of some Bibles: Abbr.
7 Flight
8 Midori on ice
9 North end?
10 ". . . ___ should I"
11 Director Lee
12 Cross shape
13 Shell food?
14 *"Seated Woman, Wiping Her Left Side"*
15 Like 43-Down's design for 23-/29-Across
16 Org. setting workplace rules
17 Swedish company with a catalog
18 Drops from the sky
19 Gospel singer Franklin
24 Flambé, say
25 ___'acte
29 Castle security system
30 Bygone channel
31 "No seats left"
32 Use (up), as time
33 One for the money?
34 *"Tableau 2"*

36 Good lookers
37 Fated
38 With 43-Down, what 23-/29-Across was
39 Player of one of the women in Robert Altman's "3 Women"
40 Site of Spain's Alamillo Bridge
42 Jewelry firm since 1842
43 See 38-Down
44 U.S.P.S. deliveries
45 Latin 101 verb
47 Drinks of liquor
48 Sixth-brightest star in the sky
51 *"Mandolin and Guitar"*
56 Start of a common run
57 Joy of "The View"
58 Showing surprise
64 Words from Charlie Brown
70 Dog-___
71 Many a perfume
75 Epps of "House"
78 Shrub that may cause a severe allergic reaction
80 Leaden, in London
84 Angela Merkel's one
85 Place for a stamp
86 Sorts
89 School popular in the 1920s
91 Autumn ESPN highlights
92 Sue Grafton's "___ for Ricochet"
93 Common middle name for a girl
94 Scholarly
96 Code-cracking grp.
98 "Time out!" signal
99 Old defense grp.

by Elizabeth C. Gorski

100 Turkish bigwig
101 "The Antipope"
103 Early spring feast
104 Just love
105 Life preserver, e.g.
107 Spanish tidbit
108 Skinny
111 B.O. purchases
112 "Head and Shell"
113 Roman household god
114 Paris's ___ Saint-Louis
115 Medium strength?
116 "Huh?"
117 Viking ship item

ACROSS

1 "My People" writer
9 Its motto is "Under God, the people rule": Abbr.
13 ___ Errol, main character in "Little Lord Fauntleroy"
19 Violent behavior due to excessive use of banned athletic substances
20 Humana competitor
22 Time's 1986 Woman of the Year
23 Start of a wish by 112-Across on 9/21/09
25 Big name in tires
26 ___ bark beetle (pest)
27 Nita of silents
28 Wish, part 2
30 ___ of the Guard
34 Actress Merrill
36 Like the best wallets?
37 Working hours
40 Lucy's guy
42 Big wheels
43 Wish, part 3
47 [Yuck . . . that's awful!]
50 Parliament output?
51 Toward the quiet side
52 It seemingly never ends
53 Page, e.g.
54 Malia's sister in the White House
57 Wish, part 4
63 Table scrap
65 Oxford, e.g.
66 Paragons
67 Garage container
71 Wish, part 5
73 ___ the Laborer, patron saint of farmers
74 Hell's Angels, e.g.
76 Aside from that

79 Prince ___ Khan, third husband of Rita Hayworth
80 Wish, part 6
84 Transition
88 Words of agreement
89 Musical sense
90 Not in operation
92 Christmas hours in N.Y.C.
93 Law, in Lima
94 Magazine for which 112-Across writes
101 Refuse
102 What can one do?
103 Actor who said "I'll make him an offer he can't refuse"
104 Tropical grassland
107 Astronomer's sighting
109 Minotaur feet
112 NBC football analyst/reporter and longtime writer
114 Flavor
117 Sudan neighbor: Abbr.
118 Kind of penguin
119 End of the wish
124 More massive
125 Magical symbol
126 Take for a spin
127 Infiltrates, say
128 Ballet jump
129 Soda bottle size

DOWN

1 Dick who was once House majority leader
2 Danny who directed "Slumdog Millionaire"
3 Windbags
4 Whirl
5 Long, long time
6 ___ Harbour (Miami suburb)

7 Sayin' no to
8 "99 Luftballons" pop group
9 Got hitched
10 Noah Webster, for one
11 "I already ___"
12 Pullover, e.g.
13 Middle-school Girl Scout
14 Draws a parallel between
15 Boneheads
16 Streamlets
17 Kind of tray
18 Hack it
21 Starting from
24 Obama's honorary deg. from Notre Dame
29 Creator of Oz
31 Dashboard stat
32 "L'heure d'___" (2008 Juliette Binoche film)
33 Historic ship whose real name was Santa Clara
35 Cockeyed
38 Nickname of the Spice Girls' Sporty Spice
39 Porcelain containers, maybe
41 Poem with the lines "Nobody'll dare / Say to me, / 'Eat in the kitchen' "
43 "___ in ice"
44 Hush-hush org.
45 Michelle of "Crouching Tiger, Hidden Dragon"
46 Memo intro
47 Contraption
48 Freud disciple Alfred
49 Canada ___
53 Chemical coloring
55 Famous deerstalker wearer

56 Shady spot
58 "___ thought"
59 John Elway, for the Broncos
60 Printer resolution meas.
61 Piazza dei Miracoli town
62 Monthly expenditures: Abbr.
64 Battery, e.g.
67 Like most music
68 It has ray flowers
69 "Sheesh!"
70 Losing tic-tac-toe combo
72 Bridge expert Culbertson
75 Member of the Brew Crew, e.g.
77 Dirty
78 Land, eventually
81 "___ all!" ("Fini!")
82 Hot topic in insurance
83 ___ Schneider, villainess in "Indiana Jones and the Last Crusade"
85 "Stop your moping!"
86 Capitalize on
87 Flight board fig.
91 Impress permanently
94 More hairy
95 Some Warped Tour attendees
96 Big name in hotels
97 Lame excuse for missing homework
98 Endearing
99 2016 Olympics locale
100 It's got mayo
101 Thin
104 Alternative to a wagon
105 Secret event of '45
106 Harvesters, e.g.

by Brendan Emmett Quigley

108 "Much ___ About Nothing" ("The Simpsons" episode)
110 Practice piece
111 Like some stockings
112 Asphalt, e.g.
113 Run of letters
115 Germany's ___ von Bismarck
116 Nothing, in Nantes
120 Subject of many lies
121 K'ung Fu-___ (Confucius)
122 The Gateway to the West: Abbr.
123 Prefix with valent

18 COMPOUND FRACTURES

ACROSS

1 Tops
5 Quilt filler
9 Detest
14 Some I.R.A.'s
17 Some extra books
19 Softly
20 Post a modern status update
22 Eyewear providing hindsight?
24 French town
25 Restrain
26 Game in which a player may be schneidered
27 Repeated a Benjamin Franklin electrical experiment
29 Peanut-loving ghost?
32 Intermittent revolutionary?
33 Afflicts
34 "___ Can Cook" (onetime PBS show)
35 Leader against the Aztecs
36 Hearing aids, briefly
37 Christianity, e.g.: Abbr.
38 Bluff bit
40 Desert stream
41 Emulate a grandparent, maybe
43 Rare mushroom?
47 "Uh-uh"
51 Backrub response
52 It comes before the carte
53 Put away
55 Some sushi bar orders
56 Give up smuggled goods?
62 Guards against chapping

64 Area code 801 area
65 Swamp thing
66 Use www.irs.gov, say
68 Not exciting
69 1989 Madonna hit
71 High-school athletic star at a casino?
74 ___ area
75 Indian government of 1858–1947
77 Word from Antony to Cleopatra
78 Parisian roll call response
79 Barack Obama, for one
81 Noble Les Paul?
88 "As ___ Dying"
90 Man's name meaning "young man"
91 Coward with a pen
92 ___ gratification
93 Boombox button
95 Hannibal of "The Silence of the Lambs"
97 Old TWA hub: Abbr.
98 Three or four
99 "Maybe" music?
101 Dreams that don't die?
104 1946 John Hersey book
105 Runner Budd
106 Simile words
107 Japanese financial center
108 Bug that never takes a ride?
113 Deux of these are better than one
114 "As You Like It" setting
115 Hustle
116 60 minuti

117 "This I Promise You" group, 2000
118 "Bill ___ History of the United States"
119 Détente

DOWN

1 Limo, e.g.
2 Form of the Egyptian god Thoth
3 Paunch
4 Gives up on
5 What "two" meant, historically
6 iPhone download
7 Broadway, say
8 Append
9 Give ___ on the back
10 Inexpensive pen
11 Greatly reduced
12 Trading unit
13 Fairy tale sister
14 Sporty Toyota
15 River areas named for their shape
16 Mettle or metal
18 "The Human Stain" novelist
20 Big Super Bowl expense
21 Like online medical advice for kids?
23 Pompom holder
28 Had as a base
29 One of three brothers in the Old West
30 White ones are little
31 Swimmer Diana
32 Fountain order
35 Kind of bean
38 Blacken
39 Go over and over
40 Director, writer and actor in "The Woman in Red," 1984
42 Age-old robbers' target

44 Vegetable that gives you an emotional release?
45 Eng. or Span.
46 "Lux et Veritas" collegian
48 Belief of about 1½ billion
49 Pause producer
50 City near Düsseldorf
54 Bias
56 New York politico Andrew
57 Follower of each or no
58 Source of a "giant sucking sound," according to Ross Perot
59 Common cause of a 3-Down
60 Not fun at all
61 Mad man?
63 Opposite of plus
67 "Dona ___ and Her Two Husbands"
70 Lever or level
72 "The Big Country," for one
73 Sci. specialty
76 Peachy-keen
80 "Happy Days" role
82 Poker star Phil
83 Like some stock market highs and lows
84 Lone
85 Strip, sand and stain
86 Tommie of the Amazins
87 Tugboat services
89 Sammy Davis Jr. autobiography
93 Hunt's "Mad About You" co-star
94 Slips
96 They've got promise

by Matt Ginsberg and Pete Muller

97 Like many an oath
98 Dormant Turkish volcano
99 Candid, maybe
100 Botanist Gray and others
101 Popinjay
102 Mings, e.g.
103 Job precursor: Abbr.
105 97.5% of a penny
109 X
110 Manage, with "out"
111 ___ premium
112 Mint

ACROSS

1 Oriole, e.g., briefly
5 "Still waters run deep," for example
10 Microwaves
14 Bygone Toyota model
19 Prefix with factor
20 Brand with a pyramid on the package
21 Verve
22 Person with a program
23 "O say can you see" or "Thru the perilous fight"?
25 Resident of a military installation?
27 Divine
28 Lace shade
30 Place on a bus
31 Business card abbr.
32 Boxful for Bowser
33 Miss in Monterrey: Abbr.
34 Bring in
35 Alarm
36 Architect Saarinen
37 Confronting boldly
39 Singer Simon
40 Tropical fruit seller?
44 Tape holder
47 Alley ___
48 Run down, in slang
49 Collectible disks
52 Singer India.___
53 Philadelphia's historic Gloria ___ Church
54 Singer Horne
55 Lacking serviceability
57 Poet Federico García ___
59 Hair net
61 Place to get drunk in the kitchen?
63 About to get
64 A as in Austria
65 Original nuclear regulatory grp.
66 Craggy ridge
67 What overuse of a credit card might result in?
70 "That's ___" ("It's done")
72 Seasons
73 Not so cool
74 Drains
76 Like, '60s-style
78 Old brand in the shaving aisle
79 Toledo-to-Columbus dir.
80 "Casablanca" role
81 Cool
82 Put back on the market
84 Gentleman's intransigent reply?
87 Means of identifying wood
90 Dry Champagne, e.g.
91 Horseshoer's tool
95 Columnist Barrett
96 &&&&
98 This one, in Acapulco
99 Against
101 Latin 101 verb
102 Redheaded kid of old TV
103 "The Time Machine" race
104 More than the immediate future
105 Where nitpickers walk on a street?
108 Online beauty contest?
110 Obliterate
111 Nabisco product
112 Group with the 2002 hit "Girlfriend"
113 Isn't straight
114 Cobbler's supply
115 Seizes
116 Drug agent's seizure
117 Handy ___

DOWN

1 Toward the stern
2 Poe poem
3 Beef Wellington, e.g.
4 Take up again, as a case
5 High points
6 Place for a rivulet
7 Porthos, to Aramis
8 Produce
9 Bygone Buick
10 Indian bovine
11 Part of many fancy dish names
12 Part of a book . . . or something to book
13 Scornful expression
14 Tallow ingredient
15 Blue Angels org.
16 Sci-fi weapon
17 Vacation place, often
18 Boulevard, e.g.
24 Impedes legally
26 Whip
29 Sent a message to shore, say
33 Guard
34 Heavy sheet inside a book's cover
35 Away's partner
37 ___ Motel
38 Home ___
39 Pauses during speech: Var.
41 Had the upper hand
42 Score just before winning
43 Bit of fluff
44 Back-room cigar smokers, say
45 United charge
46 Back up
49 Object of a scurrilous attack, maybe
50 Like surveyors' charts
51 Most withered
52 Makes flush
54 Cambodia's ___ Nol
56 54-Down, e.g.
58 Goldsmith, for one
60 Crude transports
62 College world
65 Utterances around baby pictures
68 Moccasin decoration
69 Diner manager/waitress in "Garfield"
70 Shirts and blouses
71 Rice ___
75 "Je vous ___"
77 Gibson necessity
82 Most dilapidated
83 Muscly
84 Cara ___ (term of endearment)
85 Sherry-like wine
86 Takes out of the will, say
87 Basis of 85-Down
88 "Night of the Living Dead" director, 1968
89 From one end of a battery
92 Cartwright of "Make Room for Daddy"
93 Group of viruses
94 Trimmed
96 Quick
97 Subject of a museum in Yorba Linda, Calif.
99 One way to fly

by Robert W. Harris

100 Fidgety
102 Till compartment
103 Cause of star wars?
104 Hosp. staffers
106 Enzyme suffix
107 Wyo. neighbor
109 __ hair

Note: When this puzzle has been completed, connect the circled letters in order from A to N to get an appropriate image.

ACROSS

1 Pair of pears
7 Young socialites
11 "___ Nagila" (song title that means "Let us rejoice")
15 Move from Los Angeles to New York, say
16 Ply with liquor
17 Helped settle an argument
21 *Tony Parsons novel [1943 song]
23 Source of black diamonds
24 Workout count
25 Like some valves
26 *Mandarin variety [1942]
27 Had brunch
28 Some dogs
29 Aminos, e.g.
31 Robert of "The Sopranos"
32 No-good
34 Lost
35 Thrice daily, on an Rx
37 Molokai and Maui: Abbr.
38 Left-wingers
40 Bread box?
41 Last non-A.D. year
44 One way to put out an album
45 "Blah, blah, blah"
47 William ___, the Father of Modern Medicine
49 Seeds might be planted in it
51 Greek god of the north wind
53 Late Saudi king
55 2001 World Series winner
57 Uranium source, e.g.

58 "Mad Men" extra
61 Stylish filmmaker
64 Pink-slip
65 Mental flashes
67 *It flows into Ontario's Georgian Bay [1961]
69 Soup server
70 9/
71 "Pretty please?"
72 Glide (over)
74 Weak-looking
75 Girl Scout symbol
77 Revise
79 Nanny's warning
81 Orch. section
82 Attack fiercely
85 Curvy-horned animals
88 Took a gander at
89 Of element #76
91 Strong joe
93 ". . . ___ saw Elba"
94 Copy job delayers
95 Hubbub
96 "Are you in ___?"
98 Faux gold
100 Billing no.
103 Beachgoer's hair lightener
104 Get 100 on a test
105 Ungodliness
108 *Laurel and Hardy flick [1949]
111 Oil source
113 Suffix with billion
114 Move from New York to Los Angeles, say
115 Lyricist born 11/18/1909 who wrote the words to the 10 songs with asterisked clues
117 Whenever
118 Dr. Alzheimer
119 Off the coast
120 Suffix with tip

121 "What's Going On" singer
122 Some wraps

DOWN

1 Greek market
2 Three trios
3 *"Omigosh!" [1938]
4 Dummkopfs
5 Show grp.
6 Narrow way
7 Shopaholic's accumulation
8 Morales in movies
9 Texas State athlete
10 It's a mess
11 *Rural jaunt [1945]
12 "Garfield: ___ of Two Kitties" (2006 film)
13 "Les Voyages Extraordinaires" writer
14 Abacus user
16 Like "Don Juan"
17 Rachel of "Mean Girls"
18 Ages and ages
19 Nobelist Hammarskjöld
20 Suffix with duct
22 Vintage Ford
26 Associate with
28 Knox and others: Abbr.
30 See 110-Down
33 Vintage sign word
34 Hollywood pooch
35 Start of an adage about forgiveness
36 Cross inscription
37 So that one can
39 Hoodwink
42 Many a 115-Across collaboration
43 Assemblies
44 Some Juilliard students

45 Maximal ending
46 *Total sham [1963]
48 *Former first lady [1945]
50 Came alive
52 Stubborn sort
54 Hwy. offense
56 Hungarian half sister?
59 *One of the Brontës [1964]
60 Cambodia's Lon ___
62 Emmy winner, e.g.
63 Hair-raising shriek
66 Div. of Justice
68 Nevada's largest county
69 See 110-Down
71 Ham radio catchword
73 Cable inits.
76 "The Wizard ___"
78 "Why did ___ this happen?"
80 Get better
83 Comes (to)
84 Swings
86 Former 38-Across
87 With desperation
90 *Toro's target [1956]
92 "Where ___ sign?"
94 Tittle
97 7-Up, with "the"
99 Indiana/Michigan natives
100 Eastern titles
101 Cardinal's topper
102 Knock it off
103 City rebuilt by Darius I
104 Photographer Leibovitz
106 Peace goddess
107 Studious crowd
109 Tandem's capacity

by Elizabeth C. Gorski

110 With 69-Down, V.I.P. in the 30-Down
112 Cry from a deck
113 Janis's comic strip hubby
115 Sporty wheels
116 Med. specialty

CAREER-DAY SPEAKER SCHEDULE

ACROSS

1 White-tailed movie star
6 Barbecue byproduct
11 "Many good nights, my lord; ___ your servant": Shak.
16 N.Y.C. airport
19 Literary work in which Paris is featured
20 County abutting London
21 Candy wafer company
22 Hosp. workplaces
23 Career Day Speaker #1: Meter maid?
25 Unwrinkle
27 Talk up
28 #2: Tea server?
30 Blues musician Baker
33 Chocolate-and-caramel brand
36 Filmmaker Martin
37 Big bin
38 #3: Golf pro?
44 Swan's shape
45 Many four-doors
46 1985–88 attorney general
47 Toast starter
49 Mendes of "2 Fast 2 Furious"
50 Growing-friendly
52 Perturb
56 Rap's ___ Wayne
57 Suffix with pant or aunt
58 #4: Tree surgeon?
63 Sex symbol once married to Vadim
66 Flightless bird
67 Button materials
68 First landfall north of Oman
70 #5: Manicurist?

74 Reeve or Reeves role
75 Gambler's holy grail
78 They take the bait
79 Warranty invalidator
82 #6: Justice of the peace?
86 Long. partner
87 ___-wolf
90 Literary creation
91 Skywalker's cohort
93 "No ___!"
94 "Aunt ___ Cope Book"
96 Play byplay
98 ___ Chao, only cabinet member to serve through George W. Bush's entire administration
100 Dillinger's derringer, e.g.
103 #7: Grocery store owner?
106 2007 Steve Carell title role
108 I's
109 Job bidding figs.
110 First of two choices
111 #8: Disc jockey?
116 "___-A-Lympics" (old TV cartoon series)
118 Bullies
119 Career of the parent who typed up the Career Day schedule?
125 Conclusion for many believers?
126 Bay, for one
127 Sideways up
128 Of interest to ornithologists
129 Grazing ground
130 Dump and road endings

131 "Midnight Cowboy" nickname
132 College classes

DOWN

1 Iota
2 Larter of "Heroes"
3 Amp plug-in
4 Honeyed pastry
5 Start of a plan
6 Old salt
7 Bouillon cube ingredient, usually
8 Sugar suffix
9 Boy toys?
10 Shakes down
11 Untouched
12 The Thrilla in Manila, for one
13 Reforestation subj.
14 Garbage hauler
15 Emerald City visitor
16 "Hey, see what I got!"
17 Meager bowlfuls
18 Club that began as the Colt .45s
24 Blushes
26 Over-the-wall wallops: Abbr.
29 Glazed fabric
30 It debuted on "E Day"
31 Fountain in front of the Palazzo Poli
32 Large body in Washington, D.C.
34 Appendage
35 16 oz.
39 Where Key's bombs burst
40 Reader of signs
41 Wagon puller, often
42 It's often played on Sunday
43 Madrid's ___ Sofia Art Center
48 Library section
51 From
53 Seconds

54 Many a bar mitzvah attendee
55 First, in Frankfurt
59 Prefix with -tect
60 Goal-oriented org.
61 Middle grade
62 Impair
64 San ___, Lone Star State city
65 Slight fight
68 Leads (by)
69 Hall-of-Famer Sandberg
71 A little over half a century in old Rome
72 "Help!" key
73 Unit of contraband
76 Equip with weapons, old-style
77 Mell Lazarus comic strip
80 Hand-held cutter
81 Functional
83 Cause of quailing
84 Comparable (to)
85 Break in a building's facade
88 World capital once under French rule
89 Spectators
92 Beatty and Sparks
95 Pesky biter
96 Mounted on
97 Approval for Juan Valdez
99 When Juliet says "O happy dagger!"
100 Animal in an exercise wheel
101 Unwilling
102 City in Mount Rainier's shadow
104 Disgorges
105 "I can get by with that"
107 Parental imperative
112 Results of 26-Down
113 Lot "souvenir"
114 Leafy vegetable
115 Author Jaffe

by Patrick Merrell

117 Skirmish
120 One likely to
    have pet peeves?
121 Dash lengths
122 ___ Maria
123 Human body
    part with
    vestigial muscles
124 Hosp. V.I.P.'s

22 CUED UP

ACROSS

1 Government pubs., say
5 Twine holder
10 Amateur publication, for short
14 What a migraine might feel like
18 Moonfish
19 Primary stratagem
20 Like much music
21 Old alpaca wool gatherer
22 Delighted exclamation?
25 Cough cause
26 Sail extender
27 Inventive type
28 Bit of attire for a carriage ride
29 Pitcher's feat
32 One all, say
33 Tame
34 "Tamerlane" dramatist Nicholas
35 V-chip target
36 Part of an Irish playwright's will?
38 Museum worker
40 Bank statement entry
42 It came up from Down Under
43 Tom of "The Tomorrow Show"
45 Fish-and-chips fish
46 Sultan's land
49 Aquafina competitor
54 Impertinent sort
56 TV character often seen in a Metallica T-shirt
58 Pipe attachment
59 Needle problem
62 Tests the water?
64 "Don't fight"
66 Game grp.
67 Many curves, in math

68 Carsick passenger?
70 Bon mot
71 Babylon's site, today
72 Conventions
73 Starting point
74 Some pieces in an archaeological museum
75 Bratislava's river
77 "Come on, guys!"
79 "Jour de Fête" star, director and writer, 1949
81 Neighbor of a shift key
82 "Little Women" woman
83 Iranian supreme leader ___ Khamenei
85 New Zealand's discoverer
89 49-Across, e.g.
91 Red leader?
93 Spanish girl
94 Causing uneasiness?
101 Not safe
103 Schools of thought
104 Drawers, e.g.
105 Plain and simple
106 Darjeeling, e.g.
108 White as a sheet
109 Germane
111 Last stage of insect development
112 Believe
113 Carryin' on, in olden times?
117 Gambling game enjoyed by Wyatt Earp
118 Paunch
119 Wake Island, e.g.
120 Turn over
121 Irish ___
122 Put in stitches

123 Poet who wrote "An' the Gobble-uns 'at gits you / Ef you / Don't / Watch / Out!"
124 Walked

DOWN

1 Bobs and such
2 Alphabetic trio
3 Florida Keys connector
4 Anger at losing one's flock?
5 Gymnastic feat
6 Conspired
7 Unlikely ballet dancer
8 Sign warning people to be quiet
9 Columbo's employer, for short
10 Whizzed along
11 Maraud
12 Tandoor-baked bread
13 Head of lettuce?
14 Krishna is one of his avatars
15 One surrounded by cell walls
16 Looks sore
17 Bald baby?
20 Bring up the rear
23 N.L. West team, on scoreboards
24 ___ four
28 "The Dark Knight," for one
29 Assns.
30 It may be declined
31 Suit
33 Absolute beauty
36 Call on a pitch
37 Nebraska senator Nelson
39 Easy chair site
41 Narrator of "How I Met Your Mother"
44 Blue

46 Superior to
47 It may feature a windmill
48 "Don't Be Cruel" vis-à-vis "Hound Dog"
50 Subjugation?
51 Bring about
52 Time's partner
53 Some tides
55 Name shared by 12 popes
57 Big gulf
58 French mathematician who pioneered in the theory of probability
59 Water park feature
60 Sura source
61 "Impossible!"
63 Positive thinking proponent
65 Legal writ, in brief
69 Clockmaker Thomas
76 German city where Beck's beer is brewed
78 "Our ___"
80 Certain X or O
82 Programming problem
84 Wood alternative
86 Get fogged up
87 Greatest flowering
88 Astronaut's insignia
90 Dolt
91 Like a butterfingers
92 Within earshot
94 Hearty drafts
95 Prevent from being reelected
96 Cleave
97 Try to avoid detection
98 Chevy model
99 Forsooth
100 It may be dramatic
102 Opportune

by Will Nediger

106 Matthew 26 question
107 Sound at a spa
109 "The Clan of the Cave Bear" author
110 Baseball G.M. Minaya
113 Montana and others, for short
114 Helios' counterpart
115 It may be said before a kiss
116 ___ Land of "Twenty Thousand Leagues Under the Sea"

WEARING O' THE GREEN

ACROSS

1 Shook, maybe
6 Quarrel
11 Animal that has kittens
16 Litterae or poetica
19 Impersonations
20 Sky box locale
21 Fish may be kept in it
22 Lovey
23 Soave ___
24 Lethargy
25 1989 Al Pacino movie
27 Trumpeter Red
28 Gang types
29 Director Reiner
30 "Understood!"
31 Roguish
32 Grandchild of Japanese immigrants
33 Tony-winning Hagen
34 13th-century invader
35 People to hang out with
38 Former U.S. Open site
41 Stable sounds
42 Went to the top
44 Relieves
45 Like some pond life
47 Bygone New York newspaper
48 Brave
49 Sitting room?
51 "Uncle Tom's Cabin" girl
52 "Shoulda, woulda, coulda" thinker
54 Soccer star Hamm
57 Chat room abbr.
58 Goes (for)
61 Dark
63 Passbook entry: Abbr.
64 N.H.L. conference div.
65 It's good when they're extended
67 Broadcasting inits. since 1970
68 Number after cinque
69 Cause of some skids
70 Get rid of
71 Calendar abbr.
72 Quick scores?
73 "Dear" ones
74 Many a state name in D.C.
75 Dyes
77 Muffin ingredient
79 Sky boxes, perhaps
81 It's for the birds
82 Thin as ___
84 Keyboard key
86 Arrived
88 Wizard's home
90 Like some covers
93 Desires
94 Mythical bird
95 Hard roll?
98 "___ Had It" (1959 hit)
99 D.C. regulators
100 "___ Breckinridge"
101 Flutist's embellishment
102 Gluts
104 Numbskulls
106 Rugged ridge
107 Trust fund babies, often
108 Titus, e.g.: Abbr.
109 Cuts corners?
110 Something to read word for word?
111 Began
112 River to the Irish Sea
113 Certain Oldsmobile
114 They can hold water
115 Practices

DOWN

1 Ohio River tributary
2 Artemis's twin
3 "Witness" co-star
4 ___ Stanley Gardner
5 Actress Cannon
6 Runway moves
7 Sings "Rock-a-Bye Baby"
8 Tow truck attachments
9 It's positive
10 Wagner's final work
11 Eclipse
12 Like stainproof fabric
13 They're fit for a princess
14 Organic compound
15 One who cries foul?
16 Last Supper guest
17 Lets on
18 Bull market necessities?
26 Be a go-between
32 Pacifier
34 Where, to a whaler?
36 Carrier at J.F.K.
37 Matadors' duds
39 Run-of-the-mill: Abbr.
40 Most overcome
42 Reds
43 Big name in brushwork
45 "Finally!"
46 Made "moonlight requisitions"
47 "ER" doctor played by Laura Innes
48 Where cows are sacred
50 Is a blabbermouth
52 Steamroll
53 Sam and Ben
54 There's no use in this
55 Does data work
56 Napping
59 Marketing device
60 Iberian Mrs.
62 Marathon mementos
66 Fall off
76 "___ cannot be!"
77 Something screwdrivers can help make
78 Small estuaries
79 Krazy ___
80 Negative reaction
82 1998 song by Rebecca Blake
83 Mold anew
84 Harsh critic
85 "Three Musicians" artist
86 They're boring
87 ". . . ___ quit!"
88 Skipped out, in a way
89 Common refrigerant
90 Bumble
91 Loath
92 Good news from lenders
96 Traffic light feature
97 Feudal lord
100 Kind of call
102 Bygone leader
103 Sleekly designed
105 Abbr. often appearing above percentages

by Elizabeth C. Gorski

ACROSS

1 ___ Beds National Monument, Calif.
5 Difficult billiards shot
10 What "p" may stand for
15 Org. with eligibility rules
19 Sale sign
20 John of song
21 Drink
22 Pequod captain
23 SIDESTEP ___ WATERFALL
25 WATERFALL ___ BOOK CLUB
27 Shark shooter
28 Big name in stationery
30 Stock figures
31 Oats, e.g.
32 Putdown
33 Places for taps
34 Nourish
37 Achilles, e.g.
39 One with a fastball?
40 Pale
41 BOOK CLUB ___ ROOM SERVICE
43 Eliminate
46 ". . . like ___ not!"
47 Decant
48 Set
49 Subterfuge
50 Steer
51 ROOM SERVICE ___ TRICK KNEE
55 Reserve
56 Hedgerow tree
58 Gardner and others
59 Got an eyeful
60 O. Henry specialty
61 Earth Summit site
62 Place to get a burger
63 Nibble
65 Dispatch boat
67 It crosses the nave
70 Some German exports
71 TRICK KNEE ___ DRY CLEAN
73 Go out
74 Scads
75 Tough
77 Push
78 Gossipy Barrett
79 "On the double!"
80 DRY CLEAN ___ ORDER FORM
84 Polish name rarity?
85 Part of an accusation
87 Puts down
88 Plumbs the depths
89 Extremists
92 Sticks around a game parlor
93 Breathing space
94 As originally found
95 Cries of agreement
97 Handouts
101 ORDER FORM ___ LINE DANCE
103 LINE DANCE ___ TIME MACHINE
105 Tribe in Manitoba
106 Place for the highborn?
107 Go back to square one
108 Singer Tennille
109 Commuter plane trips
110 Center of French resistance in W.W. II
111 Gathered (in)
112 Woman's name suffix

DOWN

1 Certain dogs, for short
2 "Pronto!"
3 Number two
4 Show concern for
5 Two-to-one?
6 One way to read
7 Bowl over
8 Junior, e.g.
9 Makes beloved
10 Letter holder
11 Parrot
12 Like some colors
13 Park Avenue, for one
14 Intermission
15 Gab
16 Carolers
17 1973 Masters winner Tommy
18 Infernal regions
24 European liberal
26 Reliever's goal
29 "The ___ of English Poesie"
32 Market town
33 What to do
34 "The evidence of things not seen": Hebrews 11:1
35 Port city of ancient Rome
36 TIME MACHINE ___ SEAT BELT
37 Lament
38 Payola, e.g.
41 Long in the tooth
42 St. Louis's historic ___ Bridge
43 SEAT BELT ___ SIDESTEP
44 1975 Wimbledon champ
45 Kind of instrument
47 Get on the horn
49 "Lady Love" singer
51 They may get a licking
52 Spooky
53 To the point
54 Reserved
55 Queeg's command
57 Get in shape
59 Nick
62 System of shorthand
63 "The Godfather" actor
64 Not manual
65 Fusses
66 Lets off steam
67 Shorebirds
68 Missed, with "for"
69 Shades of blue
72 Torpedoes
75 Like the "ch" in Bach
76 Composer's pride
78 It's played against the house
81 Goes along
82 Word that's an example of itself
83 Bedroom fixture
84 River to the Rybinsk Reservoir
85 In groups
86 Package carrier
88 Cruised the Net
89 Nada
90 January in Guadalajara
91 "It's ___ in the right direction"
93 Boo-boo
95 Prefix with photo
96 Cardinal
97 Boater's worry
98 Pellets
99 In rapture
100 Classic railroad name
102 "Whaddaya know!"
104 "La la" preceder

ACROSS

1 1983 film comedy with Bill Maher
6 Lovelies
11 Arguments
19 Now, in Nogales
20 Old drugstore name
21 Equivalent
22 Bona fide
23 Mother in "The Glass Menagerie"
24 Sawbucks
25 Subject of "The Haj"
26 Warehouse function, maybe
28 ___ T
29 Old-time actress Frances
30 With the situation thus
32 Popular fruit drink
33 Wine additive
34 Starting points
36 South Dakota
40 Female donkeys
41 "Haystacks" painter
42 However, briefly
43 They usually have yellow centers
44 Start of a count
45 Mine carrier
49 Edits
50 In toto
51 Tall, skinny guy
52 Turns
53 ___ Maples Trump
54 Washington's Sen. ___ Gorton
55 Bad start?
56 Things to chew on
57 Neighborhood convenience
59 ___-American
60 Computer add-on?
61 Items hit with hammers
62 Actor Keach
63 Plant pore
64 Maker of NBA Pro and NFL Blitz
66 Baby carrier
67 Showy
68 Pause for cold warriors
69 Bubbler
70 Migrating geese
71 Kind of chart
72 Displaying 5-Down
73 First in courage
74 They have panels
78 Least dull
79 Fruitless
80 Kayoed
81 Sports shoes, informally
82 Galoot
85 Zilch
86 It's not preferred
90 Valet employer
92 Drop off
94 Get ready to bite
95 "Lord, ___?"
96 Weaken
97 Payton of football
98 Faint dead away
99 Is unwilling to risk
100 Playing cards
101 "Crime and Punishment" heroine

DOWN

1 Florentine art treasure
2 Take after
3 This rises by degrees
4 Air on stage
5 Boor's trait
6 Bumps
7 Wood sorrel
8 Domain
9 Some legal scholars, for short
10 Blind feature
11 Certain missile
12 Like Beckett's "Endgame"
13 "The Big Heat" director
14 Apart from this
15 Challenge for a barber
16 "Who Do ___ Kill?" (1992 movie)
17 Skedaddle
18 Halvah ingredient
20 They think they're superior
27 "Indeed"
31 Mediums
33 Early jazz composition
35 Puts down, in a way
36 Men's fashion accessories
37 Just
38 Online brokerage
39 "Come back, ___" (western line)
40 Shutter
41 Director Louis
44 They're measured by degrees
45 Not dry
46 Rest stop amenity
47 Chicken Little, for one
48 Post-firing task
49 Lift off
50 Best Picture nominee of 1996
51 Urban area
53 Matisse's world
54 Word on many a button
57 "Les Trois Mousquetaires" and others
58 Bit of rubble
59 Deals with guilt
61 Photo finish?
63 The Amistad and others
65 Unenthusiastic
66 Extra horsepower, in slang
67 Open
69 Popular corn chip
70 Swell
72 English tidbit
73 Calvin Coolidge's estate, with "The"
74 Aslope
75 Writer Fallaci
76 Dairy machine
77 Kind of vine
78 Problematic
81 Commemorative marker
83 Of no importance
84 Henry's tutee
86 Cleveland cagers
87 Son of Judah
88 Abbr. on a food label
89 Brand
91 Northerner's home
93 Before, of yore

by Manny Nosowsky

ACROSS

1 Lead sharer
7 They're fare-minded
11 Farm call
15 Appointments approved by the Sen.
19 Like federal tax laws?
20 Therapeutic plant
21 Rolling rock?
22 Title role for Jodie Foster
23 "Don't mess with the Hurricanes!," e.g.?
25 Analogous
26 So
27 Capitol figure
28 Site for bells
29 Underhanded bum
30 Frigid
31 Select
33 "Howdy, ma'am," e.g.?
36 Area away from the battle
37 Tender spot?
38 Peanut product
39 Word of support
40 Dangerous answer to a sentry
41 "___ Plenty o' Nuttin' "
43 Clash of clans
46 Laertes' T's
48 Problem at exclusive schools?
55 Tanker troubles
56 Southern vacation spot
57 1920s tax evader
58 Talk up?
59 Cheats
62 Element used in electroplating
66 One from Wittenberg
67 Taking in calves?
71 Gene stuff
72 Makes a fuss
74 Fink on
75 Pinion's partner
76 They're out of this world
79 Revival technique
80 Peerless
82 Not take tailoring seriously?
87 Grouch
88 Pacific repast
89 Opening time, maybe
90 Actress ___ Dawn Chong
91 Bagel topper
94 Home of "Friends"
96 Summons: Abbr.
97 Like some shows
101 Water-carrier's motto?
106 Outlet
107 Try it!
108 Started smoking
109 Give the cook a break, maybe
111 1967 N.H.L. Rookie of the Year
112 Words from a nonfolder
113 ___ breve (2/2 time, in music)
114 Female improv?
116 Be a stool pigeon
117 Regan's father
118 Chancel wear
119 Slob's napkin
120 Hardly beauty queens
121 Like some D.A.'s
122 Silence of the staff
123 Furnish

DOWN

1 Tent tenant
2 Colorful percher
3 Reagan Supreme Court nominee
4 Lassie's lid
5 Sambuca flavoring
6 Concrete
7 Expensive spread
8 Get straight
9 "NYPD Blue" creator
10 "Told ya!"
11 White-bread
12 Cleaned up after a fall
13 Flier's home
14 Winner of 1865
15 They're not pros
16 Forgiving
17 Prude
18 Vehicle drawn by draft animals
24 Purges, in a way
29 "The Crucible" setting
32 In a well-kept way
34 Player of the Four Aces
35 Audited
37 Push (around)
42 Gerard of "Soldier's Fortune"
44 Lines at a checkout?: Abbr.
45 1949 film classic
47 Under cover, perhaps
48 "The sweet small clumsy feet of ___": E. E. Cummings
49 1957 #1 song
50 Camaro model
51 Farm call
52 Baseball's Garciaparra
53 Nautical pole
54 London area
55 Some writers work on it
59 Mathematical subgroup
60 "The Conspiracy Against Childhood" writer LeShan
61 Tally mark
63 Gulf war loser
64 Like raw diamonds
65 Approach, with "for"
67 Like a good mixer
68 Speaker of baseball
69 John or Paul but not George or Ringo
70 Gang land
73 Goya's naked lady
75 Least scarce
77 Chiefs' org.
78 Franc fraction
80 Part of C.P.U.
81 Tours turndown
82 Ivory tower, maybe
83 Having night vision?
84 Incurred
85 Big horn
86 Accord
90 Salad slice
92 "Wowie zowie!"
93 Creepy cases
95 Spicy, in a way
96 Getting the most "aws"
98 Traveled (along)
99 Hit the big time
100 Baby grub producer
102 Big bang producers
103 Booster rocket
104 .946 liter
105 Poets' feet
106 Old hat
110 The Beatles' "Back in the ___"
114 Area of Mars
115 Place to put one's feet up

by Nancy Salomon and Harvey Estes

ACROSS

1 Trim
5 Story that may hold secrets
10 Dresses for cooking
15 Arrangement holder
19 "___ to that!"
20 TV executive Arledge
21 Appearance at home?
22 Endangered antelope
23 Outer layer
24 Things that are not appreciated
26 Space between the dotted lines
27 Hardly a cold snap
29 Notice
30 I.C.U. conduits
32 Produce a 130-Across
34 Actress Sorvino
35 From the East
36 Line of thinking
38 Quiet time
43 From an earlier time
46 Important test
48 Do the same as
49 Literary connection
50 Words of caution
54 ___ Day (Wednesday)
57 Portoferraio's island
58 "Death in Venice" author
59 Register
61 Like the Owl and the Pussycat's boat
63 They're not me or you
66 Take a break
68 Govt. loan org.
69 Entices potential dieters
76 Go (for)
77 Upstate New York's ___ Lake
78 Calder Trophy awarder
79 Part of some facials
84 Complicated situations
86 Tennis's Nastase
87 Thunderbird enthusiast?
88 Unappetizing food
90 In succession
93 Flooded
95 They're fourth on the way up
97 Makeup artist's problem
98 Watered down
99 When many people get to work
104 Hebrews' first high priest
106 Say without thinking
107 Splitter who makes splinters?
109 Departed quickly
113 Can opener
116 Secure
118 Kind of smell
119 Actor Andrew
120 Popular activity for dogs
123 Built for speed
124 One and only
125 Big name at Notre Dame
126 Exquisitely wrought trinket
127 Car wash supply
128 A big person may come down with it
129 Round of four
130 Disturbing noise
131 Gut feeling?

DOWN

1 He left Oenone for Helen
2 Lady friend in Italy
3 Keep getting
4 Ultimate object
5 Musical run
6 See 70-Down
7 Despicable sort
8 How some legal proceedings are conducted
9 TD Banknorth Garden player
10 Italian tourist attraction
11 No. on a certain table
12 Result of a productive 21-Across
13 Coffee go-with
14 Wonder who?
15 Do work on the house
16 U.A.E. center
17 Since then, in song
18 Extinguished flames?
25 Some transfusions
28 Cartoon dog
31 News agency name
33 ___ cavity
35 Enjoyed to the max
37 Spotted
39 Ticket abbr.
40 Eye
41 Sticks figure
42 Ignoble
43 He played Castillo on "Miami Vice"
44 Reluctant
45 Singer with the Aliis
47 Musically connected
51 Understood
52 Chekhov and others
53 Peppery
55 It breathes
56 Blue Ribbon makers
60 Unwelcome one
62 Wound
64 Reply
65 Those seeking intelligence
67 Victims of an October 1998 sweep
70 6-Down's partner
71 Designer Picasso
72 Prince or princess
73 Not at full power
74 Complaint
75 Reason to use wipers
79 Kind of song
80 Nocturnal bird
81 "Back ___ hour" (shop sign)
82 Like some seats in a stadium
83 Diet
85 It may have a head
89 What's expected
91 Scolding
92 Destroy slowly
94 Suspension
96 Positions
100 They're not to be believed
101 Polished
102 Trading place: Abbr.
103 Conditions, in a way
105 Choice for travelers to New York
108 It's in the bag
110 Three quarters of the earth, basically
111 Macy's showcase?
112 "Mending Wall" poet
113 Attention getter

by Joe DiPietro

"HEY, MISTER!"

ACROSS

1 Passage preventers
6 "Excuse me . . ."
10 Become less reserved
14 Bewitched
18 "Tzigane" composer
19 Stiff hairs
21 A whole lot of shaking going on
22 Aglio e ___ (pasta dressing)
23 Short loin products
25 "60 Minutes" regular
27 Not so hot
28 First of "The Chronicles of Clovis"
30 They help you make your goals
31 It goes around the world
34 M.B.A. hopeful's hurdle
35 Pianist Rubinstein
36 Roughed up
37 Superman's gift
39 ___ Cob, Conn.
42 Fell off
43 Kirkstall Abbey locale
44 Defeat by looks
46 Pointed ends
47 Signal to leave, perhaps
48 Not all there
49 "River ___ Return" (Mitchum/Monroe flick)
50 Skittish show?: Abbr.
51 Like old recordings
52 Describe
53 "60 Minutes" regular
54 Like some leaves
56 1972 Bill Withers hit
58 Spiro's predecessor
59 Decisive one
61 Public Citizen founder
62 Dressed down?
63 Dress down
64 Church figure
65 Sneak ___
66 Old peso fractions
67 Architect's offering
68 Southern sibling
69 Computer support, sometimes
72 Piled out
73 Six-Day War hero
75 Some need stitching
76 Use hip boots, perhaps
77 They were big in the past
79 "The ___ Bride" (Rimsky-Korsakov opera)
81 Latin father
82 Kenny G has two
83 F.D.R.'s birthplace
85 It may move you
86 Goodbyes
87 He homered 660 times
88 Needs a ring?
89 Vast
92 Vast
93 "We will ___ undersold!"
94 107-Across state
96 Chemical-free fare
101 Goodbye
102 Peut-___ (maybe, in Marseille)
103 Done for
104 "___ Sea" (Lemmon/Matthau comedy)
105 Hospital staffer
106 Farrah's ex
107 All there
108 People guilty of disorderly conduct?

DOWN

1 Monitor letters
2 You may see a reaction in one
3 Lacto-___vegetarian
4 Non-Jews
5 Rained hard?
6 Up
7 Consideration
8 Pilot's announcement, briefly
9 Incense
10 For whom the bell tolls
11 Patricia Neal's Best Actress film
12 Zog I, for one
13 Vet's offering
14 "The Kiss" sculptor
15 Shakespeare title starter
16 Painter Mondrian
17 Kiddy litter?
20 Emerson collection
24 Went over the limit
26 Together
29 "Total Request Live" network
31 Signs
32 71-Down's predecessor
33 Numbskulls
34 Luzinski of baseball
35 ___ Magna (annual early-music festival)
37 Prefix with phobia
38 Glucose and fructose, e.g.
39 Gossip-filled gathering, typically
40 They have titles
41 Corral chorus
43 No socialite
45 Not too hard
47 Visit
48 Bar stock
51 Big name in applesauce
52 Enticed
53 Start of something big?
55 Theater area
56 Open
57 Wrap choice
58 Some are false
59 Rub
60 Catch, in a way
62 Hussies
67 Stacks for burning
68 Hide well
70 "Die Fledermaus" maid
71 32-Down's successor
73 Big name in personal planners
74 Gall
75 Grocery line?
76 Generous to a fault
78 Quaint contraction
79 Some have diners
80 Terminal tippees
81 Sand painting creators
84 Hearing aid?
85 Prefix with morphous
86 Chevy truck model
88 Bakery offering
89 Ocean menace
90 2nd-century date
91 "Zounds!"
92 "The Grey Room" novelist Phillpotts
93 Former Senate Armed Services Committee chairman
95 Shooters' org.
97 It may be taken in spots
98 Siouan speaker
99 Wagering option, briefly
100 Spanish couple?

by Elizabeth C. Gorski

GET WISE

ACROSS

1 Redemptions
8 Mitterrand's successor
14 1950s–'60s Big Apple mayor
20 Classic ball game
21 Treasure State city
22 Make it
23 Wobbly band members?
25 1960s "Death Valley Days" host
26 Punta del ___, Uruguayan resort
27 911 respondent
28 Done for
29 Apollo loved her
30 Easy ___
32 American Revolutionary leader Deane
34 Visitors from afar
35 Follow
39 Subject of war propaganda
42 Hill, to an Arab
43 It covers ground rapidly
44 Wily style of diplomacy?
47 A little behind
50 Shell thrower
51 Harmony
52 Amazon dangers
54 Curse
56 Land with a queen in Kings
58 Extracts
59 Caesar's farewell
60 Plumbing problem abroad?
62 Member of a force: Abbr.
63 One in swaddles
66 Pentagon concern, for short
68 Rodgers and Hart's "What ___ Man?"
69 Mare's-nest
70 Questionnaire datum
71 Halloween mask?
76 Like New York's Radio City Music Hall, informally
79 Sighter of the Pacific Ocean, 1513
81 Capri, e.g.
82 Reruns, to summer TV
86 Place of legend
88 Position in 20-Across
91 Tarzan's pet
92 Mountain fortresses: Var.
93 Like an Englishman in the desert?
95 Bond rating
96 George W. Bush, as a collegian
98 Quantity
99 Paths of some streams
100 Pool necessity
101 Attention-getters
103 Sea salvage aid
105 Word with car or game
107 Mata Hari was one
110 Hound
111 Together, musically
115 Call for
116 Assault with crêpes suzette?
119 Wynn of "Dr. Strangelove"
120 It's west of Sherman Oaks
121 Extraction
122 Attempts
123 Conveyed, in a way
124 Made a record of

DOWN

1 Rights org.
2 Long times in Lima
3 Spinoff group
4 Make artificially better, with "up"
5 Distant
6 Pins down
7 Quite a puzzle
8 Midwest city, familiarly
9 "Shucks"
10 Pelvic parts
11 Realizes
12 Fixed payment
13 Fairy tale locale
14 Some are critical
15 Part
16 Means of communication
17 Ivory or pink?
18 "Dynasty" star
19 Actor Auberjonois
24 Turns, so to speak
30 Modern name for the capital of ancient Galatia
31 Odd, spelled oddly
33 "___ Desire" (1953 Barbara Stanwyck film)
35 They're pressed for cash
36 Exult
37 Bore
38 Musical interval
40 Measurer of brightness
41 Millionaire's toy
43 ___-Ethiopian War, 1935–36
45 Like some surgery
46 "America, the Beautiful" pronoun
48 Constellation with Canopus
49 Some stockings
52 Settles
53 Alternatives to 747's
55 Subject of a composition
57 Relative of Camembert
60 Directions
61 Chaps
63 ___ ghanouj (eggplant dish)
64 Marble
65 What pregnancies produce?
67 Pupil's place
69 They're blue
71 Seattle athlete, for short
72 Actress Blanchett
73 Young zebra
74 Los ___, Calif.
75 ___ Cove ("Murder, She Wrote" locale)
77 Delineate
78 French journal
80 XXV Olympics site
83 Minus
84 Little ending
85 "___ who?"
87 "Gotcha"
89 Hoo-has
90 Power of old films
93 Wright brothers' craft, e.g.
94 Like a well-grounded argument
97 Didn't hesitate
100 Yuletide handouts
101 W.W. II guns
102 Subsequently
104 "Not ___!"
105 Main road
106 Initial
108 Kind of rock
109 Sound
111 Suit to ___
112 Not cheap
113 Press
114 Blue-___
117 Decked
118 USA alternative

by Nancy Nicholson Joline

30

SHAREWEAR

ACROSS

1 Beer pasteurization pioneer
6 French husband
10 You can swear by him
14 Lady of Portugal
18 An ice place to live
19 Spanish port
20 Pink-slipped
21 Periods divide them
22 Madras dress that's taken up by hitches?
24 Gown that's lost in a Florida town?
26 Uprose
27 "Airplane" co-star Robert
28 Tree in the Garden of the Hesperides
29 Female TV role played only by males
31 Overeater's worry
33 Not so taxing
35 Worldwide workers' grp.
36 Famed Bruin's nickname
38 Lexicographer Partridge
40 Hassle
42 Buttoned garment that's central to a 1970 movie?
45 ___ School (early 20th-century art group)
48 Son of Seth
50 [Pardon]
51 Wrap that's included with a landlord's sign?
53 Bird that's more than rare
54 Beloved, in "Rigoletto"
55 Detach, in a way
56 Arabic for "reading"
58 Take a chance
59 "Ed Sullivan Show" mouse ___ Gigio
61 Squeaked by
63 Cocked, as a hat
65 Borden brand
68 Quaint footwear
70 Big, as a concerto goes
71 Pursuit
72 Superlatively decided
73 Ulster, e.g.
74 Frankfurter link?
75 Brown shade
77 Large-scaled game fish
80 Brokerage offerings, for short
84 Money exchange fee
86 Underthing that's part of a bleeped phrase?
88 Pulitzer writer Sheehan
89 Spare
90 "Bewitched" witch
91 Old costume that enters a contest like bingo?
94 Animal's track
96 "Eye of ___, and toe of frog"
98 Raspberry
99 Kirk bench
100 Finishes
103 In harmony
105 Trig calculations
107 "En ___!"
109 Doesn't move
111 Adhesive
113 Waistband that's tucked in – pity, that!?
115 Thong that's covered with flaws, among other things?
118 Cane
119 "Sleepy Time Gal" songwriter Raymond
120 Befuddled
121 Strikes out
122 Perry Como's "___ Marie"
123 Hanger-on, maybe
124 Worked on a bed
125 Commencement

DOWN

1 Information unit
2 Rude review
3 Elides
4 Turns up
5 Avocations
6 They were once promoted with the slogan "Ivory tips protect your lips"
7 Ta-ta
8 Enigma
9 Final finish?
10 Cup at a diner
11 Kind of daisy
12 Vice ___
13 Japan's capital, formerly
14 Intensified
15 Protective cover that's found in an "Ave Maria" phrase?
16 Table salt, symbolically
17 Governor for whom a North Carolina city is named
19 Ariz. neighbor
23 Look at, in the Bible
25 Barbara of "Mission: Impossible"
27 Holdup
29 Popular fragrance
30 Honolulu's ___ Stadium
32 Old fashioned leggings are in—try for the impossible!?
34 Man with a nice laugh
37 Dirt
39 It might ring your neck
41 Alpine refrains
43 Plays it to the hilt
44 Hither's partner
46 Oafs
47 Dynamic prefix
49 ___ voce
52 Actress Van Doren
55 Raises
57 Former Japanese capital
60 Scraps
62 Homme ___ (statesman)
64 Water boy's task
65 Part of E.O.E.
66 Fencing actions
67 Article on a baby that's snatched up by a news anchor?
68 Early trade union
69 Ebro feeder
70 Geometry ending
72 Made, as cotton candy
73 French noble
76 Tinker's target?
78 Theologian's subj.
79 Thrust
81 Tries for a third trial
82 Pop singer Mann
83 A load
85 Iroquois Indian
87 Precincts
92 Magnetic induction unit
93 Big Florida destination
95 Thomas Gray works

by Cathy Millhauser

31

PARDONABLE CRIMES

ACROSS

1 As is proper
6 Left
10 Cornwall town on Falmouth Harbor
15 Like some dinners
19 Scenic walk
20 Flash
21 German composer Carl Maria von ___
22 Something to pay?
23 Publicly disrupting a concerto?
26 Not deceived by
27 Doing counterfeits sculpture?
28 Augurs
29 Edge
32 Blood pigment
33 It's impolite
34 Handles the reception
35 What "I" might indicate
36 Car accessory
38 Informal term of address, in Britain
39 Council honcho
40 Cricket player
42 Valentine figure
45 Catches
48 Asian kingdom
49 Difficulties for wedding planners, maybe
50 Pianist's challenge
52 Actress Skye
53 Lifeboat lowerer
55 Cryer in movies
57 Aim
58 "Last Essays of ___," 1833
59 Thou of thous
60 Animated show on Nickelodeon
61 Utmost
62 Do business
63 Canceling a newsmagazine?
66 Young newts
70 Tocqueville's here

72 Beloved family member
73 A cuppa
74 Kind of drop
75 It's eaten with a cracker
78 Startled cry
79 Mountain in Exodus
81 Meat stew, for short
82 Scriptural elucidations
84 Place to sleep, in Britain
85 Places to sleep
87 Informal letter signoff
88 At no charge
91 Sly coverup
92 Rulers with thrones
94 Rule opposed by Gandhi
95 Appliance maker
97 ___ kwon do
98 Ally in Hollywood
100 Stench
102 Mathematician Turing
103 Company report abbr.
104 Dotty inventor?
105 Pilfering from a fertility lab?
108 Its motto is "Industry"
109 Robbing factory workers?
113 Seized vehicle
114 1948 Literature Nobelist
115 Comics dog
116 Not built-up
117 Sped
118 Indiana's state flower
119 Bit of thatch
120 "The Herne's Egg" playwright

DOWN

1 P.D. broadcast
2 Score that's "saved"
3 Lao-___
4 Table extender
5 1923 earthquake site
6 Flight formation flier
7 Less at ease
8 It's declining in Germany
9 Flavors
10 Like many TV movies
11 Bank amount
12 Sinker
13 Split
14 Internet address ending
15 Gunning down a night traveler?
16 Time of early youth
17 Refit
18 It may reflect well on you
24 Big wool source
25 They have many bends
28 It's heard from the herd
29 Pushed (for)
30 Financially compromised
31 Funnellike flower
34 Woman's shoe with a stiltlike sole
37 Jawbones
39 Municipal bldg.
41 Burglarizing a museum exhibition?
43 Assembled
44 City near Gibraltar
46 Garbage ___
47 Where to set down roots?
49 Depravity
51 Suffix with differ
54 Bon ___
55 Nudge

56 Sailing
60 Bio. evidence
63 Like some lawn displays
64 Sign
65 Fannie or Ginnie follower
67 Lying
68 Attacks on horseback
69 Cut
71 Stick on a table
75 CBS, e.g., slangily
76 Feller
77 Gibbon, for one
79 Irrigation tool
80 Hamlet portrayer, 1996
83 Driver of a four-horse chariot, in myth
84 "Right Place, Wrong Time" singer, 1973
86 Citrus garden
89 Trample
90 Prosperous times, informally
91 Like many Rolls-Royces
93 Suffix on fruit names
96 Trinket stealer
98 Once-popular children's TV character
99 Hailey best seller
100 Page number
101 Hardship
105 Gondolier's need
106 Art class model
107 Swing about
109 Not square
110 "Patriot Games" grp.
111 Critic Hentoff
112 Bygone Manhattan sights

by Patrick Berry

ACROSS

1 Wanderer's words
5 What a writer might do
9 Outcropping
13 Create a solution?
17 Like part of the Arabian peninsula
18 Author Calvino
19 Somewhat, in music
20 Eyelet
21 Mockery, of a sort
22 Geological ridge
23 Insurable item
24 Writer ___ Stanley Gardner
25 Bit of a draft
26 Old-style revolutionary
28 Yarn spinner
30 Tweeted
32 Amuse with words
33 Caroler's syllable
34 That objeto
35 Feminine suffix
36 Like hair on the top of a bald person's head
38 Writes (for)
41 Recess at St. Peter's
43 On drugs
44 Oust
46 Old station wagon, in slang
47 ___ War
50 Ice picker-upper
52 Waikiki wear
54 Not adhering to the subject
57 Buds
59 Ecstasy
63 Vietcong insurgent grp.
64 Give the slip
66 Protect from floods
69 Farm team
70 Fed. budget group

71 Some Amtrak cars
73 Heavy overcoat
75 Telltale sound after "I haven't had a drop to drink"
76 Not this or that, in Spain
78 Gazing hostilely
80 Orchard pest
81 "This ___ test"
82 Contracted cost
84 Teammates
87 Bear hug
90 Black
92 "What ___?"
93 Animal with a black-tipped tail
96 Parts of a personality profile
98 Say "nothin'," say
102 Convenience outlet, often
103 Moons, e.g.
104 High hat
108 Tricky football plays
110 Homme d'___
112 Overseas price add-on
113 Dallas cager, briefly
114 It's dotted
115 Training places?: Abbr.
116 "Later!"
117 Brian of Roxy Music
118 "Later!"
119 Parapet
121 Exiled Roman poet
123 Bashes
125 Kind of boss
127 Country singer McCann
128 It has many slots
129 Clear the boards
130 White oak
131 Firewood carrier
132 Upper hand

DOWN

1 Crows
2 Strike caller
3 James Clavell best seller
4 Public house
5 Prepare to sleep
6 Tie deciders: Abbr.
7 Deadeye Annie
8 1980 Economics Nobelist Lawrence
9 Calculating sort
10 "The Sleeping Gypsy" painter
11 Start to malfunction
12 Get soused
13 "___ Believes in Me"
14 Ruin
15 Maltreated
16 Critical rocket maneuver
27 Actor Morales
29 Sales force
31 Matured
37 Aardvark features
39 Spanish silver dollar
40 Part of a sales force: Abbr.
42 Religious sch.
44 Acapulco article
45 Pull off a complete reversal
47 Parts of samba bands
48 Recently
49 Industry
51 Kind of glasses
53 Arrive, in a sense
55 Beatty of "Deliverance"
56 Pilot
58 Two-time Cotton Bowl winners: Abbr.
60 Like a tough battle
61 Fosters
62 Crate
65 Start of many Italian surnames

67 Hold to a zero score
68 Symbol of Egyptian royalty
72 Angel's favorite letters
74 Vit. info
77 Cabalistic
79 Play direction
83 Sizes up?
85 Type sizes
86 [Make way!]
88 It usually comes in stripes
89 Laugh syllable
91 To now
93 They're hard to make out
94 Occasional paint surface
95 Newsmaking brother of 1903
97 Scoffing retort
99 6-0, in tennis
100 Bizet opera title character
101 Warning to motorists
104 Certain camp
105 Drink
106 Scandal subject
107 Squared
109 Having hangovers?
111 Electronic game pioneer
120 Little fella
122 John ___
124 Pollutant
126 Play form using wooden masks

by Bill Zais and Nancy Salomon

33 REPRESENTATIVE GOVERNMENT

ACROSS

1 Fixes
5 Many a Sri Lankan
10 Herring family members
15 Visibly shaken
19 "By yesterday!"
20 ___ Kane of "All My Children"
21 Former Energy Secretary O'Leary
22 Alpine climber
23 Cooperstown nickname
24 Capital on the Willamette
25 Stripling
27 F.B.I.
30 Poor marks
31 Born abroad
32 Dangerous job
33 Not so new
36 Become less tense
38 Classified ad abbr.
41 Baseball manager Tony La ___
45 N.A.S.A.
49 Sharp feller
50 Cabeza, north of the Pyrenees
51 One way to enter
52 Causes an unearned run, perhaps
53 Pitch makers
57 Vietnamese neighbor
58 Vamp's accessory
60 Blood pressure raiser
61 Like oak leaves
62 Pie cuts, essentially
64 Salvager's gear
66 I.R.S.
72 Kvetches
73 Really enjoy
74 Term
75 Digital clock settings
76 Big belts
79 G.R.E. takers
80 Any of Yalta's Big Three
84 Groks
86 Daytime talk show name
88 Filmmaking family name
89 Prefix with sphere
90 E.P.A.
96 Some may mind this
97 Prefix with fuel
98 Pewter component
99 "___ Unplugged" (1999 album)
100 When it's low, it's good
102 One way to go
103 Flier to J.F.K.
104 U.S.A.F.
113 When printings begin
114 Debussy contemporary
115 Casino tool
117 Act the letch
118 Interviewer, perhaps
119 Kwanzaa principle
120 It's in the eye of the beholder
121 Reagan sentence starter
122 Mortimer Adler's "How to ___ Book"
123 Rose and Rozelle
124 Quits

DOWN

1 "Saturday Night Live" alum Mohr
2 From
3 Travelers in Matthew
4 Record holder
5 Bit of floorwork, maybe
6 Nejd desert dwellers
7 Leon Uris's "___ 18"
8 Clinched
9 Protect, as a document
10 Protect, as a seedling
11 "___ but known . . ."
12 Sea of ___ (Don River's receiver)
13 It may be kosher
14 Runners carry them
15 Paltry
16 First shepherd
17 Zoom, e.g.
18 Something to dial: Abbr.
26 Toyota offering
28 Doing
29 Japanese ___ (popular pet)
33 Like some judgments
34 Place for a checkered career?
35 Strong second?
36 It's hard to live on
37 Rancho units
38 "Dance in the Country" painter
39 Bit of raingear
40 Usher's request
42 Series
43 Buster, old-style
44 Declare
46 "The Dancing Couple" painter
47 Get one's fill
48 Where Regulus is
54 Tar Heel State campus
55 Siberian industrial center
56 Possible result of a sacrifice
57 Wide, to Cicero
59 In harmony
62 Add more ornaments to
63 As a preferred alternative
65 Publicizes, in a way
66 Some are mental
67 Vegetarian's demand
68 Bearded leader
69 "The Westing Game" author Ellen ___
70 Lose a lap?
71 Gain a lap?
77 Hosp. areas
78 Nurses
80 Source of sauce or milk
81 Penny-pinching
82 Dramatic beginning
83 Turndowns
85 Coffeecake topping
87 Yip or yelp
88 Approaches stealthily
91 ___ Gallery of Immortals (Greek pantheon)
92 "Generations of healthy, happy pets" sloganeer
93 Colder spots, often
94 Canute expelled him
95 A can of soda may have one
101 Fix
102 Flummoxed
103 Silk-stockings
104 Basic impulse
105 Hawk
106 Kiln output
107 Pool site, maybe
108 Nut, basically
109 All there
110 Toiling
111 Bring in
112 Cargo platform
113 John McCain, once
116 Sweden's capital?

by Matt Gaffney

G MOVIES

ACROSS

1 La Guardia posting: Abbr.
4 Pool ploy
9 Mosque officials
14 Logan's home
18 Wings
19 Bering Sea hunter
20 Shearer on the screen
21 Mrs. Charles
22 Musical version of "The Corn Is Green"?
25 Lament loudly
26 Like cardinals
27 Dump emanation
28 Port of Vietnam
30 Crown covering
31 Movie about a Mali malady?
34 Score unit
35 Snake, for one
37 Frasier's ex
38 Midlands river
40 Rebellious Turner
41 Pay
44 Pet name
47 Michael Jackson biopic?
50 Start a hole
52 Piece of work
55 Where Zeno taught
56 Latin lesson word
57 "Jennie Gerhardt" author
59 Crossword clue abbr.
60 Get into shape?
61 x
63 Asylum seeker
64 Has the stage
66 Brace
68 Applies, with "on"
70 Arias
71 Between prime and good
73 High land
77 It gets hit on the head
79 Bunch of bills
80 Teriyaki alternative
82 Crosley or Nash
83 "Atomic Leda" painter
84 Yankee insignias
85 Remove marginalia
86 Bitter biblical epic?
90 Ultimate ending
91 Worked the land
92 Got together
93 The Jetsons' dog
97 Sister of Calliope
100 500 spot
101 Take (from)
102 Subtitle of "Elvis: The Army Years"?
106 Quick responses
108 Shoe reinforcement
109 Trigger control
110 Pennsylvania Dutch dish
112 Are, in Argentina
113 Part of the "Stare Trek" series?
117 Caber tosser
118 Sniggled
119 Piece of history
120 Priv. eyes
121 Blockbuster buy
122 Exchange at Wimbledon
123 W.W. II craft
124 Co. founded by Ross Perot

DOWN

1 Property transferor
2 Was behind schedule
3 Colonel's command
4 Martian marking
5 Deplaned
6 Artist Magritte
7 In the open
8 Peak in the Cascades
9 Precious bar
10 Havana's ___ Castle
11 Altar in the sky
12 Famous movie year
13 Beach annoyance
14 Straighten out
15 Documentary about cross-dressing?
16 Concert venue
17 Be undecided
18 Mountaineer's effort
23 "When Will ___ Loved"
24 Dot follower, perhaps
29 "Exodus" character
31 Attend
32 Custard dessert
33 Broadcast
35 McCourt matriarch
36 Traveling gunslinger
39 The folks over there
41 It may jackknife
42 Fall guy?
43 Short-straw drawer
45 Superimpose
46 Sea nymphs of myth
48 Visitor for a justice of the peace
49 Winery sight
50 "Oh, ___ Golden Slippers" (classic tune)
51 Jacob of journalism
52 Expelled tenant
53 Bacon orders
54 Film about a wedding on Everest?
58 Used-car deal
62 Quiet
65 Barely beats
67 Bailiwick
69 Spoiled
72 Introductory words, maybe
74 Whimper
75 Somewhat
76 High ball
78 La Scala star
81 On the other hand
87 "To ___ and a bone . . .": Kipling
88 Potent leader?
89 Crazy prank
91 Old TV series set in Coral Key Park
94 Took a header
95 Little streams
96 Haunt
98 Queen of Hades
99 Blotter letters
100 Shrug off
102 Cavaradossi's lover
103 Synthetic fiber
104 Down on one's luck
105 Morse minimum
106 Set up
107 Kind of wheels
108 Battery component
110 Normandy battle site
111 Pet plant
114 Tony winner Salonga
115 The lot
116 Cal. page

by Richard Silvestri

ACROSS

1 Charge
5 Auricular
9 Feature
14 Environmental hazard, for short
17 "___ grip!"
18 Kind of coil
20 Lickety-split
21 Certain something
22 "My word!"
23 Champion on the ice
26 Perky name?
28 Stone landmark
29 Second edition
30 Many a college teaching assistant
33 ___ Méditerranée
34 Parts of a krona
35 Düsseldorf dessert
36 July 4, e.g.: Abbr.
39 Quatrain scheme
41 A
42 Like the sound "ng"
45 Leave
48 Daisy Fuentes or Carson Daly, once
51 Many a sailor's downfall
52 The Tatler essayist
53 ___ voce
54 One who's up a creek?
55 Affectation
57 British banking name
59 Vibe
60 Pre-calc
63 Crushed
66 Impending
67 Whetstones
69 Response to a doubter
70 G.I. journalist
72 Stemmed
74 Delineated
76 Pursue intently
80 Like improved baby shampoo
81 Las Vegas landmark
83 Whitney Houston's record label
84 Sprays
86 Senate response
87 Perón and namesakes
88 Little dog, for short
89 ___ Aviv
90 Orch. section
91 Nasdaq news, in brief
92 Theater hit of 1878
101 Hesitating
103 Wife of Abram
104 Fit to be tied
106 Red Cross offering
109 Antiquated alpine apparatus
110 Just
111 Pitch
112 "The Far Side" exclamations
113 1965 jazz album
114 Kind of flour
115 Presidential nickname
116 Obsolescent conjunction
117 Bakery offerings

DOWN

1 Work week whoop
2 "The Tortoise and the Hare" writer
3 Draw on a board
4 Cold war warriors
5 Cheri of "S.N.L."
6 140 pounds, in Britain
7 "This ___ test"
8 You've heard it before
9 Sarajevo skiing gold medalist
10 Earth, for the most part
11 Actor Kilmer
12 Legendary skydiver
13 Went sniggling
14 Releases, as a fish
15 Herr's her
16 Today it's managed
19 Not much
21 Org.
24 French corp.
25 Sprawl
27 Drum site
31 Some Algonquians
32 Up to, informally
37 Potemkin Steps city
38 Pitcher Al for the Blue Jays and Mets
39 '50s political inits.
40 N.Y.C. subway letters
41 ___ barrel
42 Makes official
43 Site of the 1973 Riggs/King "Battle of the Sexes"
44 Some Christmas decorations
45 46-Down, to Aphrodite
46 See 45-Down
47 Prominent media member
49 Biblical high priest
50 1984 Redford role Roy ___
51 Hospitalize
54 When doubled, a number
56 Not so naïve
58 1998 World Series star Ricky
60 Mall mainstay
61 The Joker player on '60s TV
62 With absolutely no spark
64 Headed up
65 Miniature
68 Tar
71 Oaf
73 Hatter affair
75 Teeth: Prefix
77 With approval
78 ___ lark
79 They intersect intersections: Abbr.
82 Annual report report
84 Laugh syllable
85 Central Park designer Frederick Law ___
89 1940 Karloff horror flick
90 Kind of column
91 Darin and Dee's "___ Man Answers"
93 Kindergarten game
94 Part of a work week: Abbr.
95 Comb
96 Old
97 Span. 15-Down
98 Aforementioned
99 Worry
100 French equivalent
101 Cpls., e.g.
102 Wine, for starters
105 Big times
107 Free (of)
108 Chemical suffix

by Martin Schneider

36 OH, NO!

ACROSS

1 His last film was "The Night They Raided Minsky's," 1968
5 Work ___
10 Gold bug?
15 Utter a few choice words
19 Part of a C.S.A. signature
20 Rear
21 As ___ resort
22 Squabbling
23 Comedian who has only one-liners?
25 Neighbor of Fiji
26 "Bye!"
27 Do-gooder's quality
28 Instructions for a bottle cap?
31 Dynamited, maybe
32 Neur. readout
34 Office squawker
35 Walkman batteries
37 Beguilement
39 Cut out
43 Where many allowances come from?
50 Like rail vis-à-vis air
51 Diminutive suffix
52 Gauche
53 South Africa's ___ Paul Kruger
55 "ER" actor
56 Rent
58 "That's a ___!"
59 Sandbags, often
63 Shepherd's locale
64 Premature
66 Silver-tongued TV newsman?
68 Duchamp's "Mona Lisa," e.g.
69 Gold braid

70 Together, in music
71 Very cold draft?
75 Washington display
79 Clear
80 Takes
81 Basketful
82 Who's minding the baby, maybe
83 '60s TV boy
85 It has many benefits: Abbr.
86 New Zealand minority
88 Remote target
89 Ranch wear
92 Exoneration for a group of actors?
96 Rampaging
98 "Uh-uh"
99 Row producer
100 Not this again!
103 Alternative to a Maxwell
106 Adventurer's stock
110 Like Erato when writing poetry?
114 Garrison Keillor specialty
116 Feodor I, e.g.
117 1920s–'30s film star Conrad
118 What many pitched baseballs do?
120 ___ many words
121 "Half ___ is better . . ."
122 In a tough position
123 ___ v. United States (classic Supreme Court obscenity case)
124 Weak poker hand
125 Coppers
126 Gobs
127 Not a good sound for a balloonist

DOWN

1 Bygone Renault
2 "Be-Bop-___" (Gene Vincent hit)
3 Budget alternative
4 Unimaginative sequel, say
5 ". . . ___ saw Elba"
6 Café cup
7 Casino request
8 British verb ending
9 Dick Francis book "Dead ___"
10 Theatergoer's choice
11 Johnny Mercer's "___ My Sugar in Salt Lake City"
12 "La vita nuova" poet
13 Home of the Norse gods
14 Positions
15 Living end
16 Golden Spike locale
17 In ___ (as found)
18 "Immediately"
24 Like the laws of kosher food
29 Well product?
30 Dreamboat
33 See
36 Stranded on a mountain, say
38 Sporty truck, for short
40 First name in modern dance
41 Certain fishermen
42 The willies
43 Japanese fish delicacy
44 ___ Bator
45 Crane site
46 Daisy chains
47 Scuffle
48 Free restaurant serving
49 Exclusive

54 Infamous traitor
57 Mask
59 Scams but good
60 Touched ground
61 Baked beans, e.g.
62 Threaded metal fastener
65 London streets, in a manner of speaking
66 Hors d'oeuvre topper
67 "___ the lookout!"
69 Big name in book clubs
71 "The Lord of the Rings" hero
72 Flower
73 Patsy's "Absolutely Fabulous" pal
74 Heavy blow
75 Origin
76 Four-star
77 Holder of ancient riches
78 "It Must Be Him" singer, 1967
81 ___-guided
84 "Take your pick"
86 Plan (out)
87 Nix
90 Satisfy
91 New York's ___ Lakes
93 Swallows up
94 Engages in baby talk
95 Heads
97 Antique shop deal
101 Part of a train
102 "Let ___ Cake"
104 Stand for a portrait
105 Word go
107 Chihuahua canines
108 ___-Unis
109 Actor Green and others

by Nelson Hardy

110 Canal cleaner
111 Annapolis sch.
112 Former capital
of Romania
113 Stretcher
carriers, briefly
115 Sked figures
119 Playwright
Levin

ACROSS

1 Place to change
7 Film festival site
13 Powerful cliques
19 Cottonwood trees
20 Cousin of a meadowlark
21 Feminine
22 Some bomb squad members
23 Lunar craft
24 Moved with a davit
25 Start of a quote
28 Home to many Swiss banks
29 "___ Little Tenderness"
30 Nautical ropes
31 Istanbul currency
33 Leader of a flock
36 Itch cause, perhaps
40 Tore
44 Quote, part 2
48 "L'chaim," literally
50 1943 conference site
51 They're taken in punishment
52 Historian Durant
53 Elroy's pooch
54 Member of a sting operation?
58 Gentlemanly reply
60 Accelerator bit
61 Visits from Carry Nation
62 Atlanta-to-Miami dir.
63 & 65 Irish writer and author of the quote
67 Legal ending
70 Gap
72 Venue for the Blues Brothers, for short
73 Music shop fixtures
76 Checkers masters
80 Patricia of "Betrayal"
82 They sit near the violas
83 Two-handed lunches
84 One who's not out of bounds?
86 Nervous ___
87 Quote, part 3
92 One, in Köln
93 Jeanne d'Arc et al.: Abbr.
94 Cockeyed
95 Saddlery needs
97 Aligned
98 Stiff bristle
100 Allegro ___ (very fast)
105 End of the quote
111 Like some elephants
113 Environs
114 Runoff spot
115 In progress
116 Like meringue
117 Sites for fights
118 Book of Changes
119 Least hale
120 Sire, e.g.

DOWN

1 West Indies language
2 Wahine's welcome
3 Cakes with kicks
4 "Don't make ___!"
5 ___ motel (tryst site)
6 Part of N.A.A.C.P.: Abbr.
7 Pigments
8 Sheikdom of song
9 Stealth warrior
10 Network terminal
11 T.V.A. product
12 Muralist José María ___
13 End users?
14 Wacky
15 Ramadan observance
16 Captivated by
17 Partner of steak
18 Lead role on TV's "Providence"
21 ". . . it's ___ know"
26 Not esto or eso
27 Put ___ (ask a hard question)
32 Project conclusion?
33 LuPone role
34 Oklahoma county seat
35 Scuttle
36 Makes fuzzy
37 Prosodic foot
38 Play a key role?
39 Caesar's existence
40 Doesn't fold
41 Pumice features
42 Name in a Beethoven opus
43 Vietnam's Ngo Dinh ___
45 Gain entry
46 Beat, as the heart
47 Entreated
49 Marco Isl.'s locale
53 British Petroleum acquisition
55 Something to cash in: Abbr.
56 Tilter's need
57 Emulated Ananias
59 Comet competitor
64 Biddy
65 Big name in book publishing
66 Venerable one
67 Gastroenteritis cause
68 Knitter's buy
69 Test track features
70 Winter blankets?
71 Council city of 1409
72 Ten Commandments word
74 Beluga yield
75 Skilled
76 Michael Moore's "Downsize ___!"
77 Gun, slangily
78 Colleague of Dashiell
79 Horde
81 Matriarchal figure
85 Really big shoe?
86 Vezina Trophy org.
88 Serving up whoppers
89 Floodgate
90 Whooshed
91 Smack
96 Most of Libya
97 Grand name
98 Place for hospitality
99 They're pointless
101 Break off
102 Île de la Cité locale
103 The U.N.'s Kofi ___
104 Clarification preceder
105 Attached to
106 "___ known then . . ."
107 Prefix with valence
108 Actor Martin of "Hill Street Blues"
109 Carrier to Ben-Gurion
110 Kind of door
111 Violinist Kavafian
112 Rare polit. designation

by Elizabeth C. Gorski

ACROSS

1 Swiss Mrs., maybe
5 Comparable to a wet hen
10 They're developed by rowing
14 Whip
18 O.K. Corral fighter
19 Get a rise out of?
21 Town on the Vire
22 Nestlé pet food brand
23 1983 movie cause of heartburn?
25 With 119-Across, country lunch customer of song?
27 Ruhr industrial hub
28 Baldwin, Guinness, etc.
30 Clinch
31 Sweet barbarian?
35 Bee's target on a flower
38 First name in architecture
39 Fleece
43 System starter
44 "Ta-ta"
46 MTV hosts
48 Whaler, for one
50 Fast-food snack?
56 River connected by canal to the Volga
57 Movie dog
58 Vegetable fats
59 Weirdos
61 Greek penultimates
65 Wayside stop
66 Hindu melody pattern
67 ___-com
68 Be a klutzy chef?
75 Globetrotters founder Saperstein
76 Past
77 Past
78 Peak of myth
79 Do a kabob job
81 "Dilbert" creator Adams
83 Iona College player
87 Jot
88 Won't fit, as a sash?
93 Place for Cicero
95 Double header?
96 Early Irish assembly site
97 Certain win, for short
98 Explorer Bering was one
99 Gave the slip
102 Satirize
104 Risk getting clawed?
110 Girlish
114 Strainer
115 Additional
119 See 25-Across
121 Midwest native American on TV?
124 "You Bet Your Life" sponsor De ___
125 Game-ending declaration
126 TV's ___ Lee
127 Giant chemicals corporation
128 Kind of leopard or goose
129 Offshore
130 Predilection
131 Hourglass part

DOWN

1 Luau, e.g.
2 Stands roars
3 God seen on "Xena: Warrior Princess"
4 Cheery
5 H.S. subject
6 Dry, in Versailles
7 Taj ___
8 St. Teresa's home
9 Cut
10 L.A. sked abbr.
11 People: Prefix
12 Drug-free
13 Swedish mezzo Anne ___ von Otter
14 Robert Burns was one
15 "Blondie" boy
16 Gush
17 Conflicted
20 Recess
24 Solid
26 One of the King Sisters of '40s music
29 Electronic control systems
32 Andrews Sisters, e.g.
33 Month after Nisan
34 Chain hotel, for short
35 Layer's lair
36 Unoriginal reply
37 Crotchety one
40 Actress Wood of "Diamonds Are Forever"
41 Mrs. Marcos
42 Conditioned reflex researcher
45 Pope Urban II, originally
47 Culottelike garment
48 Papyrus and such
49 Vile
51 Weapon in the game Clue
52 Film director Petri
53 City near Mt. Rose ski area
54 Get ahold of
55 Gem State
60 They may be checked
62 Presently
63 Trespass on
64 Take care of
68 Islamic militant group
69 Let up
70 "Romeo and Juliet" setting
71 Let out
72 Borodin title prince
73 "Forget it, Little Red Hen!"
74 Spread unchecked
80 Somalian model-turned-actress
81 Priers
82 Part of amatol
84 Like Woody Herman's sax
85 Town ENE of 53-Down
86 Where the Rhone and the Saône meet
89 George Ade's "The Sultan of ___"
90 The Oscars, e.g.
91 Graceful galloper
92 Cane material
94 It may be made of buffalo skins
100 Cane, e.g.
101 It may be passed
103 Beast that Apollo slew
105 Forster subject
106 Miss Marple finds them
107 Novelist ___ Tennant
108 1996 Madonna role
109 PC troubleshooters, for short
110 Overlook
111 Presently
112 The Eagles' "Take ___ the Limit"
113 Indian Ocean vessel
116 Burrow
117 Like "Star Wars"
118 Place to go for a spin
120 "___ minute"
122 Islet
123 "That's news to me!"

by Cathy Millhauser

39 RARE BIRDS

ACROSS

1 Drams
5 Step on it!
10 Anjou alternative
14 Acted like a baby
19 Flu source
20 ___ legomenon (word that appears only once in a manuscript)
21 ". . . ___ dust shalt thou return"
22 "Step on it!"
23 Bird with a devoted following?
26 "___ of Winter" (1992 Eric Rohmer film)
27 Endures abuse
28 Cowardly bird?
30 Not taboo
32 Word in alumni notes
33 Kind of flute
34 What's place, in a comedy routine
36 Howls
38 Masterful
42 Paradigm of easiness
44 ___ polloi
45 Nasty fall?
47 Be extremely expectant
48 Zapping
52 Bird barber?
56 ___ Smith
57 Climb
58 Exchanged items, maybe
59 Look up to
60 Carson National Forest locale
61 They may be left hanging
63 Creature mentioned by Marco Polo
66 It's in 19-Across
67 Embarrassed bird?
70 Tony winner Neuwirth
71 Letters that please 42-Down
72 Six-time Super Bowl coach
73 Stand for
74 Part of many a disguise
76 Fabric finish?
77 "Death in Venice" author
78 They use horseshoe crabs as bait
79 Bird with a severe drinking problem?
85 Swear by
86 Mt. Apo's locale, in the Philippines
87 Piecrust ingredient
88 Cologne cubes?
90 Bambi's aunt
91 Quarterback Humphries
92 Make out
94 Ravel wrote a piano concerto for it
98 1995 British Open winner John
100 You might say it when you get it
102 1954 Edgar Award winner
105 Celebratory bird?
111 "Steps in Time" autobiographer
112 1938 hit "I ___ Anyone Till You"
113 Bird on the links?
115 Moon of Uranus
116 "Women and Love" author
117 Library lack
118 Like some ears and elbows
119 '70s–'80s sitcom title role
120 Breeze (through)
121 Like wheat and barley
122 Show wild instability

DOWN

1 It took effect on Jan. 1, 1994
2 Father of biblical twins
3 Healthy-looking bird?
4 It has a lustrous face
5 Certain Muslim
6 Jet Propulsion Laboratory site
7 It has long arms
8 Dance partner
9 Lay out
10 Base caller
11 Clock or cat preceder
12 Pack
13 "The Private Eyes" co-star
14 Perot prop
15 Some boat motors
16 Kind of testimony
17 Perry's progenitor
18 Unnatural blonde, e.g.
24 Slithering strikers
25 Land in un lac
29 Golfer Geiberger and others
31 "In" place
35 Honeymoon haven
36 47-Across catcher
37 Sports Illustrated's 1974 Sportsman of the Year
39 Part of a vamp's costume
40 First Lady before Eleanor
41 Pliable leather
42 Backers
43 Tuition check taker
45 Domestic
46 "Der Blaue Reiter" artist
47 Studies
49 Poet Sor Juana ___ de la Cruz
50 Navigation abbr.
51 Sneaker
53 Branch of sci.
54 French orphan of film
55 "Once in Love With Amy" songwriter
60 1960 chess champion
61 Wedding planner
62 Arab name part
63 Bird on a night flight?
64 Moon of Uranus
65 Plane producer Clyde
68 Rain drain locale
69 Cherokee Natl. Forest locale
70 Wax unit?
72 Town on the Vire
75 Bit of a bray
76 Like some warehouses
77 Producer: Abbr.
79 Drilling expert: Abbr.
80 Horse bit
81 Charlottesville sch.
82 Yodeler's place
83 Bit of hope
84 Audiophile's purchase
89 Bonn boulevard
92 Father of Phinehas
93 Harmonizes, briefly
94 Cause of weird weather
95 Fastened, in a way
96 Cruz ___, Brazil
97 In the neighborhood
99 Felicitously
100 Adrien of skin care products

BAD clue
DNF

by Nancy Scandrett Ross

101 W.W. II general
    ___ Arnold
103 Often-missed
    humor
104 Not yet
    familiar with
105 "Kapow!"
106 Kumar of "The
    Jewel in the Crown"

107 His horse had
    eight legs
108 Karmann ___
    (car)
109 Big prefix in
    banking
110 Sufficient, once
114 Alexander
    ingredient

ACROSS

1 They're stuffed in delis
6 Train
11 Kids' game
19 Jiggers?
20 Uncertain
21 Like pigs' feet
22 Julia Roberts/Hugh Grant film
24 Best-selling 1969 album
25 Willa Cather heroine
26 John, Paul and George: Abbr.
27 Part of U.N.L.V.
28 Like 47-Down's bubbles
29 Kay Kyser's "___ Reveille"
30 He was Plato in "Rebel Without a Cause"
31 Emphatic type: Abbr.
33 Electrify
35 Sneaks one past
37 Radar gun wielder
39 Where Eliza Doolittle met Henry Higgins
45 Imagined
48 Dispositions
49 Have ___ at
50 Marmalade-loving bear
54 Rama VII's domain
55 Gastronomic capital of France
56 ___ artery
57 At another time
59 Split
61 Refreshment stands
63 Köln's river
65 ___ four
66 Organ with a drum in it
67 Theme of this puzzle
70 ___ Mochis, Mexico
73 Restaurant stack
74 Sinner's motivator?
75 "Fiddler on the Roof" setting
77 Eyeballed
80 Adventure
81 Sound
82 Felt bad about
83 Counterfeiters' nemeses
86 "Upstairs, Downstairs" setting
89 "Fables in Slang" author
90 Semi drivers?
93 Hardly hardworking
94 Coarsely abusive language
97 Censor's subject
98 Spot for a parade
102 Nev. neighbor
103 Tel ___-Jaffa
104 Not in the strike zone, maybe
106 Jeff Lynne's grp.
107 Exemplar of grace
110 Tire trapper
112 Change pocket
114 Capacitates
116 "___ Blues" (1924 Paul Whiteman hit)
119 British press, figuratively
121 Like some discussions
122 Party, e.g.
123 Needing kneading?
124 Certain bike
125 Friday's creator
126 Full

DOWN

1 It's hung and beaten
2 Unexpected, in a way
3 Jot
4 Re
5 They may need guards
6 Come too
7 Shakespearean ending
8 Tag line
9 Bird, once
10 One-named fashion designer
11 Sunscreen ingredient
12 Finance workers, for short
13 One up, e.g.
14 In-case connector
15 SALT II signer
16 Yours, in Tours
17 New Jersey's ___ University
18 Countercurrent
21 Polo clubs
23 Pellagra preventer
32 She married Mickey
33 Fellow students, e.g.
34 Breathed
36 They're kept behind bars
38 Hoisting devices?
40 "Mahalo ___ loa" ("Thank you very much," in Maui)
41 Go places
42 Harry Belafonte song phrase
43 Swelled heads
44 What one little piggy had
46 Like pigs' feet
47 Island entertainer
50 Peak discoverer
51 Inter ___
52 French Christian
53 Incessantly
55 Decision-making method
58 "The Nanny" butler
60 Fender benders, e.g.
62 Short composition
64 Star bursts
65 Chefs aim to please them
68 Mace source
69 Post-delivery handout
70 Mother of Helen
71 Of the 66-Across
72 ___-eyed
73 Kind of student
76 University of ___ (the Golden Hurricane)
77 Excite, slangily
78 Quattro or Cabriolet
79 Striptease
84 Track challenge
85 Reversed
87 High-cholesterol concoction
88 Former first family
90 Pulled off
91 John
92 Didn't tip
95 Department store section
96 Develop
99 Soften
100 Comic John
101 Made introductions, maybe
105 Power statistic
107 Place on the schedule
108 Film editing effect
109 Grace period?
110 Ill-bred
111 Reconditioned, e.g.
113 Kick
115 Spanish tar
117 Drillmaster's word
118 Murder ___
120 Bowie collaborator

by Nancy Nicholson Joline

41 "SUB" TITLES

ACROSS

1 Plantation workers
7 Where Renata Scotto debuted
14 Like some eggs
21 Heartthrob's fan
22 Call up, as reservists
24 Having missed the boat?
25 "Goose Feathers of Monte Cristo" by Alexandre Dumas
27 Cook's collection
28 Finger ___
29 Many millennia
30 Company
32 Traffic director
33 Wallet fill
34 Accounting acronym
35 "Exodus" hero
36 Chocolate treat
38 J.F.K. regulators
41 More than zero
42 Soybean paste
43 "Liberate My Sons" by Arthur Miller
46 Two-time Smythe Trophy winner
47 Never, in Nürnberg
48 Blanket
50 Bikini, e.g.
51 Urban bell site
52 Unruffled
54 Filmdom's Mr. Chips
56 Grimace
57 Remain unmoved
58 ___ Gatos, Calif.
59 Hydrolysis atom
60 Iroquois foes
62 Old potentate
63 Horrible one
66 Printers' problems
68 Stay glued to
71 Busby Berkeley's real last name
72 Actress Archer
73 Steve Martin's "All ___"

74 In working order
75 Carnival city
76 Papal hat
77 Whoop-de-___
78 Munchkin
79 Loop loopers
80 Veteran
82 Milky Way maker
83 Classic cars
84 "From where ___ . . ."
85 Mudslinger
86 Having the upper hand
88 Bohemian
89 Newspaper page
90 Hall-of-Famer born in Panama
91 System starter
92 Grp. making case studies?
93 Reduces
95 Wise guys
96 Edmonton skater
98 Hit the tarmac
102 Produce protection
103 Singer Neville
104 Stewart and Washington
106 Siam suffix
107 Acapulco gold
108 "The Leap Luck Club" by Amy Tan
111 ___ free
112 Geom. point
113 Lovey
114 "Oh, uh-huh"
115 Suffix with ball or bass
116 Wine combiner
117 O'Hara estate
118 Publisher Henry
120 Jamaican sectarian
123 Hendrix hairdo
124 Mexican art
125 Cheapskate
128 "The Second Gratitude" by Walker Percy
131 Earnest

132 Oldest permanent settlement in Ohio
133 Right, in a way
134 Steamed
135 Natural tint source
136 Joined

DOWN

1 Bankers' errors
2 "Oklahoma!" girl
3 Not flashy
4 Marine eagles
5 Makes the calls
6 B.O. sign
7 "Tardy at Eight" by George S. Kaufman
8 It's said with a snap of the head
9 Tommy gun
10 Pres. Obama, to the Joint Chiefs
11 "___ santé"
12 Emmy-winning actress Metcalf
13 26 for Fe: Abbr.
14 ___ favor
15 Amoeba feature
16 Comparable to a cucumber
17 Gab
18 "Aspiration Man" by Gore Vidal
19 Previous to
20 ___ Plaines
23 D.D.E.'s oversight, once
26 Grow, in a way
31 Leaky
34 Feline ennead
35 Neck of the woods
37 Breathing sound
39 Riyadh resident
40 Host
42 D.M.V. part
43 Mickey and Huck
44 Woe of Genesis 12:10
45 Siouan tribesmen

49 Dazzling eyeful
51 Miss America accessory
53 Word of regret
55 "The Pekoe Towers" by J. R. R. Tolkien
57 Percentage
61 Full of chinks
62 Holds back
63 King of Judea
64 Old-womanish
65 "Much Ado About Virtue" by William Shakespeare
66 Bury
67 So far
68 Parody
69 "___ well"
70 Cross
72 Pointed
74 "An Individual Not Taken" by Robert Frost
76 Street performers
78 Food processor
81 Not live
82 Spanish wool
84 Locale for 1999 solar eclipse watchers
86 ___ tricks
87 Track event
88 Put down
90 Nag
92 Budget rival
93 Stage piece
94 Frigid finish
95 "If He Walked Into My Life" musical
97 "___ a roll!"
99 Going to seed
100 Put off
101 Nuts
103 Spartan
105 Pay tribute to
108 "Dear John" letter writer
109 Community club
110 Erin Moran TV role

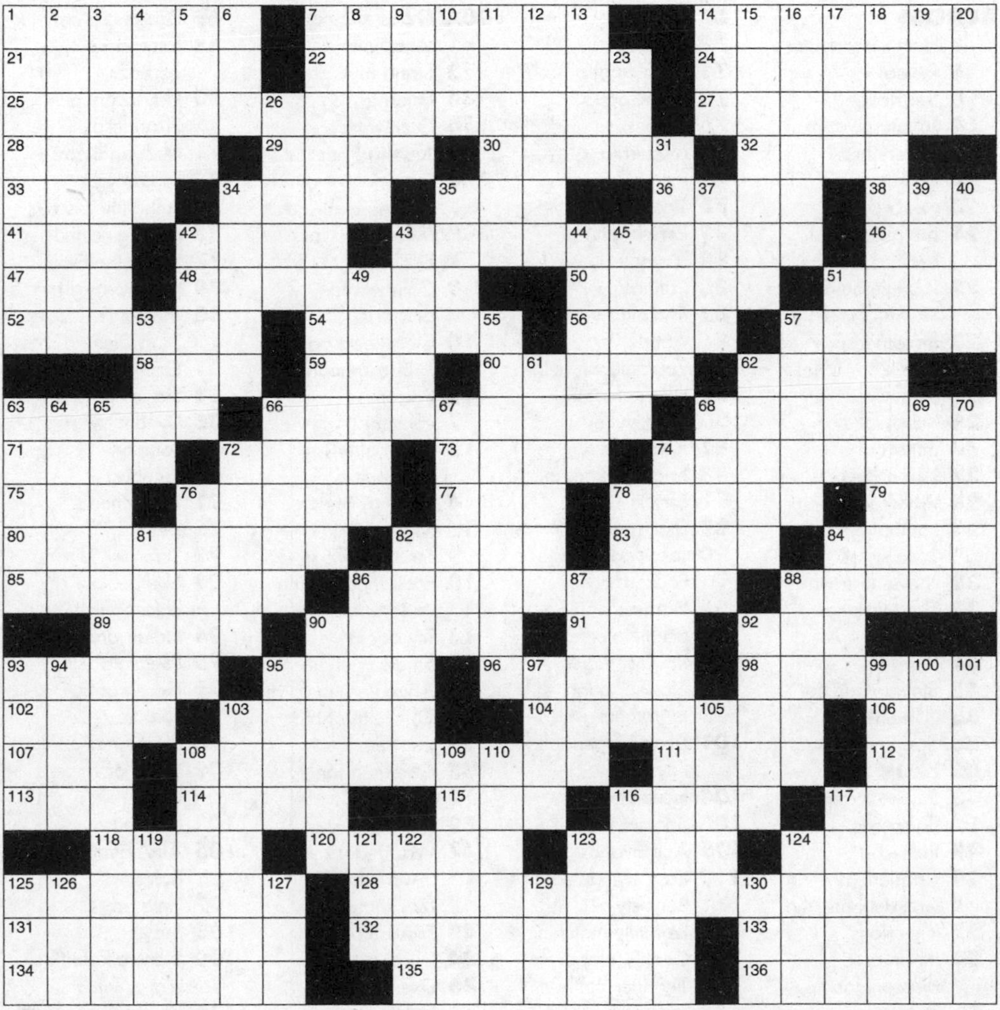

by Randolph Ross

116 ___ the races
117 Circus performer
119 Fairy tale start
121 Banking convenience
122 Roe source
123 About
124 Bring to tears
125 Nine-digit no. issuer
126 Word before ear or horn
127 Embarrassed
129 ___ Gardens
130 Vietnam's ___ Ranh Bay

No Holds Bard

ACROSS

1 Morse code bits
5 Reveals
10 Legislation
14 Toughie
19 Israel's first U.N. representative
20 ___-Lodge
21 No quick trip around the block
22 ___ Kristen of "Ryan's Hope"
23 Increased pay rate, Bard-style?
25 Angry reaction
26 Your place or mine
27 Like some guesses
28 20th-century combat, Bard-style?
31 Move, in a way
32 The Mustangs of the N.C.A.A.
34 Ride, so to speak
35 Stew ingredient
36 "Uh-uh!"
38 Spring times
40 Legit
43 Empathic remark, Bard-style?
47 Inched
49 Charles who was dubbed "the Victorious"
50 Abbr. on a discount label
51 Auto purveyor, Bard-style?
57 Pulver's rank, in film: Abbr.
58 Pack away
59 Synchronous
60 Heiress, perhaps
61 Sales people
63 Kicked off
65 It may fill a lib. shelf
66 "Kramer vs. Kramer" director Robert

67 Hunks
69 Bamboozles
71 Card combo
73 Travel agt.'s suggestion
75 Moderator's milieu
76 Time to act
79 Person with a day
80 Rating giver
82 Eshkol once led it: Abbr.
84 Zoological mouths
85 Hierarchy, Bard-style?
87 First word?
88 Knock the socks off
89 Marner's creator
90 Takes advantage of, Bard-style?
94 Harness ring
97 Scuffle memento
99 Rocker Nugent
100 Black and tan ingredient
101 Like Chippendale furniture
104 Hunter's quarry
106 Book of the Apocrypha
110 Easy schedule, Bard-style?
114 Perfectly matching
116 Capt.'s inferior
117 Two-liter bottle contents
118 Miserly, Bard-style?
120 1973 Rolling Stones hit
121 "Be that ___ may . . ."
122 Customers: Abbr.
123 N.Y.P.D. employee
124 Spring purchase
125 France's Coty
126 Titter
127 Informal shirts

DOWN

1 Ward off
2 Stand for
3 Overplay
4 Carnival treat
5 Tuckered out
6 Stuntmen's woes
7 Folding challenge
8 Military E-1 or E-2, e.g.
9 Convertible, perhaps
10 Of a heart part
11 Public announcers
12 Edison contemporary
13 Manipulates, as data
14 Loading site
15 Minnesota's St. ___ College
16 Six-winged being
17 Access
18 Try again
24 Singer Merchant
29 Animals with calves
30 Opposite of bid
33 ___ tree
37 Qualified for the job
39 Age
41 Warmed up the crowd
42 Like some glass
43 "Your turn"
44 Durable wood
45 Like many Harlemites
46 Soviet co-op
47 Kind of block
48 Contemptible newspaper
52 Density symbol, in mechanics
53 Attached, in a way
54 Forsakes
55 Prefix with system
56 Half a cartoon duo
59 Summon up
62 Fore-and-aft sail
64 Balzac's Père ___

66 Puts in a blue funk
68 Pie chart section, perhaps
70 Playwright Pirandello
71 Medicinal amt.
72 ___ de vie
74 Antiquity, once
75 Having no master
77 Slangy suffix
78 [bo-o-o-ring!]
80 Vietnam's ___ Dinh Diem
81 Combat zone
83 Stone name
86 Dynamite component, for short
91 "Sprechen ___ Deutsch?"
92 Dab
93 Skelton catchphrase
94 Indian drums
95 "Seinfeld" role
96 Goren gaffe
97 "No ___!"
98 Sharpened
102 Prize for Page or Cage
103 Embraced
105 All-American name
107 Held up
108 Busy
109 Sidewalk Santas, e.g.
111 Pound, in Piccadilly
112 Versatile vehicles
113 "Now!"
115 In ___ (actually)
119 Break the ___

by Fred Piscop

ACROSS

1 Out
7 Greeting from Pooh
12 Accumulation
17 Ventilating slat
18 Neighbor of Turkey
21 ___ Belt (constellation feature)
23 Good fight, in old Rome?
25 Teller of secrets, in a saying
26 Hockey's Mikita
27 Diplomatic trait
28 Smash really bad
30 They give sum help?
31 Costing a fish two fins?
34 Anesthetic, once
38 Hotel room fixtures, for short
39 He hides in kids' books
40 Taken ___
41 This, to Luis
43 Gumption
45 Classic prefix
48 "Oops!" to a paramecium?
51 Trunk with a chest
52 Author O'Brien
53 Digs of twigs
54 Regarding
55 The Flintstones' pet
56 Holiday music
57 Biblical food fight?
59 Know-it-all
62 "Tom Jones" script writer John ___
66 Fix firmly
68 Basic shelters
69 World's longest wooden roller coaster, located in Cincinnati
71 What a citizen like Galileo had?
73 Did lining
74 Feature of some winds
76 Express regret
77 Squire
81 Word on some Procter & Gamble lotions
82 He "spoke" for Bergen
84 Cutups at a record company?
86 Parked oneself
87 Fixes firmly
88 "The other white meat"
89 Certain thallophytes
90 Seed scar
92 Whack
93 Rescuers
95 Cadillac driven by Monica's interviewer?
101 Covered for court
102 Hightail it
103 One's own, for a starter
104 Unprofessional, slangily
108 Edgar and Hugo, e.g.
110 Unusual brass polish?
113 Social surroundings
114 Coastal town crier
115 Parenthetical lines
116 Twisty-horned antelope
117 Some stars
118 Ones sticking their necks out to entertain?

DOWN

1 Celebrants' wear
2 Grate stuff
3 Selene's counterpart
4 Hunter a k a Ed McBain
5 U.S. trading partner, formerly
6 A hydrogen atom has one
7 Get cracking, in a way
8 Mountain crest
9 K–O filler
10 Moolah
11 Whopper toppers
12 Cry with catches
13 Subject to court proceedings
14 1997 basketball film
15 Musicians' behavior, in the end?
16 New York hoopster
19 Speck
20 Pre-med course: Abbr.
22 Cinco follower
24 Celtics' Archibald
29 Olympics athlete Carl
31 Polynesian carving
32 British poet laureate Nahum
33 Prefix with second
34 Songwriter Sammy
35 Shawm descendant
36 Raven sounds
37 C.D., for one
41 Deserve
42 Slide specimen
43 Word ending many company names
44 Stem
46 When Plácido Domingo was born
47 Welcome sites
49 Tropical vine
50 Laura who played Dr. Weaver on "ER"
51 Quartet on a Quattro
52 Verve
55 Saul's successor
56 Indian valuable
57 He was more than a neigh-sayer
58 Dried, maybe
60 Of a pelvic bone
61 Cathartic drug
62 Others at the Alhambra
63 N.F.L. coach Don
64 An obese Lugosi?
65 Mind
67 Animal handler
70 Lemur's hangout
72 Imitation
75 Voiced pauses
77 Java neighbor
78 "Tantum ___" (part of a Eucharist hymn)
79 Purim's month
80 Applications
82 Aspersion
83 Ices, perhaps
84 Know-nothing
85 "B.C." abode
87 Cheer
88 It's saved by e-mail
91 James Michener narrative
92 Thick-trunked tree
93 Skirt feature
94 Ho's hi's
95 Streetcar
96 Mandel of "St. Elsewhere"
97 Takes steps
98 Libertine
99 String quartet member
100 Teen faves
104 Entice
105 Abbr. on egg cartons
106 Spin tail?
107 Pianist Dame Myra
109 Nord's opposite
111 Scolding syllable
112 Phenomenon such as ESP

by Cathy Millhauser

44   JUST TRY ME!

ACROSS

1 1957 Literature Nobelist
6 A milk drinker may have one
14 Booms
19 There may be a spat about it
23 Brimming
24 Six-liter bottle
25 Dickensian schemer
26 Vandals
27 Smiling reporters from earthquake sites?
29 Russian roulette and chicken?
31 Branch
32 Grig's digs
33 Union agreements?
35 Gerry Adams's org.
36 Lord of the East
37 Title woman of a 1962 Roy Orbison hit
39 Hot
40 It's best when it's broken
42 Buoyant
44 Moore of old TV game shows
46 Oprah in "The Color Purple"
49 Sun follower?
50 Take control of
51 Expecting
53 Oval home
55 Affixes
57 Drips drops
58 Sperm banks?
62 "Vissi d'arte" singer
66 Parting words
67 Pulitzer poet Dugan
68 Change a letter, perhaps
69 One who delivers on campus
70 Bubbly entertainer?
71 Wingdings
73 Winner in 1967: Abbr.
74 "Long," in Hawaiian
76 Donkey's years
77 Calypso instrument
79 Tangles
81 Kind of special

83 "Jabberwocky" word
84 Summer house?
85 Silver spur, so to speak
86 Gershwin's first hit
87 "Sleepy Time Gal" lyricist Raymond
88 Senselessness?
91 What fueled Macbeth?
96 Endangered state bird
97 Epiphanies
98 Oscar-winning "Nashville" tune
99 Put in stitches
100 Meal starter
102 Breed
103 Expert in martial arts
104 Series ender
105 1979 James Bond movie
111 Rapprochement
112 Pres. who once coached Yale football
113 Dopey picture?
115 Watch in astonishment
117 Private line
118 It flowered during the reign of Louis XV
120 Controversial school subject
123 "How to Murder Your Wife" star
124 Bearcat
125 "My Friend Flicka" author
126 Cat's reaction to a vet shot?
128 Chilly
129 Marquand sleuth
131 Expire
132 Quarters, say
133 Entered
136 Words of dedication
138 Triumphant
140 Trailer
141 "Across" or "Down," in a crossword
142 Object of advances?
144 First name in old westerns
146 Nonkosher sandwiches
149 Rock blaster

150 Stud ___
151 Cough (up)
152 Coming from both sides
154 Rossini's "Count ___"
155 "The Last Supper," e.g.?
158 Handwriting on the wall for Mark McGwire?
163 Popular New Age singer
164 "Dumb & Dumber" destination
165 Prepare to take off
166 Stabber
167 River Kwai locale
168 Pad paper?
169 Broadcasters
170 Buttinsky

DOWN

1 Intrigue
2 Plugged in
3 Publication since 1952
4 R.M.N. and J.F.K. were once in it
5 ___-wolf
6 Stephen King white-knuckler
7 Like 25-Across
8 Careers
9 Career
10 General assembly?
11 French business abbr.
12 Laugh sound
13 Holmes's Miss Venner
14 There's an arrow in its logo
15 Introduced
16 Basketball center
17 Fills with joy
18 Support for Hillary
19 "___ La La" (Manfred Mann hit)
20 Kind
21 Where to walk very carefully
22 Bacon bits?
28 Off-the-wall
30 Infamous Spanish collar
34 Low beams
38 Finish treating the puppies?

40 Ornamental stone
41 Herman Wouk's Youngblood ___
43 Like a young sheep that avoids wet pavement?
45 Browned in deep fat
47 Runner who was called "The Buckeye Bullet"
48 Worthy
51 They may be dry or baked
52 Hardly a symbol of spontaneity
54 Patronage
56 "The Quiet Man" setting
58 "Young Frankenstein" actress
59 N.L. batting champ of 1966
60 Webb address?
61 Pleasant place to drive
63 Second banana
64 Scam artist
65 First name in detective fiction
69 Another time
72 Meandering
75 It's often twisted apart
78 It precedes lunes
80 Hike
82 Cavernous opening
85 Flips out
86 "The Guns of Navarone" actress
88 Subject of a 1986 Tad Szulc biography
89 Words repeated by Jolson and Cantor
90 Rattle
92 Foreign prince
93 Basket elevation
94 Uris book, with "The"
95 Terrace surface, perhaps
101 Fox relative
104 Root of diplomacy
105 Bergman's last role
106 Brewer's aid
107 Cole Porter miss
108 Wise man
109 "Frasier" dog
110 Makes out

by Bob and Sharon Klahn

114 Potential prizewinner
116 1930 discovery
119 University of Wales site
121 Producers of tieups at work?
122 Indian craft
126 Cobra killers: Var.
127 It's heard at a snap
130 Children's game classification
132 He played the Wiz in "The Wiz"
133 View at the Tate Gallery
134 Mocha inhabitant
135 Melon tree
137 Whom Paris left for Helen
139 On the double
140 Spruces up
143 Leave one's coach
145 "What the Butler Saw" dramatist
147 E. C. Bentley detective
148 "Playboy of the Western World" playwright
152 Blue books
153 "Jour de Fête" star
156 Beat it
157 Losing ground?
159 Hill dweller
160 TV Guide notation
161 Mole
162 Vein glory?

ACROSS

1 Like some transit
6 Pessimist's lack
10 Unlikely class president
14 Times when headlights are turned on
19 Saudi neighbor
20 "Couldn't have said it better myself"
21 Tony's cousin
22 Winning
23 Mustang feature, maybe
25 Skylarking
27 Harvard hater?
28 Columnist Herb
29 Horse halters
31 They're found on palms
32 Home of Tivoli gardens
34 Revel
35 Brunch cocktail
36 Occasion to stand up
37 Star turn at La Scala
38 Bits and pieces
39 Mosquito breeding ground
43 Crow's home
47 45 ___
50 Orchestra section
51 Pushed
53 Like some chances
54 Muse for D. H. Lawrence
57 One after another?
58 Travel guides
60 Star's rep: Abbr.
61 Louisiana, the ___ State
63 Photo session
64 Jollity
66 It's known as "Insurance City"
70 Kind of offender
71 Narodnaya is the tallest of them
72 Came from behind
74 Part of Kramden's guffaw
75 Tony-winning dramatist Hugh
77 Ever so slight
79 Relatively rational
80 Royal educator
82 Mate bees with fleas?
83 Clemson mascot
85 White-bearded grazer
86 Cold buffet slice
88 Airline entree?
92 José of dance
94 Targets of men who make passes
95 Shared airs
98 1982 Richard Pryor comedy
100 Scuba gear
102 Hit a hard drive that's caught, in baseball
104 Oranjestad native
105 Jumpy
106 Whence the Magi, with "the"
107 Oriental tie
108 Leveling
110 Tumble-down
113 Help a forgetful actor
114 Role model, maybe
115 Cut and paste
116 Observant one
117 Whirling
118 ___ Noël
119 Ellipsis
120 Commercials

DOWN

1 Like a boxer before a bout
2 Necklace item
3 "Carlito's Way" actor
4 Press, so to speak
5 From a mold
6 N.H.L. goalie Dominik
7 Overcast sky, say
8 Nugget size
9 Climbs aboard
10 Hide-and-seek proclamation
11 Tropical wood
12 Holders of glasses
13 Cool, modern-style
14 Habitually humiliated person
15 Springs
16 British guns
17 "Charmed Lives" author Michael
18 1974 Sutherland/Gould spoof
24 Calculus
26 "Just for the thrill ___"
30 Part of Q.E.D.
33 Nanas' daughters
34 Madrid museum
35 Ways
37 One way to start
38 Molten metal channel
40 "I can't ___ satisfaction" (Rolling Stones lyric)
41 Hoaxes
42 Fiber that travels well
44 Bothering
45 Draftable, maybe
46 Ambulance staffers: Abbr.
47 D.D.E., for one
48 Readies the oven
49 Fictional Mrs.
52 Kind of wing
55 Spare change?
56 Like base 8
58 "Grab ___!"
59 Welcome sight for a castaway
62 At the close of
63 One trying a hiccups cure
65 Where John Wooden coached
67 "Guys and Dolls" writer
68 Plays
69 Hardly Mr. Right
70 Hera's mother
73 Joanne of "Red River"
76 "Goody!"
77 Orchestra section
78 Roe
81 Relative of turquoise
83 Fooled around
84 Salad slice
87 Stronghold
89 Places for trophy displays
90 Beach shades
91 Get the point
93 Like some old records
96 Grew fond of
97 Certain apartment
98 "___ words were never spoken!"
99 "Amadeus" star
100 Drift
101 Go fish
102 Lives on
103 Stadium sections
104 Start of an incantation
105 ". . . under the whelming ___": Milton
106 Give forth
109 Nada
111 Hornet's nest
112 One with a beat

by Nancy Salomon

ACROSS

1 Wild place?
5 Here, elsewhere
8 Zimbabwe's capital
14 Plow puller
18 Doozy
19 Narrow margin of victory
21 They may come from Qom
22 Big Indian
23 Dull routine
24 "Good Stykeeping" award?
27 Garlicky dish
29 Princess of Nintendo games
30 Three-time Wimbledon winner
31 Report from a Pamplona beer bash?
37 Relative of a mandolin
38 Some are wicked
39 Financial backer
42 Simps' syllables
46 Shoot for
47 Humped ox
51 Gem symbolizing the soul
53 Kind of jacket
54 Biblical particle?
56 Fumbles for words
57 Popular analgesic
59 "___ boy!"
60 Set free
61 Chew the rag
62 Burst into laughter
64 Franklin and Jefferson, for two
65 Understudies for a star of "The Piano"?
70 Nickers?
73 Bring back to life, in a way
74 Whup
77 Oppenheimer development
78 Elhi orgs.

82 Timex competitor
83 Kachina doll carver
84 Containers of gourmet ice cream?
86 Application blank info
87 Scottish ___
89 Souvenir buys
90 Coarse-grained
91 Fast time?
93 Symbol of authority
94 Pizzeria order
95 Not up
97 Feeling ill, simply put?
107 Divert
109 Silly
110 Regulars' requests
111 Uneasy feeling regarding have-nots?
117 Thumbs-down reactions
118 Complex division
119 The Sandwich Islands, today
120 Georgia Senator until 1997
121 Yellowfin, e.g.
122 The King of Egypt sings in it
123 91-Across ender
124 Véronique, e.g.: Abbr.
125 Cut down

DOWN

1 Defeat
2 Methuselah's father
3 Stiff hairs
4 Terrified ones
5 Be firm
6 Rimsky-Korsakov's "Le ___ d'Or"
7 Maker of the Amigo S.U.V.
8 Poet Doolittle
9 Thundering
10 The "so few" of 1940: Abbr.
11 It makes men mean

12 Shred
13 Second sight
14 Lucky strike
15 Like some roofs
16 Cracked open
17 Oast filler
20 Extra-wide
25 Unser Jr. and Sr.
26 McCarthy's quarry
28 Comedian Poundstone
32 Logician's abbr.
33 "Middlemarch" author
34 Priests
35 City named for an Indian tribe
36 Classified listings: Abbr.
39 Far from ruddy
40 March Madness org.
41 Stare, like a tourist
43 Oscar-winning actress Miyoshi
44 Sanctuary
45 Frère's sibling
46 Singer DiFranco
47 Pueblo builders
48 Diner sign
49 Jolly old chap
50 Instruments from 119-Across
52 Root beer brand
55 Express doubt about
58 Rock's Reed
62 Sauce style
63 Kind of dispenser
64 Clear, in a way
65 Apples, e.g.
66 Townie
67 Pol's concern
68 "Barnaby Jones" actor
69 Numeral in a Uris title
70 Slew
71 Anne Nichols hero
72 Stop listening, with "out"

74 Related
75 Eat like ___
76 "Great shot!"
78 Romeo's rival
79 Wrist-radio wearer
80 Befuddled
81 Onetime lottery org.
83 Recruits, in a way
85 Troy Aikman's alma mater
88 Encourages
92 Espied, to Tweety
94 Appear
96 "The ___ Identity" (Ludlum novel)
97 Actor Dennis
98 Court org.
99 "Socrate" composer
100 Biblical land of riches
101 Never, in Nuremberg
102 Nascar broadcaster
103 Big bills
104 "Le Bestiaire" artist Dufy
105 "Uncle Vanya" woman
106 Blue-book filler
107 Light hue
108 Certain bond, for short
112 Any ship
113 Regulatory org. since 1958
114 Injection reactions, maybe
115 Maze runner
116 Where Windsor is: Abbr.

by Brendan Emmett Quigley

ACROSS

1 See above
7 Refuse
12 Less cool
19 Three-time hockey M.V.P.
20 End product
22 Artist known for his street scenes of Paris
23 Actor getting bad press?
25 Destroy a person
26 Light opening?
27 Gymnast's perch
28 Barely beat
30 Actress who's cold?
34 Karate schools
38 Scriptures volume
41 Suffix added to large numbers
42 Son, sometimes
44 They may be picked out
45 Actress with punishing roles?
49 Sack
50 Tool points
51 Begin liking
52 Grampuses
53 "The ___ the limit!"
54 Seconds
55 Article in Der Spiegel
56 Fan sound
57 Slip-up
58 [Boo-hoo!]
59 "Min and Bill" Oscar winner
64 Manilow song setting
65 State-of-the-art
66 Actor who plays terrorists?
69 Edward Jones Dome player
72 A pluviometer measures it
74 Come before
75 ___ breve
76 Go around
78 Tiny particle: Abbr.
80 It comes in sticks
81 Hitter of 660 career home runs
82 Start of a selection process
83 Mrs. Dithers, in the comics
84 Pull out
87 Word processing command
88 Telephone ___
89 Actress famous for boxing?
91 Read the U.P.C.
92 Dead accurate
94 Hideaway
95 Equals
96 Baby food
97 Actress in a dressing room?
102 One may be silent
104 St. Paul's architect
105 Grp. with holes in its organization
108 Sri Lanka's capital
111 Actress with the keys to a city?
116 Patron saint of shoemakers
117 Impeach
118 Gelcap alternative
119 Do-nothing's state
120 June of "The Dolly Sisters"
121 Says scornfully

DOWN

1 Fünf und drei
2 Miss Marple's discovery
3 Eastern royal
4 His #4 was retired
5 Big step up from the bleachers
6 Gave a darn?
7 It may be organized
8 Roaster, perhaps
9 "What would you like to know?"
10 Suffix with hand or fist
11 Strips blubber
12 Urbanite's vacation spot
13 Langston Hughes poem
14 More dignified
15 Ford failures
16 France's Belle-___
17 "Boola Boola" singer
18 Ex-Yankee Guidry
21 The Hambletonian, e.g.
24 Heyerdahl craft
29 Lady of Spain
30 Jackson and James
31 Its business is growing
32 Laughfest
33 Words after "yes"
35 Actor with a special way of talking?
36 Initials, maybe
37 Common thing
38 Bunco artist
39 Firebird
40 Actress who does the twist?
43 Julio, e.g.
45 It had the earliest parliament on the European continent
46 They're sometimes split
47 Textile trademark
48 Like some love affairs
53 Forest runner
57 Archaic attention-getters
60 Aquanaut's base
61 Dict. listing
62 "Saving Private Ryan" craft: Abbr.
63 Tampa-to-Orlando dir.
64 Some liqueurs
66 Punster
67 British surgeon Sir James
68 Chopin piece
70 Three-time placer in the 1978 Triple Crown
71 "Free" people
73 Station closing?
75 Comedian, e.g.
76 Framed
77 Actor Reeves
78 Feldspar variety
79 Fremont National Forest site
83 Midwest city, on scoreboards
84 Mark for life
85 Assam silkworm
86 Screwballer Hubbell
89 Sound system components
90 Unearthly
93 Peace of mind
95 Scribe
98 Gulf of Finland feeder
99 Registration datum
100 Dernier ___
101 "Endymion" writer
103 Power stats
105 "Here Is Your War" author
106 One on the move
107 Stratagems
108 Early third-century date
109 First or second, e.g.: Abbr.
110 Capp diminutive
112 Color TV pioneer
113 Informal British address
114 Sussex suffix
115 Tad's dad

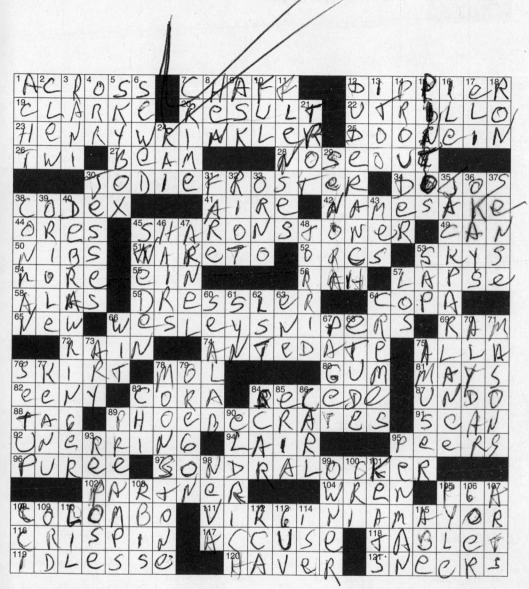

by Lloyd E. Pollet

ACROSS

1 Telephone user
7 Obeyed "Down in front!"
10 Everybody
13 Clean the last bit
18 Not straight up
19 A "man that is not passion's slave," in Shakespeare
21 Home of Kansas Wesleyan University
22 Antic
23 Energize
24 Roswell visitors?
25 Cry from Homer Simpson
26 System of measuring cereal by weight?
28 When repeated, an island NW of Tahiti
29 Down
30 ___ while
31 Cracker Jack surprise
32 Big name in real estate
33 Where diners use dinars
34 Prison library's contents?
38 Baseball fig.
39 Stared off into space
41 Sticky stuff
42 Place for a pad
43 Reeve role
44 Family's coat of arms, say
47 In a group of
49 Not yet actualized
52 Ordinary worker
53 Mayan ruin site
57 Grayish
58 Columbus's birthplace
59 Ship salvager's aid
60 Actress Thurman
61 Forbidding
62 Unhip cabbie with passenger?
65 OS/2 company
66 Play bumper-cars
67 "There's ___ In My Soup" (Peter Sellers comedy)
68 Frighten
69 "My ___!"
70 Sit in the bleachers
72 Overhauled
73 Himalayan kingdom
75 Impressionist
76 More sullen
78 Reagan Cabinet member
79 Original Stoic
81 Swiss snowfield
82 Garment industry innovator
87 Line in a voting booth: Abbr.
88 Complain at restaurants?
92 HarperCollins book division
93 Common desk items
94 Kind of tracks
95 Lobster eggs
96 ___ Xing (street sign)
97 Propeller-head
98 The Merry Men in Sherwood Forest?
103 Hospital V.I.P.'s
104 Took to the stump
105 Musical embellishment
106 Family men
109 They're called "transfers" in Britain
110 Condition sometimes treated by hypnosis
111 Pilgrim's goal
112 Perfect places
113 Ringed?
114 LAX monitor info
115 Most like Iago

DOWN

1 Fort Peck, for one
2 First name in dance
3 "The Naked and the Dead" star
4 Island in a Scottish bay?
5 Grp. with standards
6 Business solicitor
7 33-Across, once
8 Top-notch
9 Fictional teen sleuth Belden
10 Diagonally
11 English professor's deg.
12 Leopold's partner in crime
13 Southeast Asian natives
14 Actress Lena
15 Gun with a silencer?
16 Rattle
17 Bible reading
20 Name on a fridge
21 Clip joint?
26 200-milligram unit
27 Straddling
28 Auction action
29 Exhausted
35 Of the breastbone
36 John ___
37 Fenced-off area
40 Cartoon dog
42 Flesh and blood
45 Lycanthrope's catalyst
46 Waterskin
47 Wing-shaped
48 Bébé watcher
49 Hideouts
50 Music org.
51 Mostly-empty spice rack?
52 Pressed one's nose to the glass
54 Surg. study
55 Planetary shadow
56 Irish P.M. ___ de Valera
58 Doggedness
59 Took places
62 One way to explain a coincidence
63 Algae product
64 Pop singer from Nigeria
69 Emotional scene with actor Grant?
71 TV's "___ Sharkey"
72 Evasive answer
73 Greeted a shepherd
74 Part of H.M.S.
77 Miner's quarry
78 Duncan ___
79 Numbers on letters
80 Went back on stage
81 Laplander, maybe
83 Watch words?
84 Be situated above
85 Goes downhill
86 Objective
88 Potters' needs
89 Flip comment?
90 Chevalier
91 Cheapen
99 Hall-of-Famer Coveleski
100 Performer who fills the club

by Patrick Berry

101 Tarpeian Rock's
location
102 Pare,
say
106 Preamble to
the Constitution?
107 Stanley Cup
org.
108 Primed

PLURAL PERPLEXITY

ACROSS

1 Lets up
7 Rosé alternative
13 Rogue
18 Rossini setting, in España
20 Ancient galley
21 Funnies format feature
22 Start of a verse
24 Where matches are booked
25 Done, for Donne
26 Embedded, in a way
27 1969 Series winners
29 Arab League member
30 Conical-toothed tool
32 Verse, part 2
36 Bargain hunters look for them
39 Nero's title: Abbr.
40 Inveigled
41 Most reliable
45 Start of a recipe direction
48 Place to hibernate
49 Verse, part 3
53 Clayey deposit
56 1951 N.L. Rookie of the Year
57 Suffix with tyranno-
58 Big number, slangily
59 Cal. page header
61 Skydived
64 Verse, part 4
70 Like some sculptures
72 Shine, in commercial names
73 Titillates
74 Verse, part 5
79 Becomes less high, with "up"
80 Indeed
81 Sch. founded by Thomas Jefferson
82 Drone, e.g.
84 Capital of Moravia
85 King Mongkut's realm
88 Verse, part 6
93 Noted Turner
95 Stocking shade
96 Table with a map
97 Metal marble
101 Long-jawed fish
103 Actress Kelly of "Chaplin"
106 Verse, part 7
112 Collars
114 Vexed
115 Prefix with phobia
116 They may compete with boxers
119 Prompt
120 Ace, maybe
122 End of the verse
126 1996 Madonna musical
127 Cricket teams, e.g.
128 Rushed at
129 The Haggadah's read here
130 Bar food
131 Way out

DOWN

1 Nancy, the first woman in Parliament
2 Take off the top
3 Reluctant
4 Hall-of-Fame pitcher Keefe
5 Big South Conference college
6 Pivot around
7 Telephone part
8 A fleur
9 Sphygmomanom-eter's place
10 French cathedral city
11 Roast host
12 Grow grinders
13 Where one might take off on a vacation?
14 Early American colony
15 Feeble
16 Gun wielder, say
17 Did some shaving
19 Kind of D.A.
20 "America" pronoun
23 Old verb ending
28 Smooth, in a way
31 Medium for announcements
33 He played Yuri in "Doctor Zhivago"
34 Salon creation
35 Check
37 Director Jean-___ Godard
38 Málaga Mrs.
42 Capt.'s aide
43 Attempt
44 Bull's head?
46 Like some errors
47 SEATO part
49 Hula dancers
50 Daewoo competitor
51 Shorthand system inventor
52 Island north of Montecristo
54 Parents, e.g.
55 Lake of Four Forest Cantons
56 "Home to Harlem" novelist Claude
60 Bas-relief medium
62 W.W. II action locale
63 Morse code click
65 Grp. that sang "Do Ya"
66 Sentences
67 Abbr. in ages
68 Sticky stuff
69 Applied well, as sunscreen
71 Great Lakes fish
75 Level
76 Prego rival
77 Mort from Montreal
78 "Waiting for the Robert ___"
83 Fraction of a joule
86 Personal account
87 ___ fides (bad faith)
89 Sharp quality
90 Squad
91 Special person
92 Musician Brian
94 Brown of Talk magazine
97 Pinches
98 Flourish
99 It moves in a wink
100 Emulates Rembrandt
102 Spring cheepers
104 Unbranched flower cluster
105 Corrupt practices
107 Happy-go-lucky song part
108 Shack
109 Treat for Rover
110 Entreaty for Rover
111 Congers and kin
113 Origins
117 Gala
118 Portmanteau pollution mixture
121 Besmirch
123 "The Loco-Motion" singer Little ___
124 Was a bellwether
125 Are all wet

by Cathy Millhauser

ACROSS

1 Inferior
10 Puzzle page favorite
15 S. Amer. land
19 Like some addresses
20 Communist's belief
22 Part of a blouse that touches the waist?
23 The real scoop about lipids?
24 They're better than F.G.'s
25 Portion of a drag queen's wardrobe
26 Bumptious
27 Toy company that launched Rubik's Cube
28 Bad ___
29 Snowmobile parts
31 Professional with an x-ray machine: Abbr.
33 Underage child of a military officer?
38 Nonsense of a market pessimist?
44 Affirm
45 Oven maker
46 Caught in ___
47 Biblical birthright seller
48 Oscar winner Hunt
50 Glad Wrap competitor
51 Pianist Dame Myra
52 Missy Elliott's "___ What I'm Talkin' About"
53 Toil of a Broadway show?
55 Match for a bad guy?
58 Owns
59 Fine-tune

60 Italian port on the Adriatic
61 Make ___ of
62 Sam's Club competitor
64 Yes
68 Watchdog org.?
72 Fixes
74 Hair behind the ears, maybe
75 E-mail directive: Abbr.
78 What can produce a "boing!"?
82 Ardor of a new employee?
84 Bookstore sect.
85 "Our Gang" affirmative
86 Stop early
88 Botulin, e.g.
89 "___ la Douce," 1963 film
90 Charlie's Angels, e.g.
91 Tally mark
92 Torn
93 Comeback of a Japanese game?
95 Singer Johnny's gallop?
98 It can be measured in gigs
99 So
100 "Yo!"
101 Over
105 Molière's Harpagon, e.g.
108 Prosperity
110 Go the other way
113 Privilege of liberals?
115 Road in Yellowstone?
118 Become level
119 Darlin'
120 Give it ___
121 Say yes
122 Reason to take Valium

DOWN

1 Trampled
2 Accidents
3 "___ Alive!" (1974 thriller)
4 One looking for a lift?
5 Wilts
6 Comic Rudner
7 New Testament book
8 "The way of nature"
9 Popular street name
10 Patriot Putnam of the American Revolution
11 When planes are due, for short
12 Equivocator's choice
13 Child-raiser's cry?
14 Start of a cheer
15 City WNW of Stillwater
16 François Truffaut's field
17 West Point rival, for short
18 ___ nitrate
19 Polo Grounds legend
21 Words sung before and after "is just"
26 Literally, "fish tooth"
28 Rambunctious
29 Lewis Carroll creature
30 Hawaii's ___ Coast
32 Habiliments
33 "Happy Days" character
34 Province of central Spain
35 Villain in "Martin Chuzzlewit"
36 "National Treasure" group

37 Turkish hospice
38 Believers in the spiritual unity of all people
39 Roadside sign abbr.
40 Obscure
41 Gas bill info
42 Roofing items
43 Yearns (for)
49 Refuse holder
54 It's pitched
56 Times gone by
57 Current
60 Be angry
63 It's kept within the lines, usually
65 Sully
66 "At the ___ Core," 1976 sci-fi film
67 Laredo-to-Fort Worth dir.
68 Comparable in size
69 Veep after Hubert
70 Destinations of some limos
71 Perfecto, e.g.
73 One taking a quick look
75 Handyman
76 Squeeze-dry
77 Al ___
79 Must, informally
80 Ukulele activity
81 Playable
82 ___-totsy
83 Venture
87 Erymanthian ___, fourth labor of Hercules
94 Artist Max
96 Pure
97 Restrained
99 Sports car since '53
101 Italian wheels
102 Moola
103 Miles away
104 ___-bitty

by Bill Zais

106 "The Lay of the Host of ___" (old Russian epic poem)
107 Elisabeth of "Leaving Las Vegas"
108 Small warbler
109 Makes (out)
110 Speeds
111 Alamo battler?
112 1,000 smackers
114 Actor Stephen
115 West Coast hrs.
116 Wow
117 "Riddle-me-___"

ACROSS

1 Words "beautifully marked in currants" in "Alice in Wonderland"
6 Common ___
9 Make an example of
13 Destination in Genesis 8
19 With 105-Across, what the answer to each starred clue starts with
21 *Again
23 *Baseball's Willie Mays, with "the"
24 *Fiancé
25 Glycerides, e.g.
26 Football Hall-of-Famer Ernie
28 Home of Faa'a International Airport
29 Lie
30 Jury pool
31 Watch-crystal holder
32 Villain
33 Ring results, briefly
34 Bigwig
38 "Awesome!"
41 Next-to-last round
42 Little of France?
43 St. Louis, e.g.
44 Brawl motivator
45 Crunch's title
46 Rod holders
50 Photocopier choice
51 Hollow-point ammo
53 *Metal used for swords
55 Stage awards
56 Butlers and maids
57 Be about to fall
58 *Symbol of rejoicing for someone's long-awaited return
61 *Brownish-orange
65 Lady-in-waiting in "Othello"
66 Lovers of expensive furs may put them on
67 West Coast wine city
68 *Kind of ratio
72 Divine
74 New York's ___-Fontanne Theater
75 Supermarket lines?
76 "We Need a Little Christmas" singer
77 Hoop grp.
78 Alma mater for Neil Armstrong and Pat Nixon: Abbr.
79 Close of day, to poets
80 Gutter locale
81 Thomas Mann's "Der ___ in Venedig"
82 Attempts
85 With 20-Down, airshow activities
86 Jim who wrote "Ball Four"
88 Indy champ Bobby
90 Dentist's concern
91 ___ of vantage (good position for viewing)
96 Split
98 Split
99 Like wiping one's dirty mouth on one's sleeve
100 *Decelerating
102 *Composer's due
104 *Whatever happens
105 See 19-Across
106 Cantankerous
107 Not including
108 Inexact fig.
109 Magazine holders

DOWN

1 Mississippi quartet
2 ___ of thousands
3 "___ Remember"
4 "Real Time" moderator
5 Tip reducer?
6 Variety of leather
7 Exercised power over
8 All the parts of a column except the bottom
9 Stick
10 Accustom
11 Actress Harper
12 Diplomats' place: Abbr.
13 Ball handler?
14 "Not I!" hearer
15 Titular Verdi role
16 Laugh-a-minute
17 Both: Prefix
18 Curling goal
20 See 85-Across
22 Author of the Oprah's Book Club selection "We Were the Mulvaneys"
27 I's opposite on a clock
30 Improvises
31 Bar personnel
32 Light from a headlight
33 Rears
35 Cracker topper
36 What 35-Down may do
37 Jessica of "7th Heaven"
38 Done with
39 Tourist mecca near Venezuela
40 Relinquish
41 Passing remark?
42 Sch. fair organizer
46 Schumacher of auto racing
47 The "E" in H.R.E.: Abbr.
48 Violinist Mischa
49 This, in Havana
50 Cox's call
52 Spot
53 Manhattan street leading to the Williamsburg Bridge
54 Guarantees
56 Sensory receptor in the ear
59 "Mon ___!"
60 Loud, abrupt sound
61 Dog of old comics
62 Denier's reply
63 Aerobics technique
64 Winning
66 +
68 +
69 Impair through inactivity
70 Atahualpa, e.g.
71 It may be + or –
72 Act of kindness
73 Soothsayer's subject
76 "Death in the Afternoon" figures
80 Muse of music
83 Creator of "Hägar the Horrible"
84 Hero
85 Part of many a Halloween outfit
86 Noble partner
87 Fictional TV planet
89 ___ Fleming, central character in "The Red Badge of Courage"
90 Dots on a map
91 Home of 67-Across: Abbr.
92 Top
93 Not so friendly
94 Capital of East Flanders

by Henry Hook

95 Fits (inside)
96 Reed instrument: Abbr.
97 Pork cut
98 Liver in Lyon
99 Braggadocio
100 "No seats left"
101 FedEx competitor
103 Still

ACROSS

1 Theme of this puzzle
9 Accord competitor
15 Is afflicted with sigmatism
20 Emphatic refusal
21 Tulsa native
22 French pen filler
23 Film (1954), actress (2003)
25 Nothing, to Nero
26 Brief
27 Comments around cute babies
28 East ender?
29 "We can't delay!"
30 Visually assess
31 Morsel
33 Fish in fish and chips
35 Isabel Allende's "___ of My Soul"
36 Florence-to-Rome dir.
37 Director (2003), actor (1962)
39 Interject
40 Rests
41 12 meses
42 Low tie
44 Like the Wild West
47 Pen with a cap
48 Abbr. at the bottom of a letter
49 Places for runners
52 Work ___
53 Granny, in Gelsenkirchen
55 China's largest ethnic group
57 Nineveh's kingdom
59 Smeared
61 Film (1992), actor (1958)
64 Follower of weekend news, briefly
65 ___ bran
66 Friend in a western
68 "The Age of Anxiety" author
69 Rent
70 Philosopher Kung Fu-___
71 Actor (1934), actor (1995)
73 Destination of the Bounty in "Mutiny on the Bounty"
76 Comedy club annoyance
78 Olive ___
79 Troll dolls, once
81 Beau ___
82 Milo of "Ulysses"
83 Kind
85 "___ Diaboliques"
87 Big pan
89 Lead role in "La Cage aux Folles"
91 Venezuelan export
92 Object of veneration in ancient Egypt
93 Cool
94 Actress (1986), director (1962)
98 Mail order option, for short
101 Sport jersey material
102 Author Huxley
103 Wallop
104 Kwik-E-Mart owner on "The Simpsons"
105 Pantomime, say
107 Tahoe, e.g., for short
108 Future school?
109 See 113-Down
111 Soil improver
112 Actress (1983), supporting actor (1999)
116 Humble
117 Rebel
118 Checks
119 Surgical aid
120 Jerks
121 Forensic experts

DOWN

1 Investment options, for short
2 Dolls
3 Password, e.g.
4 Reactions to fireworks
5 N.F.L. guard Chris
6 Overawe
7 Santa ___
8 Spin
9 Rus. and Ukr., once
10 Response to "pow!" in cartoons
11 Big name in grooming aids
12 Winter wear
13 Detective superintendent Jane of TV's "Prime Suspect"
14 Knack
15 Jay that chatters
16 At first
17 Film (1993), actress (1987)
18 Ready
19 Three-time French Open champ, 1990–92
24 Household item with a neck
29 One flying over Hawaii
31 Stakes
32 Linda Ronstadt's "___ Easy"
33 Villa in Mexico
34 Like the inside of a sphere
37 Gat
38 ___ alai
40 Slender
43 Org.
44 Basutoland, today
45 World books
46 Song (1942), supporting actress (1994)
47 Capital known as the Venice of the East
48 Swamps
50 Informal eating place
51 More racy
54 Sierra Club founder
56 Prized horse
58 Elated
60 Area between hills
62 Geezer
63 Inspiration
67 Kind of vow
71 Reunion gatherers
72 "Us" or "them" in "It's us against them"
74 "Didn't we just have that?"
75 Global energy company
77 Make the beds, dust, etc.
80 March around camp, e.g.
84 Term of respect abroad
86 ". . . as old as yonder ___": James Joyce
88 Late news?
90 Part of a Latin 101 conjugation
91 Works
93 Mother of Paris
95 One of the Alcotts
96 "It's ___!"
97 Swarmed
98 Tibetan or Afghan
99 First act in a revue
100 Pressure
101 Taj ___
106 Junkie
108 Solicits orders (for)
109 Girl in Tennessee Williams's "Summer and Smoke"

by Nancy Nicholson Joline

110 Worms, e.g.
112 Jrs. no more
113 109-Across's
    old radio
    partner
114 Fire
115 Truck part

ACROSS

1 Offer for an R. J. Reynolds brand?
8 Rules, for short
12 1970 Simon & Garfunkel hit
19 Away from a teaching post
20 Forster's "___ With a View"
22 Joining
23 Cube holder
24 IUD part
25 Realm of Otto von Bismarck
26 1802 acquisition of 25-Across
27 Settles on, in a way
28 Top of a platter
29 Papa pad?
32 Composes
34 Org. that oversees quadrennial games
37 Sporty Mazda
38 Canola and sunflower oil?
41 Best fraternity pledge tormentor?
45 Jack who said "Just the facts, ma'am"
47 Rugged coastline feature
48 "My!"
49 Casual attire
52 Not the most exciting school athletes?
56 Social gathering with the Rockettes?
59 "Like a Rock" singer Bob
61 Cosmetician Lauder and others
62 Get decked out
63 Waste maker
65 Puts up again, as bowling pins
67 Squiggly letter
68 Got sober?

70 Flutter
73 Shows past the doorstep
75 Student of Bartók
76 The lion in "The Lion, the Witch and the Wardrobe"
78 Clap hands on
81 Pan-fry
83 C.I.A. noggins?
85 Hit boxer John with a haymaker?
87 "___ Calloways" (Disney film)
89 "Damien" subtitle
90 Mount Rigi, e.g.
91 Head set
93 Fog in Zürich?
96 How-to films for a dairy farm?
100 ___ nerve
102 First song on "More of the Monkees"
103 ___, meenie, miney, mo
104 Side view of salmon?
109 "Soon It's ___ Rain" ("The Fantasticks" song)
111 Reliquary
112 Temple of Isis locale
116 Facial growths
118 Phrase of agreement
119 Words heard after opening a gift, maybe
121 Hazel, e.g.
122 Ice Cube né ___ Jackson
123 It started around 1100 B.C.
124 Do a mailroom task
125 Professional org.
126 Transcribe some Dickens?

DOWN

1 Colorful carp
2 Enough, for some
3 Plaudits, of a sort
4 "Sure, I'm game"
5 Exposed
6 One of Donald's exes
7 Susan of "Looker"
8 Train storage area
9 ___ Tubb, the Texas Troubadour
10 Nabber's cry
11 Rather, informally
12 Silver prizes
13 Physicist Fermi
14 ___ Real, Spain
15 The "se" in per se
16 The King's "princess"
17 Common pasta suffix
18 Eastern title
21 Like some Sp. nouns
27 "The Sopranos" Emmy winner Falco
30 No man's land, in brief
31 Vladimir Putin's onetime org.
33 Michael of R.E.M.
34 Wagner heroine
35 Extras
36 Mooches
39 It commonly follows a verb: Abbr.
40 Disrespect
42 Salespeople, informally
43 Lukas of "Witness"
44 Sheet music abbr.
45 Locks on a dome
46 Chef Lagasse
50 Cornerstone abbr.
51 Must
53 Winners' signs
54 August hrs.
55 Some football blockers: Abbr.

57 "See ___?"
58 Plane part
60 Signs a lease
64 "Julius Caesar" setting
66 Deejay's bane
68 Classic soft drink with orange, grape and peach flavors
69 Shad delicacies
70 "So-Called Chaos" singer Morissette
71 Like Niels Bohr
72 Kind of inspection
73 Orch. section
74 Old French coin
76 Means of defense: Abbr.
77 Come across as
78 Canned meat brand
79 "And that's ___" ("Believe you me")
80 Christina in the 2005 revival of "Sweet Charity"
82 Speech stumbles
84 Informal greetings
86 Zoo feature, in England
88 Finnic language
92 Fashion inits.
94 Ring bearer
95 Here, on the Riviera
97 Fife player
98 Bread for tacos?
99 Plywood layer
100 ___ Book Club
101 7, 11 and 13
105 Bologna bone
106 Mandela's native tongue
107 Hijacked cruise ship Achille ___
108 Bar at the bar
110 "I'd hate to break up ___"

by Patrick Blindauer and Tony Orbach

113 Having a taste of the grape
114 Run up —
115 NASA cancellation
116 Econ. measure
117 Your and my
119 Snap
120 Cyrano's nose

ACROSS

1 Upper end of a soprano's range
6 Life work?
9 In support of
12 Bishopric
19 Basketballer nicknamed the Diesel
20 Attribute (to)
22 Joins up
23 Concave button
24 "Over my dead body!" / Alert [split]
26 Exchange words? / New beginning [merger]
28 ___ Maria (coffee liqueur)
29 Gift-wrapper's need
30 Strummed instrument
32 "___ my doubts"
33 Animated film character voiced by Matthew Broderick
35 Fine fellow
36 Undecided, you might say
38 Deal (out)
39 Annoying obligations / "No need to check" [split]
42 1980s "NBC News Overnight" anchor / Feared insect [merger]
44 At full speed
45 "Mazel ___!"
46 "The History ___" (Tony-winning play)
47 Harsh
48 Return flight destinations?
52 Off-limits
55 Get down
56 Plant manager?
58 Figure just above the total
59 Black hole's boundary / Despite the fact that [split]
62 Group migration
64 Like Eton attendees
65 Author of the "Earth's Children" series
66 Social reformer Lucretia
67 "Great Scott!"
68 A little cross?
70 Double sugar / Travel freely? [merger]
74 Get dressed (up)
75 "Feh!"
76 Insects found in trunks
77 Takes off
78 Bag
80 In the cooler
81 Unread messages, usually
83 Mountain SE of ancient Troy
85 It has many sides
86 Commuter's source of entertainment / Actor John or David [split]
90 Martini ingredient / Delta site [merger]
94 Burt's "Stroker Ace" co-star
95 "The Seagull" ingenue
96 Water, to Watteau
97 Fictional blue humanoid
98 Aggressive patriot
99 Fishtank accessory
100 Prefix with potent
102 MapQuest suggestion: Abbr.
103 Franz Liszt, e.g. / Didn't go straight, maybe [split]
106 "Come back now, y'hear?" / Park employee [merger]
110 TV journalist Van Susteren
113 Commentator
114 Using company resources
115 Great white ___
116 Took too long, as a meeting
117 Superhero name ender
118 Broke bread
119 Finger-lickin' good

DOWN

1 ___ polloi
2 Overnight site
3 Patrician
4 Della sells hers in "The Gift of the Magi"
5 See 26-Across
6 Keen producers
7 Quarantine
8 Scale's range
9 Taylor's deputy on TV
10 Kimono securer
11 ___ room
12 Gap filler?
13 Occupy
14 Blast furnace input
15 Peacemaker maker
16 #1 hit for Marty Robbins
17 Add surreptitiously
18 Some phosphates, e.g.
21 Observance
25 See 24-Across
27 Modern political acronym
30 Navajo enemy
31 See 42-Across
33 Abrupt increase on a graph
34 Assuages one's guilt
37 Prepares, in a way, as chicken
39 Adult insect
40 California county with Point Reyes National Seashore
41 See 39-Across
43 Origin
44 Complete
47 It's not needed in hydroponics
49 It's clipped at both ends
50 Philippic
51 Game similar to bridge
52 Really appeals to
53 Earthly paradise of Celtic legend
54 Caviar source
55 W.W. II light machine gun
56 See 70-Across
57 Bleeped word
60 Reagan's first secretary of state
61 See 59-Across
62 Pros who practice
63 Violinist Itzhak
66 Four-legged female
69 Napped fabrics
70 "Goodbye, Mr. Chips" star
71 ___ Sea, connected to St. George's Channel
72 It's split
73 At a distance
76 ___ bourguignon
79 See 90-Across
81 1953 3-D film starring Fernando Lamas
82 Earlier
84 Seat separator
85 See 106-Across
86 Stop up
87 Some campaign fund-raisers

by Patrick Berry

88 See 86-Across
89 Cereal grass
90 Himalayan cedar
91 ___ Quimby, girl of children's lit
92 Chinese province bordering Vietnam, Laos and Myanmar

96 Change genetically
94 ___ franca
98 2007 title role for Ellen Page
101 "___ be O.K."
103 Chemistry Nobelist Otto
104 See 103-Across

105 Precinct
107 ___ landslide
108 Country singer McGraw
109 What retroviruses contain
111 Preschooler
112 To some extent

ACROSS

1 Place for bluegrass
7 #1 on the charts
12 Blast
20 Kia sedan
21 Café con ___
22 Certify
23 Broad comedies involving hogs?
25 Like traditional Catholic Masses
26 N.H.L.'s Tikkanen
27 Entertainment center at many a sports bar
28 Where bluejackets go
30 Movement that inspired '60s fashion
31 Good viewing spot for a canyon
32 Bickering
33 Bookcase lineup
34 Beautifully illustrated report of a computer failure?
39 Clark's partner
40 It's put on some houses
41 "It'll ___ you"
42 Stockholm-bound carrier
45 First-year J.D. student
46 Makes eyes at
49 All-time top-selling Atari video game
51 Cake maker's boast
53 Short-legged, thickset horse
55 Not badgering, say
56 Flood survivor
57 Nursery rhyme call sung to an old French melody
60 Short breaks
61 French director's comment about his submission to a film festival?

67 Wide-headed fastener
68 Smears
69 Ang Thong resident
70 How some kids spend the summer
73 "Peer Gynt" mother
74 Bird call on a farm?
79 They're developed by a muscleman
82 Lip cover
83 Nebraska county with an Indian name
84 Super Bowl XLII M.V.P. Manning
85 Gen. Lee, in brief
86 Loyal
88 Lobster claw
89 A Simpson without access to his volume of the "Odyssey"?
94 Rocker Morissette
96 Till compartment
97 Succulents that soothe
98 Easy wins
99 Starter starter?
100 Sign that's often lit
101 Film editor's job
104 Most heterogeneous
106 Former Tennessee senator's Halloween costumes?
109 Prestigious
110 Curt
111 Name on some euros
112 Sources of a cosmetics oil
113 King in 1 B.C.
114 Body-sculpting undergarment

DOWN

1 Be down
2 Narrative writing
3 Razor brand
4 Cartoonist Browne
5 Breakfast menu heading
6 Brave words?
7 Mason of a sort
8 Griffin who loved game shows
9 Virginia is in it: Abbr.
10 Cover
11 Redcoat's ally
12 Do for a V.I.P.?
13 South American tuber
14 Creatures with three hearts
15 Opening remarks at a coffee makers' convention?
16 Paying guest
17 "Do ___?"
18 Baseball catchers
19 Time on la Côte d'Azur
24 Banking initialism
29 ". . . to name just a few": Abbr.
31 Not straight
32 Seller's terms
33 Symbol of blackness
34 Coup start
35 Clinton's attorney general
36 Pitcher
37 Give ___ up
38 Also addresses, as with an e-mail
42 Long-necked instrument
43 Opposite of reject
44 Payroll dept. ID's
46 Light wind?
47 Sacred cup
48 Christine of "Running on Empty"

49 French cleric
50 ___ consequence
52 Check holder: Abbr.
53 Monthly charge
54 Couple in a rowboat
57 Tournament passes
58 ___ Boy, classic figure in Japanese anime
59 One of Dumas's Musketeers
61 "___ Inside" (slogan)
62 Louis Vuitton competitor
63 Rat-___
64 Some Wharton alums
65 Tooth holders
66 Hawaiian Punch rival
67 Sticky stuff
71 Where a dope unloads a ship?
72 Words on a deathbed, maybe
74 Bass ___
75 Popular snack cakes
76 Talked-about twosome
77 Part
78 Tree in bloom in a van Gogh painting
80 Five-dollar bills, slangily
81 Photocopier option: Abbr.
82 Fraternity members
86 Highest grade
87 Was not cooped up
88 Love
89 Whence the line "To sleep: perchance to dream"
90 Stopped fasting
91 Vented

by Elizabeth C. Gorski

92 Minnesota's St. ___ College
93 Fabrics that shimmer
94 Stood
95 Led Zeppelin's "Whole ___ Love"
99 Norms: Abbr.
100 ___ buco

101 Bloke
102 ___ Reader
103 Bygone autocrat
104 Touched
105 "Didn't I tell you?"
107 Clearance rack abbr.
108 Valedictorian's pride, for short

ACROSS

1 Track figure
8 Din-din
12 Nautical line
19 Ally makers
20 Search high and low
22 Like some grievances
23 Home of the newspaper Haaretz
24 Electrical engineers and news anchors?
26 World travelers and wine connoisseurs?
28 Wrestling locale
29 Cheer greatly
30 Some Millers
31 It may be pinched
32 Zealous
34 Business card abbr.
35 Oriole or Blue Jay, for short
36 Completely bungle
38 Hercules or Ulysses
39 Eyed
42 Classic Hans Christian Andersen story, with "The"
44 Geologists and music video producers?
46 Meal crumb
47 Congestion site
48 Some volcanic deposits
52 College students and mattress testers?
57 Greeted
58 Outdoor cover
59 Robert who introduced the term "cell" to biology
60 Where the antihelix is
61 Under
64 Itinerary word
65 Choir stands
67 Despicable sort
69 Executed
70 Stop
72 The Gamecocks of the Southeastern Conf.
73 Machinates
76 Prominent D.C. lobby
78 Wallop
79 Twelve ___
81 Supercool
82 Old West outlaws and aspiring thespians?
85 Bit of gridiron equipment
87 Obviously sad
88 Boffo
89 Beat-era musicians and orthopedists?
91 Show on the small screen
96 Home of the Rachel Carson National Wildlife Refuge
98 PC screens, for short
99 Certain investigators, for short
100 Champ just before 36-Down
101 Tough spot
102 Lavishes gifts (on), say
104 U.N. chief ___ Ki-moon
105 Desex
106 Huge, in poetry
109 Shak. is its most-quoted writer
110 Fort Knox officials and pop singers?
113 Comedians and parade directors?
116 Defeat in a derby
117 Office newbie
118 "___ joking!"
119 Lettered top
120 Set out
121 Cold war inits.
122 Activity in which spelling counts?

DOWN

1 Like a guardian
2 Kept from home
3 Flew
4 Bay ___ (residents of Massachusetts)
5 Walter ___, author of "The Hustler"
6 Prince in "The Little Mermaid"
7 Answer
8 Mortgagee's concern
9 Sharp
10 Craggy peaks
11 Boulogne-___-Mer, France
12 For all to play, in music
13 With 105-Down, a short play
14 Salon option
15 Cambodian money
16 Florid
17 Stroked
18 Car with an innovative "rolling dome" speedometer
21 Ad-libs and such
25 Honcho
27 Western tribe
32 Stepped aside, in court
33 Gave
36 1976–80 Wimbledon champ
37 Not touch
38 Sounds of anger or jubilation
40 Factory shipments: Abbr.
41 Hurdle for some college srs.
43 Sharpeners
44 Estuary
45 Assist in shady doings
47 Blood ___
49 Extravagant
50 Mournful
51 Sudden floods
52 Much smaller now
53 Exterminator's option
54 Gangster's gun
55 Nickname once at 1600 Pennsylvania Ave.
56 Hurried
57 Member of the familia
62 Needing bleach, say
63 Campaign feature
66 Eked (out)
68 Feels indignant about
71 Egg holder
74 Religious pilgrimage
75 Rebounds and steals
77 Hurt so bad
80 Fruit-flavored soda
83 ___ Magica
84 "Essential" things
86 A.T.M. need
87 Without oomph
90 Certain chamber group
91 Oversee
92 Heat-related
93 On
94 Dog after the winter, e.g.
95 How Calvin Coolidge spoke
96 You can say that again
97 Lacking scruples
99 Less accurate
101 Kids
103 Expressed delight
104 Some South Africans
105 See 13-Down

by Robert W. Harris

107 Symbol of thinness
108 Attire not
for the modest
110 Striped animals
111 Wands
112 Prefix with zone
114 "Imagine that!"
115 Note to be
used later

ACROSS

1 Lively, in mus.
5 101, in a course name
10 "Little ___ in Slumberland" (pioneering comic strip)
14 One on two feet
19 Literature Nobelist Morrison
20 Word on a wanted poster
21 He's seen on the ceiling of the Sistine Chapel
22 Serengeti grazer
23 Pedicurist's need
26 Antics
27 Zingers
28 Toot one's horn
29 Scrooge's nephew in "A Christmas Carol"
30 Wearer of uniform #37, retired by both the Yankees and the Mets
34 Entered pompously
38 Clears
39 Relating to flight technology
41 Carnival site
42 "Inka Dinka ___"
43 Close overlapping of fugue voices
45 Prince ___, Eddie Murphy film role
47 Caboose, e.g.
48 Frolicking
52 Whispering party game
54 Vardalos of the screen
55 Diva's delivery
56 Holiday celebrating deliverance from Haman
59 Narrow inlet
60 Textile factory fixture

62 ___ fide
63 Lingo suffix
64 Unfortunate development
65 Bone-dry
66 Divider of wedding guests
68 Champion figure skater Irina
72 Leaves for lunch?
75 Author Janowitz
77 Professor 'iggins
78 Picassos and Pissarros
80 55-Across, e.g.
81 Bewitched
83 Penlight battery size
84 ___ radiation
86 DeMille output
87 Early millennium year
88 Manual transmission position
91 French dome toppers
93 Big shot after making a big shot, maybe: Abbr.
94 Kind of question
95 Peter Shaffer play based on the lives of Mozart and Salieri
98 "___-haw!"
99 Make haste
100 Like sugar vis-à-vis Equal
102 H.S. subject
106 Heartbreaking situations
109 Kitchen implement used with a little muscle
112 In the mail
113 K.G.B. predecessor
115 Popular Toyota
116 Users of 118-Across

118 Bats, balls, gloves, etc.
122 False appearance
123 Capital of Italy
124 Annie of "Ghostbusters"
125 Blade of Grasse
126 Lugged
127 Zenith
128 Company-owned building, e.g.
129 Sch. research papers

DOWN

1 Place for a fan
2 Writer Peggy known for the phrase "a kinder, gentler nation"
3 Actually existing
4 Stately dance with short steps
5 Tempts
6 Elite athlete
7 Error indicator
8 Suffix with adverb
9 Hit TV show with the theme song "Who Are You"
10 Port west of Monte Vesuvio
11 Fall setting
12 A, B and C
13 Mantra syllables
14 Come-hither look
15 Coming-clean words
16 Protective mailer
17 Music producer Brian
18 License to drill?: Abbr.
24 Milano of "Who's the Boss?"
25 Carbolic acid
29 Top-rated TV series of 2001–02
31 Consort of 21-Across
32 Capone henchman

33 "They're in my hot little hands!"
35 BlackBerry rival
36 Land of Ephesus
37 Acknowledge tacitly
40 Heads in the Pantheon?
44 Variety
46 Poet Omar ___
48 Rhyme scheme of "Stopping by Woods on a Snowy Evening"
49 "Star Trek: T.N.G." counselor Deanna
50 Some business attire
51 Yellow Teletubby
53 Composer Satie
57 Letters before many a state's name
58 Brush up on
61 Whiteboard cleaner
64 Subj. that deals with mixed feelings
67 Bearing nothing
69 Japanese eel and rice dish
70 "King Lear" or "Hamlet": Abbr.
71 Boxer's measurement
73 Touched down
74 Medics
76 Nonbeliever
79 Classic Dana fragrance for women
81 Representations of a winged woman holding an atom
82 Big name in skin care products
84 Entire range
85 Amazon parrot

by Paula Gamache

89 Opener for a crystal ball gazer
90 Dine at a diner
92 F equivalent
96 Not dis
97 Declaim
101 Estimated: Abbr.
103 Chemical cousin
104 Lug: Var.
105 Online protocol for remote log-in
107 Discontinue
108 Absorb
110 Like lip-glossed lips
111 Deserves
114 Cause for an R, perhaps
116 Badge holder: Abbr.
117 Status ___
118 Main
119 Day ___
120 Dawn goddess
121 Divisions of gals.

COULD YOU REWORD THAT, PLEASE?

ACROSS

1 Rocker Ocasek and others
5 Dwellers along the Dnieper River
10 "A ___, petal and a thorn" (Emily Dickinson poem)
15 Rtes.
18 1969 self-titled jazz album
19 United We Stand America founder
20 Eastern seaboard rte.
21 Greek discord goddess
23 Tax break for Gumby?
26 Publication read by drs.
27 "Steady ___ goes"
28 Motor levers
29 Abjures
31 Money replaced by the 49-Down
33 "Bien sûr!"
34 Primitive wind instruments
35 Blessing for a shipboard romance?
40 Without compassion
41 Indisposed
42 Be indisposed
43 Architect whose epitaph says "Reader, if you seek his monument, look around you"
44 It's short for a long car
47 World's longest wooden roller coaster, at Kings Island
51 Battery type
52 "Hawaii Five-O" airer
55 Bridge writer Culbertson
56 Perhaps doesn't believe witty Rogers?
58 "Let's ___!"
59 Like some single-sex schools
61 Near-grads: Abbr.
62 Dinner plate scraping
63 ___'acte
64 "On First Looking Into Chapman's Homer" poet
65 Tribe originally from the Deep South
68 Wood shop device
69 Rigor of a fever
70 "Yoo-___!"
72 "Alley ___!"
73 "Oh, please"
75 Enough to hold a lotta iPod tunes
76 End-game maneuvers?
80 Turncoat
81 Somalia neighbor: Abbr.
82 Modern address
83 Zero interest
84 W.W. II vessels
85 Choice marbles
87 End of some 82-Acrosses
88 "Hands Across the Sea" composer
90 Writer ___ Rogers St. Johns
92 Excavate in the white cliffs?
99 "A Little Bitty Tear" singer, 1962
101 United
102 Flamenco cheer
103 Current gauge
104 1910s–'20s Dutch art movement
108 Like many "Survivor" contestants
109 Short ride
110 Drab Oriental fabric?
113 Word before or after "on"
114 Was a good Samaritan to
115 Rock genre
116 Blink ___ eye
117 Born abroad
118 Musts
119 Plant swelling
120 Communism battler, with "the"

DOWN

1 Summarizes
2 "Maybe"
3 Minor league baseball category
4 Greet someone
5 Hot Springs, e.g.
6 March fast?
7 Metropolitan ___
8 What people are saying, briefly
9 Promotion
10 Apt. overseer
11 Mechanics give them: Abbr.
12 Taro dish
13 Like half of all terminals
14 Leader with a goatee
15 Say "hallelujah!"
16 Sketch sewing-kit stores?
17 British fruitcake
22 Fresh
24 "Same here"
25 Prime minister raised in Milwaukee
30 Snail shell shape
32 Personification
34 "Be a ___!"
36 Kind of alcohol
37 Expressed wonder
38 Hops drier
39 "Apologia pro ___ Sua"
43 Kelly or Whitman
44 Waste of a sort
45 Crooked
46 Clown's parade memoir?
48 Twaddle
49 31-Across replacer
50 Decamp
51 One of the four elements
53 Toweling-off place
54 Urban grid
56 Start to lead?
57 "Holy moly!"
60 Onetime telecom giant
63 Listener
65 Friday, for one
66 Dictionary, often
67 Where private messages may be sent?: Abbr.
68 Delay
70 Towel stitching
71 Olive ___
73 Dear ___ Madam . . .
74 Breath: Prefix
76 1990–'91 war site
77 Shortly
78 Braided
79 Wood shop device
84 Night owl's TV fare
86 "The House of the Spirits" author, 1982
87 Grunts
89 ___ law (early legal code)
90 Cause to blush
91 Criticize harshly
92 ___ Melodies
93 "I ___ appreciate . . ."

by Daniel C. Bryant

94 In installments
95 In hijab, e.g.
96 "L'chaim!"
97 Figure skater Sokolova and others
98 Little stinger
100 Steakhouse shunner

104 Not natural
105 Terminal figs.
106 Leap on a stage
107 Good soil
111 Summer offering
112 20-Across terminus: Abbr.

ACROSS

1 Polish Peace Nobelist
7 Story development
10 Tongue of Jung: Abbr.
13 Variety show potpourri
18 Scrubs
19 Head of Great Britain
20 Where "I shot a man" in Johnny Cash's "Folsom Prison Blues"
21 Something to believe in
22 Foul weather condition?
25 1980s U.N. ambassador Kirkpatrick
26 Date
27 Sounded wowed
28 Plume source
29 Child protector?
30 Some moralizing about getting off a balance beam?
34 Quitter's assertion
36 Former Giants giant
37 Saloon door sign
38 "Do your thing, Jack the Ripper"?
43 Provides tools for, as a crime
46 Hefty competitor
47 Matériel
48 Hardships
50 Numbskull
54 Cheerful chorus
55 Wampum
57 Classic soft drink
58 Apartment 1-A resident, maybe
59 Sophistication of clubs like Sam's and BJ's?

62 Wool source
66 Title for Michael Caine
67 Declines
68 Concerns of someone who's choking?
75 Prepare
76 Used a bus, e.g.
77 March master
78 Fraction of a min.
82 Delta 88, e.g.
83 Asian shrine
85 Mid 10th-century year
86 Another, in Andalucia
87 Bruce who played Watson
88 Her Royal Daunter?
91 Eucharist plate
94 Suffix with ball
95 Take off, as a brooch
96 Coleslaw-loving children?
104 ___ nothing
105 Player of filmdom's Mr. Chips
106 With all one's strength
107 Welsh rabbit ingredient
110 Airbus, e.g.
111 Find chewing gum under a desk, perhaps?
114 Passage practices
115 Chihuahua drink
116 Prominent Chihuahua feature
117 Samantha's cousin on "Bewitched"
118 In other words
119 Bygone map letters
120 Hook shape
121 Texas team

DOWN

1 Rolls of dough
2 Broadway Rose-lover
3 Crosses the international date line from east to west
4 Work measurement unit
5 James I and Charles I
6 Northeast state of India
7 1979 film parodied in "Spaceballs"
8 Sonata movement
9 Subordinate person
10 Sci-fi, e.g.
11 Over
12 Swiss dish of grated and fried potatoes
13 Place in Monopoly
14 Continue
15 Doing the same old same old
16 Joint parts
17 Insertion in an operation
20 Just
23 Even if, briefly
24 More humid
31 Bagnold, Blyton, Markey, etc.
32 Postal creed word
33 Some NCOs
34 Rock's ___ Pop
35 Popular pop
39 '50s teen star
40 Incenses
41 Car financing co.
42 "As we have therefore opportunity, let ___ good to all men": Galatians
43 Tommie ___, 1966 A.L. Rookie of the Year

44 Nobel physicist Niels
45 Actor Bana of "Munich"
49 Prelims
50 Import tax
51 Magnum ___
52 "Coming Home" co-star
53 Stacking contest cookie
56 Puzzled (out)
58 Metal refuse
59 Sideless wagon
60 Nonexistent
61 Seals are part of it
62 Do that's picked
63 Advent song
64 More than nudge
65 9 to 5, e.g.
69 Go on too long
70 Venetian V.I.P. of yore
71 Wannabe's model
72 Rx writers
73 Judy Garland's real last name
74 "La ___ Bonita" (Madonna song)
78 Diamond center
79 Efficiency device
80 ". . . ___ saw Elba"
81 Mass. neighbor
83 Worrisome engine sound
84 Highway or Pet lead-in
87 Like a relative notified in an emergency, maybe
89 ___ while
90 Preserves fruits
91 Sans a healthy glow
92 Remove by cutting

by Cathy Millhauser

93 Porterhouse alternatives
94 Honshu metropolis
96 Banana liqueur drink shaken over ice
97 Old Norse works
98 Magician Henning and others
99 Run up
100 Oral flourishes
101 Starfleet V.I.P.'s: Abbr.
102 Japanese yes
103 "Once You ___ Stranger" (1969 thriller)
108 TV host known for his mandibular prognathism
109 History chapters
112 Word between two surnames
113 Leftover for Rover

ACROSS

1 Thing in a case
4 1960s–'80s Red Sox legend, informally
7 In the cellar
11 Org. that promotes adoption
15 "Poor venomous fool," in "Antony and Cleopatra"
18 Pumpkin-picking time: Abbr.
19 "Sons and Lovers" Oscar nominee Mary
20 Expected
22 King of comedy
23 Going rate?: Abbr.
24 1941 Henry Luce article that coined a name for an era
28 Barcelona Olympics prize
29 Tevye creator ___ Aleichem
30 Eight-time Norris Trophy winner
31 Protein acid, informally
32 Have ___ to pick
33 Celine Dion's "I'm Your Angel" duet partner
34 Closeout come-on
39 Designated driver's drink
40 Badges, e.g., in brief
41 ___ candy (some pop tunes)
42 Work of Seigneur de Montaigne
43 "Your Moment of ___" ("The Daily Show" feature)
45 Truncated cones, in math
49 Streaming
52 Novel that ends "Don't ever tell anybody anything. If you do, you start missing everybody"
61 Not to mention
62 Atlas section
63 "Roll Over Beethoven" band, for short
64 1990s–2000s English tennis star Tim
65 Rocky Mountains resort
66 Wide-eyed
67 First principles
70 "I'm king of the world!," e.g.
71 Exceeded the speed limit?
72 "Tancredi" composer
75 Artful deception
78 State quarters?
80 Actress Ullmann
81 Suffix with billion
82 1972 Harry Nilsson hit
90 Windsor, e.g.
95 Switch finish?
96 Absorb a loss
97 1984 Heisman winner
99 Orient
100 Chickadees' kin
101 Laughing gas and water, chemically
103 Mess up
104 Lover in "The Merchant of Venice"
106 Genuine: Ger.
107 Prime eatery
111 Sloughs off
113 You can't take it with you
114 Upstate N.Y. sch.
115 Tribute in jest
118 Managed
119 Sneak a peek
121 Boot part
125 Stanley Cup finalists of 1982 and 1994
131 Couple
133 Long-legged wader
134 He played Krupa in "The Gene Krupa Story"
135 "You did it!"
136 Lorenz Hart specialty
137 Pricey sports car, informally
138 Head of a special government inquiry
143 Hard wood
144 Math. class
145 Actress Watts
146 Home on "Gilligan's Island"
147 Inflation meas.
148 On the other hand
149 Charles de Gaulle alternative
150 Varsity QB, e.g.
151 Sign at a smash
152 Possessed

DOWN

1 "Number 10" Abstract Expressionist
2 Made a comeback?
3 "A Streetcar Named Desire" role
4 "Dee-lish!"
5 "These ___ the times that . . ."
6 Closed (in on)
7 Money
8 Botanist Gray
9 Center of many revolutions
10 Certain X or O
11 Subbed (for)
12 Dive
13 Glances
14 "___ takers?"
15 Spanish sherry
16 Offshoot
17 Snap
21 Mother of Judah
25 Popular portal
26 Kupcinet and Cross
27 Application letters
29 Some namesakes: Abbr.
32 Without obligation
35 Change of a mortgage, slangily
36 Paul Bunyan story
37 Ministry of ___, in "1984"
38 Ryder Cup team
40 Time ___
43 Tase
44 When many get a St.-Tropez tan
46 Biblical queendom
47 Joint part
48 Royal Navy foe of 1588
50 Willow used in basketry
51 Hills of Yorkshire
52 Spree
53 Monster hurricane of 1989
54 Libido
55 Lowly workers
56 Do voodoo on
57 Skull and Bones members
58 Latitude
59 Bleeth of "Baywatch"
60 Unabridged
67 Executive's charter, maybe
68 Infiltrator
69 Flat-bottomed boat
73 Despot ___ Amin
74 Lead-in to "the above" or "your business"
76 Like some twins
77 ___ center
79 Mystery element
82 Leaps across the ballet stage
83 "Vega$" star Robert
84 Nick Nolte movie based on a Kurt Vonnegut novel
85 Some advanced researchers, for short
86 Traditional almanac data
87 Bikini blast
88 Sorry sort
89 Parisian "to be"
91 Jean who wrote "Please Don't Eat the Daisies"
92 "So long, dahling"
93 "The fix ___"
94 Virginie ou Pennsylvanie
98 Subject of the book "Many Unhappy Returns": Abbr.
102 ___ Zagora, Bulgaria
104 Infant's food

by John Farmer

105 "Certainement!"
108 Mussorgsky's "Pictures ___ Exhibition"
109 Contact lens solution brand
110 Venture
112 ___ Miguel, Azores Island
116 Sting's last name
117 "Hannah Montana" star Miley Cyrus, for one
119 32-card game
120 Charges (up)
121 "Into the Wild" actor Emile
122 Home of Gannon Univ.
123 Author of the "Elements," ca. 300 B.C.
124 Past records?
125 Singh on the links
126 Demean
127 Bad guys
128 Name
129 Filmmaker Joel or Ethan
130 Jaded figure
131 2006 neologism meaning "to demote"
132 Author Rand
138 "May ___ now?"
139 Bust
140 ___ Pérignon
141 Comic Philips
142 "___ Father . . ."

ACROSS

1 Program executors, for short
5 Miracle-___
8 Tribal council makeup, often
14 Casual attire
19 Like the carol "Away in a Manger," originally
21 Wine sometimes blended with Cabernet Sauvignon
22 Be
23 Turn away
24 Foot, slangily
25 2% alternative
26 *Long, long time
28 Loot
30 Yank or Tiger
31 Half-baked
32 *Stick with a needle, maybe
34 *Absence at a nudist colony?
41 What a Tennessee cheerleader asks for a lot?
42 Stuck
43 Neighbor of Ga.
44 *Bugs
50 Jazzy Jones
51 *Wee
54 Below par
55 X-ray ___
56 "What a moron I am!"
57 Gawk at
58 Whatchamacallit
60 Monterrey mister
62 Suffix not seen much in London
63 Least bold
65 Like the answers to the 10 asterisked clues, more often than any other English words, according to a 1999 study
69 Narrative
71 ___ choy (Chinese vegetable)
72 Contract specifics
73 Luster
74 Tip of the Arabian Peninsula
76 Massage target?
77 Spicy cuisine
81 Debt acknowledgment
82 *Conspicuous
86 Trying period for a doctoral student
87 *Supplant
91 Clean air org.
92 Baseball's ___ league
93 Gen ___
94 *Doggedness
97 *Oblige
103 Commotion
104 Series of rounds
105 Is undecided
107 *Event
113 Root used in perfumery
115 Farmer's ___
117 Attempts
118 T-shirt style
119 Follows
120 Like some pens
121 Swift's "A Modest Proposal," e.g.
122 Plain
123 Alternative to dial-up
124 French noblemen

DOWN

1 Symbol of happiness
2 Long-haired sheepdog
3 Regulated bus.
4 Writer/illustrator Silverstein
5 Mustang competitor
6 Photoshop options
7 Tops
8 Ambulance figure: Abbr.
9 Many August babies
10 Disarming words?
11 Rocker John
12 Violinist's need
13 Pen, to Pierre
14 1950s Braves All-Star pitcher Burdette
15 Relaxes, in a way
16 It's bowed
17 Archipelago part
18 Cubic meter
20 Laredo-to-Galveston dir.
27 "Bro!"
29 Cliff
33 Spanish "a"
34 Karl Marx's one
35 Alphabet quartet
36 Expose
37 Product with TV's first advertising jingle, 1948
38 Word of encouragement
39 QB Manning
40 "Illmatic" rapper
44 Most massive
45 The whole wide world
46 Show up again
47 Judged, with "up"
48 They're seen in many John Constable paintings
49 ___ machine
51 Orator's no-no
52 Restaurant chain since 1958
53 Close, as a relationship
56 Laura of "Jurassic Park"
58 Some shampoos
59 Running mate with Dick
60 Like cotton candy
61 Commercial come-on
62 Type
64 Ticklish one?
65 Freeze
66 Target of many a Bart Simpson prank call
67 Rice-A-___
68 Marmalade component
69 Without adjustments
70 Dynasty of Confucius and Lao-tzu
75 Trendy
77 Olive or apple
78 Goldie of "Cactus Flower"
79 Actor Baldwin
80 "Ah, yes"
83 O.K. mark
84 When Earth Day is celebrated: Abbr.
85 ___ profundo
86 Anthem contraction
88 Rare imports, maybe
89 Crucial sleep stage
90 Cock-a-doodle-doo
92 Examination
94 Opposite of "nod off"
95 Marked permanently
96 Parish priests
97 Previously mentioned
98 Toes' woes
99 Parish priests
100 Matriarchs
101 ___-garde
102 Brusque
106 Ooze
108 Dorm heads, for short
109 "Heavens!"

by Oliver Hill

110 International chain of fusion cuisine restaurants
111 Course after trig
112 Somme times
114 Heavens
116 Literary inits.

Poplar Music

ACROSS

1 Craving, slangily
6 Crèche figures
10 Impromptu Halloween costume
15 Spray withdrawn in 1989
19 Try to steal the scene, maybe
20 "Darn it!"
21 Mountain chain
23 Nick name?
24 1977 Dolly Parton song for tree fanciers?
26 Bridal collection
28 Not ___ many words
29 Nominal promotion of a military officer
30 Sugar substitute?
31 Modern pentathlon event
32 Inner circles
33 1965 Yardbirds song for tree fanciers?
39 ___ volatile
40 Bellowing
41 Nirvana seeker
42 World capital, founded in 1538, formerly known as Chuquisaca
44 Suffix with myth
48 Went like a shot
50 1957 Jerry Lee Lewis song for tree fanciers?
53 Outer limits
54 Stand
56 Rush hour sounds
57 Port of Iraq
58 One trillionth: Prefix
59 Rossini subject
60 Air Force athlete

61 1964 Bobby Goldsboro song for tree fanciers?
68 It's spotted in the wild
69 Like a lot of Australia
70 Lay on the line
71 Brain parts
72 Tippy transport
74 Bank deposit?
75 Old-time oath
79 1982 Joan Jett and the Blackhearts song for tree fanciers?
82 Jazzy Nina
84 Altar procedure
85 "Sesame Street" regular
86 Beaufort scale category
88 Neighbor of Chad
89 Flight formation
90 1959 Chuck Berry song for tree fanciers?
92 Source of some coffee
96 Italian bread
98 Source of creosote
99 Sugar or flour
100 Doozy
101 Do police work
107 1978 Linda Ronstadt song for tree fanciers?
110 Palate part
111 Sing "Bye Bye Birdie," e.g.
112 Hurt badly
113 16th-century English dramatist George
114 Badlands sight
115 Exorcist's enemy
116 Red army?
117 Sp. misses

DOWN

1 Witty remark
2 "A Jug of Wine . . ." poet
3 Off-limits item
4 Words of reproach
5 Strand
6 Key fort?
7 Stretch
8 Ashram leader
9 Chemical suffix
10 Teatime treat
11 Theater audience
12 For this reason
13 Dot follower, often
14 Tito Puente played them
15 "Sink or Swim" author
16 Permission
17 Sign of spring
18 Go into hysterics
22 ___ Lad, doughnut shop on "The Simpsons"
25 Cry of dismay
27 Insignificant amount
31 "A Letter for ___" (Hume Cronyn film)
32 ___ Jr., West Coast hamburger chain
33 Discombobulate
34 Mill material
35 Cross
36 Thanksgiving serving
37 Enters cyberspace
38 Dungeons & Dragons character
39 Sing like Fitzgerald
42 Impassive
43 Nut holder
44 "___ else fails . . ."
45 ___ Systems, networking giant
46 Helpful pointer
47 Musical Rimes
49 Underlying meaning
51 Place for an easel

52 One way to be taken
55 R.N.'s station
58 Purple stuff, perhaps
59 Power of film
60 Happy gatherings
61 Play-by-play partner
62 Theodor Escherich's discovery
63 Ledger entry
64 Anacin alternative
65 ___-Poo of "The Mikado"
66 1970s–'80s baseball All-Star Manny
67 Rap star ___ Jon
72 Chick on the piano
73 Rough condition to face?
74 Criticize
75 Eastern ruler
76 Energetic
77 From the top
78 Laura of "Blue Velvet"
80 Ran through again
81 Give the once-over
83 Cliques
87 Prizes
90 Sufficient, informally
91 Dance specialty
92 Dickens title starter
93 Soul singer Lou
94 Via ___ (Roman road)
95 Be noisy
96 Words before bed or rest
97 Not at all familiar
99 E-mail annoyance
100 "The Informer" author O'Flaherty
101 Kind of meeting in "O Brother, Where Art Thou?"
102 Give off
103 Camper driver

by Richard Silvestri

104 Something one
can never do
105 Salmon tail?
106 Actress Charlotte
and explorer John
108 Grand ___,
Nova Scotia
109 John's "Pulp
Fiction" co-star

63 DONE WITH EASE

ACROSS

1 Rooter at the Meadowlands
8 Lean and bony
15 Superman, to his father
20 Common solvent
21 Filled
22 Acid in proteins
23 State of a bottle-fed baby?
25 Woody Allen title role
26 Afternoon hr.
27 Construction bit
28 Bleacher
30 Comme ci, comme ça
31 Was visibly irked with
35 Shower with flowers, say
36 Soft drink brand
38 A platform in front of Elsinore, in "Hamlet"?
44 Contemporary of Duchamp
47 "Doctor Faustus" novelist
49 Jazz virtuoso Garner
50 The toe of a geographical "boot"
51 Massage therapist's office?
55 Like a Rolek watch
57 Fashion designer Bartley
58 Brown alternative
59 "You can ___ horse to water . . ."
61 Sentimentality
62 "Puppy Love" singer, 1960
63 Jawaharlal Nehru's daughter
65 Rouge roulette number
67 Group of yo-yo experts?
70 One willing to take a bullet for Martin or Charlie?
76 Neighbor of Hung.
77 Fixes firmly
79 Shade on the French Riviera
80 Calypso offshoot
83 Actor Alain
86 It has banks in Bern
87 Urban area in a Cheech Marin film
89 1965 Peace Prize recipient
91 Little Bo-Peep's charges?
94 Catty comments?
95 87 or 93
97 Turn on an axis
98 Alphabet trio
99 Musicians at a marsh?
103 Numerical prefix
105 Corrosive chemical, to a chemist
106 Strong and deep
108 Oversight
112 Limo feature
117 "Road" picture partner for Bob
118 "Same here!"
119 "The joke's ___!"
120 St. Paul sixth graders?
125 Indonesian island
126 Victimizes
127 Brewing needs
128 Do
129 Calendar divisions
130 ___ Row

DOWN

1 ___ Kádár, 1950s–'80s Hungarian leader
2 Low-price prefix
3 "The Love Boat" actress Lauren
4 Squash, squish or squelch
5 Head
6 Gloucester's Cape ___
7 Chick
8 Cuban-born jazz great Sandoval
9 Fix
10 3.9, e.g.: Abbr.
11 Final: Abbr.
12 Gift with a string attached?
13 Over
14 Fix-up
15 Buzzers
16 Green card, informally
17 Leslie Caron title role
18 Home of the Chisholm Trail Expo Center
19 Front of a mezzanine
24 ___ big way
29 Casually showed up
31 Land west of Togo
32 The less you see of this person the better
33 Intro to business?
34 Alpine region
37 German biographer ___ Ludwig
39 ___ of the above
40 Romaine
41 Online periodical, for short
42 Warsaw Pact counterforce
43 Automaker Ferrari
44 Key of Elgar's Symphony No. 1
45 Get the class back together
46 ___-boo
48 "Bye Bye Bye" band, 2000
52 Cousin of a camel
53 "Aren't I amazing?!"
54 Skirt type
56 Called
60 Good blackjack holdings
63 Like G8 meetings: Abbr.
64 "There's no such thing ___ publicity"
66 Subdue
68 "My man!"
69 Resort to violence
71 "Three cheers" recipient
72 Ideal sites
73 Like some pyramids
74 Lined
75 Don, as a sari
78 "Luncheon on the Grass" and others
80 Well
81 Baby-bouncing locale
82 Sanyo competitor
84 Words to live by
85 Hornet, e.g.
87 Extracted chemical
88 "___ of Six" (Joseph Conrad story collection)
90 Hrs. on the 90th meridian
92 Addie's husband in "As I Lay Dying"
93 Stretch . . . or a hint to this puzzle's theme?

by Tony Orbach and Patrick Blindauer

96 Shop grippers
100 "And I'm the queen of England"
101 Director Mark of "Earthquake"
102 Particles in electrolysis
104 Slide presentation?
107 Amazon ___
109 They might be bounced off others
110 Troubadour's stock
111 Wimp
112 Scribbles (down)
113 Body of troops
114 "Well, I declare!"
115 Summer hangout
116 Poop
118 Seaborne lackey
121 Org. interested in schools
122 Albany is its cap.
123 That's "that" in Tijuana
124 Pro ___

ACROSS

1 Site of campus workstations
6 Ancient pueblo dwellers
13 Norm of "This Old House"
18 Muse with a wreath of myrtle and roses
19 Together
20 Tell things?
21 Bill formerly of the Rolling Stones
22 Fight imaginary foes
24 Richard ___, 2002 Pulitzer winner for Fiction
26 ___ B'rith
27 Sylph in Pope's "The Rape of the Lock"
28 Pressure, of a sort
32 "Sixteen Tons" singer, 1955
36 Do better than
37 In the capacity of
38 X-ray units
41 Nails
42 Notch shape
43 "Would you like to see ___?"
45 Italian restaurant chain
47 Game pieces
48 Some badge holders
49 "Alice in Wonderland" sister
50 It's a laugh
51 Each
53 "Lawrence of Arabia" composer Maurice
54 ___-doodle
56 Start of the names of some health care plans
58 Daily grind
60 Place for a vine
61 Bent over
63 How headings are often typed
65 Surfing spot
66 Immigrant's class: Abbr.
68 "Survivor" setting, often
69 Blood-typing letters
70 Fire
72 Some M.I.T. grads: Abbr.
73 Buster?
75 Certain T-shirt design
77 Sure application spot
79 Drug-free
80 National Chili Mo.
81 Blue shade
83 "Pearly Shells" singer
85 Refrain syllables
86 Loud laugh
88 Take to Vegas, maybe
90 Valuable find
92 Mideast call to prayer
93 Airport with a BART terminal
95 Steer
97 Kids
98 Kind of score
99 "Deadwood" figure
100 Untouched
101 Meaningless amount
103 Quick stumbles
104 Dealer's handout
107 Starts, as rehab
110 Upper ___
111 Shade provider
114 Outplays
115 Former L.A. Ram who holds the N.F.L. record for most receiving yards in a game (336)
119 Response to "Any volunteers?"
123 Pretends
124 "Back door's open!"
125 Explorer of sorts
126 To date
127 In order
128 Post with a column

DOWN

1 Missal location
2 "Geronimo!," e.g.
3 Escape
4 Defender company
5 Test extras
6 Electrolysis particle
7 Match ___ (tie game, in France)
8 Aardvark
9 ___ Phillips, who played Livia in "I, Claudius"
10 Old film pooch
11 "Fan-tastic!"
12 Suffix in some pasta names
13 Hosts
14 To the point
15 Opening track of "The Beatles' Second Album"
16 Cobbler's tool
17 Eds. read them
19 "No problem!"
20 Oscar-winning Brody
23 Jack of "Eraserhead"
25 Good nickname for a cook?
28 Galley marking
29 Peripatetic sort
30 Einstein subject
31 Short-billed rail
33 Push for more business orders
34 House of Lancaster symbol
35 Jilts
39 Sloping surfaces next to sinks
40 Pacifier
44 Cheese ___
46 Good farming results
48 Klinger portrayer on "M*A*S*H"
52 ___ pro nobis
53 Awarding of huge settlements to plaintiffs, in modern lingo
55 Some greetings
57 Zoologist Fossey
59 Early anti-Communist
62 Mix
64 The Nutmeg State: Abbr.
66 Hug
67 Marathoner Alberto
71 Control: Abbr.
74 Actor James
76 Indian tribe encountered by Lewis and Clark
78 Sign of the cross
82 "Were that so!"
84 Plain as day
87 Excellent debt rating
89 Rappel down
91 Edsel driver's gas choice
93 "Bambi" author
94 Monastery figure
96 Sovereign's representative
99 It's a trap
102 Approves
105 Thicket
106 Faust, e.g.
108 Old Treasury offering
109 Nation of ___
112 Month in which Moses is said to have been born and died
113 Aloe ___

by Brendan Emmett Quigley

115 Fourth-most populous state, just after N.Y.
116 French article
117 Turkish title
118 Press (for)
120 VII octupled
121 Many a toothpaste
122 Suffix with direct

When this puzzle is done, the seven circles will contain the letters from A to G. Starting with A, connect them alphabetically with one continuous line, and you'll get an image of a 39-Across.

ACROSS

1 How architects' models are built
8 Lou Bega's "___ No. 5"
13 Ottoman V.I.P.'s
18 Foyer item
19 Plug in a travel kit
21 It may give you a cold shoulder
22 Alarming
23 *1969*
25 Auditioned for "American Idol"
26 Italian town known for its embroidery
28 End of a plumb line
29 Law assignment
30 Garbage hauler
32 "True"
35 Neighborhood next to N.Y.C.'s East Village
37 Ecuador and Venezuela are in it
39 [See instructions]
41 Relating to a blood line
45 Sub systems
47 Suffix with urban
48 *1973–85*
50 Moles' production
52 Subj. for bilinguals
54 Like some video, to cable customers
55 Warhol's "___ of Six Self-Portraits"
56 Lambs' kin
58 Aside (from)
61 "Smooth Operator" singer
62 French seas
63 Powder site, maybe
64 First mate
65 "Put ___ writing!"
67 Layer
68 *1987–89*

71 Figures at many a wedding reception, briefly
74 Kite flier's wish
75 Muscle mag displays
76 Sneaky
77 Semitic deity
78 Med. plans
80 Gut course
82 Alexander Hamilton's last act
83 "By the power vested ___ . . ."
84 Aches
86 N.B.A.'s ___ Ming
88 Ventured (forth)
90 Writer born May 28, 1908
93 Speech pauses
95 Surprisingly
96 Brings out
97 Offering from St. Joseph
99 Willy Wonka's creator
100 ___ buco
102 Mexican beer
103 A great deal
105 "Lost" filming locale
108 Global currency org.
110 2003 best-selling fantasy novel by teen author Christopher Paolini
113 Beethoven's third?
115 *1995–2002*
119 New Jersey city, county or river
121 Name-drop, maybe?
122 Least restrained
123 Artist Watteau
124 Ward off
125 Singer Jones and others
126 Piano players' hangouts

DOWN

1 Old propaganda propagator
2 Ocean menaces
3 *1962–67, 1971*
4 Attire with supersized pockets
5 "Exodus" hero
6 ___ 9, first spacecraft to land softly on the moon
7 Deviled things
8 Chairman's supporter?
9 Natl. Poetry Mo.
10 Brief encounter?
11 Programme airer, with "the"
12 Knee sock material
13 Wood shaper
14 Like some wrestling
15 Tennis star Mandlikova
16 Edwards and others: Abbr.
17 Eye doctor's concern
19 Shakes up
20 Hungers
24 On
27 California's ___ Valley
31 "___ #1!"
33 Title for 48-Across and 3-Down
34 Lennon's mate
36 Nears, with "on"
38 "The Allegory of Love" writer, 1936
40 Kurchatov who oversaw the Soviet atomic bomb project
42 Lowly one
43 Composer of "Dido and Aeneas"
44 Spearheaded
45 Sign of approval
46 White-collared thrush: Var.
49 Authorizes

51 Butterfly experts, perhaps
53 March 25, in the Christian calendar
57 It can be fragile
59 Residences, in slang
60 Drs.' org.
64 Ship-to-ship communication
66 In song, "Once you pass its borders, you can ne'er return again"
68 Fights
69 Cable TV inits.
70 Baton Rouge sch.
71 *2006–*
72 Bond common to the answers to the six *italicized* clues
73 Runners' locales
74 It's full of holes
77 Rock guitarist once married to Goldie Hawn
78 Commander
79 Plan for dinner
81 1998 Sarah McLachlan hit
82 Alpha
84 Disapproving cry
85 Bluesy Smith
87 Night lights
89 Rich soil
91 Homeland protection org.
92 Main mailbox locale: Abbr.
94 Sweater flaw
98 Castle and Cara
101 Game played with a 40-card deck
104 "Romanzero" poet
105 Phone co. employee
106 Suffix with billion
107 Jalopy

by Elizabeth C. Gorski

109 Univ. house
111 Autumn birthstone
112 Second start?
114 Clinches
116 Hanna-Barbera art
117 German direction
118 ___ Na Na
120 Disco guy on "The Simpsons"

EXTRA SYLL-UH-BLES

ACROSS

1 Diane of "Alice Doesn't Live Here Anymore"
5 Picture holder
10 ___ alai
13 They may be big fellers
17 Prefix with business
18 West African coins
20 On one's ___
21 World capital formerly a pirate stronghold
22 Waistband sold in stores?
24 Issue to avoid
26 Bad things to share
27 Wiser from an ethical perspective?
29 Miller brand
30 Two points?
31 Wellborn folks
32 Fighting force trained by Pavlov?
38 Qualifying races
39 Auto superseded by the Rambler
40 Actress Susan of "L.A. Law"
41 Leading man?
45 Some cloisonné pieces
46 Distresses
47 Put through demeaning rituals
49 City just west of Silver Springs
50 Salon selections
51 Kilo- times 1,000
52 Mardi ___
54 Skirts worn by both men and women
56 Freelance autopsist?
59 Renaissance painter Uccello
61 Lady Bird Johnson's given birth name

62 Private
63 Catchy song parts heard on "Name That Tune"?
66 Country with a camel on its coat of arms
67 Sign
68 Captain Hook's mate in "Peter Pan"
69 X3 and X5 maker
72 Pack carriers
73 T. ___ Price (investment firm)
75 Intervals
76 Animation
77 Minus
78 Club wielders' grp.
79 Stud farm visitor
80 Crème de la crème
81 Stones and brickbats?
86 Appointed
90 Attorney general during Reagan's second term
91 "Metropolis" director
92 Store that peddles political influence?
95 Like glass doors, often
98 Its bite is worse than its bark
99 Boiled lobster's feature?
102 Be part of the opening lineup
103 High dudgeon
104 Ankle covering
105 Barrett of gossip
106 Lots of talk
107 Smidgen
108 Only beardless one of the Seven Dwarfs
109 Fall around Christmas

DOWN

1 Testing facilities
2 Flu symptom
3 Washes without water
4 Record keepers, of a sort
5 Mobile phone company
6 Bottom of the barrel
7 Weave's partner
8 Rimbaud's "___ Saison en Enfer"
9 "___ the Wanderer" (1820 gothic novel)
10 Composer Pachelbel
11 Gone from the company, maybe
12 Like many large cos.
13 Evildoer
14 To the rear of
15 It's in the spring
16 Alibi
19 Premium vodka brand, for short
21 N.F.L. star Grier
23 Bug-ridden software releases
25 Miniature
28 Down Under jumper
30 Buchanan's secretary of state
32 Sound of a failure
33 Lifesaver
34 Architect Jones
35 Ornamental piece of drapery
36 Timber-dressing tool
37 Actress Witherspoon
41 Squirrels' cache
42 Word to which a common reply is "Bitteschön"

43 "Tattered Tom" author
44 Ensign holder
46 Bacterium that needs oxygen
47 Submit
48 John of "The Addams Family"
49 Self-descriptive fruit
51 Cheek teeth
52 ___ Park, historic home near Philadelphia
53 Vin color
55 Organic compounds with nitrogen
56 French aristocrats
57 Nudge
58 Founding member of the Dadaists
59 Place to keep Mace
60 Not quite right
63 Get better
64 Slowly
65 Motivate
69 Fighting words
70 Fly-catching aid
71 Depression causes
74 Granola tidbit
75 Willing
76 Appliances with lids
78 Belarus port
79 Think that might is right?
80 It may come with attachments
81 Not just sit there
82 Projected onto a screen
83 Last number in a column
84 Ohm of Ohm's law
85 Queen of mystery
86 2005 Best Picture winner
87 ___ Sorrel (woman in a love triangle in "Adam Bede")

by Patrick Berry

88 Available by the pint, perhaps
89 Rubberneck
93 Alter pieces?
94 ___ Roberts, first inductee into the Romance Writers of America Hall of Fame
95 ___-Ball
96 Inadvisable action
97 Chew on
100 Per la grazia di ___ (by the grace of God)
101 Brand at a gas station

ACROSS

1 Bear-named villainess in Superman films
5 Cause of a full stop for sailing ships
13 Ritzy Rio neighborhood
20 Column on a questionnaire
21 Blasted, with "on"
22 Wreaked havoc on
23 They tremble in the slightest breeze
25 Apple pie order
26 Strip
27 Hoedown sites
28 Geneviève, e.g.: Abbr.
29 Beginning of a cowboy song refrain
30 Loathing
31 "Star Wars," e.g.
32 Parliamentary measure of 1774
35 It's pitched
36 Abbey area
37 Introductory course?
39 Grassy plains
40 Ten-millionth of a joule
41 Too much ink
42 Arctic bird
43 Run out
44 Period in which we live
47 Addams who created the Addams family
51 Drang's counterpart
53 Sidesplitter
54 Word before and after "yes"
55 Reason for lights going out
56 Trio of comedy
58 Takes off
60 "All ___"
62 Mrs., abroad
63 Recoiling from
65 Pursue
68 Hikes
69 Compound that's subject to tautomerism
70 Vending machine tricker
72 Packard's partner
73 Scintillas
75 Chess opening?
77 Canine cry
79 Cries shrilly
80 ___ Mawr
81 "The Spirit of Australia" sloganeer
84 Engorge
86 Wildly
87 Implements using fulcrums
88 Red, e.g., once
91 Credit card magnet
94 Birthstone for some Libras
95 Stage direction
96 Relative of Welsh
97 Daughter of James II
99 Shadow
100 Attacks
101 Tea holder
102 Grasp
103 Teem
105 Washing machine setting
106 Title girl of a Willa Cather novel
109 Graham Greene novel set in Saigon, with "The"
111 Woodworker, at times
112 Without paraphrasing
113 Pig product
114 Backwoods valleys
115 Freezing mixtures
116 Scroll holders

DOWN

1 Two wiggling fingers, maybe
2 Drunkard
3 White-hot
4 Invite to a movie, say
5 Classic 1965 novel set on the planet Arrakis
6 Arts and Sciences major: Abbr.
7 Gypsum variety
8 Amount to take
9 "It Happened One Night" director
10 Mideast city that was once a British protectorate
11 Monocle, basically
12 Members of 82-Down
13 Ready to blow
14 Like forget-me-nots
15 Gardner of "Mogambo"
16 Where G.I.'s fought Charlie
17 "Ararat" director, 2002
18 Doc
19 Mavens
24 Computing-Tabulating-Recording Co., today
28 Slangy greeting
31 Primer pooch
32 Wharves
33 South African who twice won the U.S. Open
34 Hidden drawback
36 El ___ (1942 battle site)
37 Glide
38 "___ House," 1983 Madness hit
41 Is a second-story man
42 Stuffed shirts
43 Really mean
44 What, to Camus
45 Capital on the Dvina River
46 Suffix with zillion
48 Low-cost stopover
49 Stops on le métro
50 Word next to an arrow, maybe
51 Daze
52 Cozy and warm
55 St. Lawrence and others
56 In Harry Potter books, nonmagical offspring of wizard parents
57 Treaded transport
59 Sign of a brake problem
61 Patrick of "X-Men"
64 Place between hills
66 Fruit named for its appearance
67 Fever causes
71 Spray under the sink
74 1973 #1 hit for the Rolling Stones
76 Tour de France stage
78 Close
81 More upset
82 Sawbones' org.
83 Play a sax solo, maybe
85 Hosp. staffer
88 1988 Tracy Chapman hit
89 Just for the heck of it
90 Offers
91 Sport with a service line
92 Seek aid from
93 Many a tux
94 Beginning of all New York ZIP codes
95 Wild animal ID

by Will Nediger

96 Battle of ___ Bay, 1898
98 Gets warmer
99 Karate-like exercises
100 The Beatles' "And I Love ___"
103 Plaintiff
104 Lean and sinewy
105 Solitaires, e.g.
107 It's well-supplied
108 Palm Springs-to-Las Vegas dir.
109 Home shopping channel
110 Watch unit: Abbr.

ACROSS

1 Fills to almost overflowing
8 Unposed photo
14 Search blindly
19 What some shoot in a golf round
20 Decked out
22 Alternatives to Yodels
23 Memo about Stephen King's "Christine"?
25 Bob Marley's "___ the Sheriff"
26 Drop from the invitation list, say
27 Dig in
28 Staple figure in origami
30 Emmy-winning Ward
31 Meeting of the minds?
32 Memo about an inveterate perjurer?
37 Like the Honda Element
38 BBC : Britain :: ___ : Italy
39 Part of ½
40 Want to undo
41 Absentee
44 Kind of line
46 "Now I see!"
48 Memo about a dating guide?
50 Way around Paris
53 Contingencies
54 MSN rival
55 Board
57 An essay may be on one
61 Loon
64 Memo about where tariffs are imposed on incoming ships?
68 In the slightest
69 Mocks
70 Apple gadget
71 Memo about stores for animal appendages?
74 Falls on the border
76 Strategic W.W. I river
77 Mower part
78 Wee bit
79 D.C. bigwig
80 City on the Ruhr
82 Memo about a religious outpost for prisoners?
88 1492 voyager
91 Editorial take
92 Have mercy (on)
93 Bearded beast
94 Source of wool
99 Timecard abbr.
100 Flirtatious sort
101 Memo about why to buy an air purifier?
105 Box office sign
108 Canned
109 Lightly moisten
110 Journey part
111 "Right on!"
112 Ready to roll? . . . or not ready to roll?
114 Memo about a lyricist?
119 Top echelon
120 Ignore the usual wake-up time
121 Clothing chain since 1994
122 It's distracting
123 John James Audubon, e.g.
124 "Ain't gonna happen!"

DOWN

1 Short and often not sweet
2 Some are Dutch
3 Give some zing
4 Hoity-toity type
5 Special ___
6 Fourth members of a musical group
7 At will
8 Inflexible, as some rules
9 Suffix with stock or block
10 Go-ahead signal
11 ___ Malfoy, Harry Potter antagonist
12 Buries
13 Special military assignment
14 4, on a phone
15 "Arrested Development" actress Portia de ___
16 Candy bar whose name is an exclamation
17 It may be used for banking
18 They're left behind
21 1958 hit whose B-side was "La Bamba"
24 Articulate
29 Biggest section in a dictionary
32 Rice-A-___
33 All of a crowd, maybe
34 When repeated, Mork's TV sign-off
35 Prefix with byte
36 Whaling adverb
37 Kid's greeting
41 Threefold
42 Proves otherwise
43 Like Albany or Chicago
44 Low-___
45 Bordering on
47 Frank
49 One of a comedic trio
50 LeBlanc of "Joey"
51 One with a pole position?
52 General on a Chinese menu
56 Long lines on a timeline
58 Turkey is part of it
59 Music players
60 Rule before a revolution, maybe
62 Popular table wine
63 Clay, by another name
64 No longer working: Abbr.
65 Specialized fishermen
66 Grand ___, setting for "Evangeline"
67 HDTV maker
69 King ___ Carlos of Spain
72 Figure-watchers' figs.
73 World Cup cheer
74 Where Forrest Gump did a tour
75 "Gotcha," to a beatnik
78 Boom maker
81 Put (away)
83 K–12 grades, collectively
84 ___ loading
85 How a ringtone may be set
86 Discman maker
87 ___ Ed
88 Like many nonanimated Disney films
89 Banished
90 Having digits
95 Isr. neighbor

by Jeremy Newton

96 They do impressions
97 First Ford
98 Invariably
100 Filet type
102 Schiller's "___ Joy"
103 Babydoll
104 Old western actor Van Cleef
105 Makeup applier's boo-boo
106 One of the Canterbury pilgrims
107 Ham ___
111 Years in old Rome
113 Old Ottoman title
115 Univ. in Troy, N.Y.
116 Family nickname
117 Shine, in product names
118 Fingers

CHAIN REACTION

ACROSS

1 Third Crusade siege site
5 Citadel trainee
10 Where houses traditionally have no walls
15 Isn't idle
19 Leeway
20 Like galleys
21 Run ___ of
22 Great Lakes salmon
23 FOOD COURT ___ CIRCUIT BOARD
25 CIRCUIT BOARD ___ ROOM SERVICE
27 Music may come in it
28 Stock market worker
30 Like some sacrifices
31 Stove option
32 Is for a group?
33 Clothing lines
34 Life's partner
37 ___-midi (French time of day)
41 Like many dorms nowadays
42 Laughable
43 ROOM SERVICE ___ LIGHT TOUCH
46 Code unit
49 Covert sound
50 "Beetle Bailey" character
51 What greedy people want
52 Cause someone's insomnia, maybe
54 "Git!"
55 LIGHT TOUCH ___ BELL PEPPER
57 Pet animal of Salvador Dali
58 Sponge
60 Sylvia Plath poem that begins "I know the bottom, she says. I know it with my great tap root"
61 Weightlifter's rep
62 Impassioned
63 Corporate division
65 Fabric border
68 Give up
69 Young newt
70 Some dates have one
71 Long-armed Sumatrans
73 BELL PEPPER ___ BRUSH FIRE
76 Was idle
77 Track take
78 "It's been real"
79 Protection
80 Iota
81 "Father ___," hit 1990s British sitcom
82 BRUSH FIRE ___ SMART CAR
84 Songwriter Carole Bayer ___
85 "Comin' ___ the Rye"
86 French word before deux or nous
87 Dialogue units
88 Bore
92 Third-century year
94 D-Day mo.
95 Tale of a trip to Ithaca
96 Shaped, as wood
100 Julia who starred in "Sabrina," 1995
104 SMART CAR ___ PIANO BAR
106 PIANO BAR ___ TRAILHEAD
108 Composer Thomas
109 Irving Berlin's "___ My Heart at the Stage Door Canteen"
110 Tennessee teammate
111 Final Four game
112 Tomorrow's opposite: Abbr.
113 Send
114 Some seconds
115 Too: Fr.

DOWN

1 Tennis lobs, e.g.
2 Prince Albert, for one
3 Gift that might cut
4 Newly developed, as technology
5 Pullover shirts
6 Dweller along the Mekong
7 Once, old-style
8 Mugful
9 Work of prose or poetry
10 More conservative, as investments
11 In front of, in dialect
12 Farm call
13 Best, in a way
14 Played the enchantress
15 Gulf of Guinea capital
16 Alternatives to RCs
17 ___ park
18 Blisters, e.g.
24 "Stop it!"
26 Place for an opinion
29 Code unit
34 Give insider info
35 Protect
36 TRAILHEAD ___ COUNTERTOP
37 Turkey's tallest peak
38 Read carefully
39 Throw a fit
40 Heaven on earth
41 Vikki who sang "It Must Be Him"
44 Soap plant
45 Some camera lenses
46 COUNTERTOP ___ POST OFFICE
47 Oaxaca gold
48 Hanoi holiday
50 Teahouse treats
52 Cut decoratively
53 Brass
55 Heavy hitter
56 Area around the mouth
57 A tremendous supply
59 2, 4, 6, 8, etc.
63 Calyx part
64 They were seen at Black Power meetings
65 Like Iran's Ahmadinejad
66 Satan is often seen with one
67 Records
70 Bull or Buck, e.g.
71 Make a choice
72 Paris's ___ La Fayette
73 Farm tower
74 Ball in a basket
75 "Syriana" actress Amanda
78 Tote
80 It's in front of a mizzen
82 Something to pop
83 Write on a BlackBerry, maybe
84 Eat noisily
85 Recipe abbr.
88 Fee for many a doctor's visit
89 Put on a pedestal
90 City on the Rhone
91 Key
92 Split
93 Garçon's handout
94 Bordello patrons
97 Channel for interior decorators

by Pamela Amick Klawitter

ACROSS

1 City once called Eva Perón
8 Jim Belushi's costume in "Trading Places"
15 Cross stock
19 Napoleon's relatives
20 Woo
21 Reform Party founder
22 Impatient kid's plea at a zoo?
24 Minneapolis suburb
25 Four: Prefix
26 Wipe out
27 Animal with an onomatopoeic name
28 More kempt
29 Big name in computer printers
31 Worrisome type at a china shop?
33 X-rated
36 Sea route
39 "That hurt!"
40 Count with a severe overbite
43 Villa ___ (town near Atlanta)
44 Dwellers along Lake Victoria
48 Seeking the right women's tennis attire?
50 Love overseas
51 Maker of the old Royale
52 "Get it?"
53 Insinuating
54 Warning sign on a pirate ship?
57 Gold medalist skier Hermann
59 Miss Piggy's pronoun
60 "Presto!"
61 Source of some inside humor?
67 Name on a plane
69 The dark side
70 Young hog
71 Tree doctor?
75 City WSW of Dortmund
77 Geom. point
80 24-hr. convenience
81 Dope
82 Your basic "So this guy walks into a bar . . ."?
85 Disastrous drop
88 Rabbit's title
89 Certain hand-held
90 ___-majesté
91 Brand-new to the language
93 Gulf
94 Use of steel wool, e.g.?
98 Palate appendage
101 Butch Cassidy, for one
102 ___ crow
103 Peaks
105 Swingers' stats
109 "Be that as ___ . . ."
110 Cheez Whiz you could blow up?
113 What a rake does
114 Thaw
115 Traveler's temptation
116 Once, in the past
117 Hellish
118 Bears witness

DOWN

1 In case
2 Workout aftermath
3 Churchyard unit
4 Jack who wrote the lyrics to "Tenderly"
5 Intend (to)
6 Nursery items
7 Cartoon dog
8 Father of Deimos and Phobos
9 Apple or pear
10 Comedic Philips
11 Punch with a kick
12 Take apart
13 Become blocked, in a way
14 Christie contemporary
15 Took a two-wheeler
16 "A Masked Ball" aria
17 Music for a baseball team?
18 Movie lover's cable channel
21 Have a quick look from the hallway, say
23 Geiger of counter fame
28 Alternative to J.F.K. and La Guardia
30 Rain hard
31 "___ teaches you when to be silent": Disraeli
32 Prepare to chat, maybe
33 Some hand-helds
34 Golden pond fish
35 Be something special
37 Padded
38 Laugh, in Lille
41 Type of eye surgery
42 Practically pristine
44 Thurman of "Kill Bill"
45 "When You ___ Love" (1912 tune)
46 Actress Patricia
47 Concession stand purchase
49 Opera's ___ Te Kanawa
50 Settled (on)
54 Luau fare
55 Converse competitor
56 Holler's partner
57 Use shamelessly
58 Gray area?: Abbr.
59 Co. with a butterfly logo
61 Nature's aerators
62 Nikita's no
63 White wine apéritif
64 Soyuz launcher
65 Lots
66 South Pacific kingdom
67 "Voice of Israel" author
68 Org. with peace-keeping forces
72 Stock ticker's inventor
73 1958 Best Actor David
74 "___ Day" (1993 rap hit)
75 Flush (with)
76 Arid
77 Perfume brand
78 Boxing stats
79 There are 435 in Cong.
82 Seed cover
83 Ben-Gurion carrier
84 Author portrayed in the miniseries "The Lost Boys"
86 Indiana city near the Michigan border
87 Spoils
88 Illegal record
91 Sly
92 Boneheaded
94 Deceit
95 Out-and-out
96 When doubled, sings
97 Something to believe
99 Roxie's dance partner in "Chicago"

by Tony Orbach and Patrick Blindauer

100 "___ or lose . . ."
103 Lead-in to girl
104 Battle of Normandy city
106 Streisand, to friends
107 "___ first you don't succeed . . ."
108 Orch. section
110 Wallet items, informally
111 Darth Vader's boyhood nickname
112 Chess piece: Abbr.

ACROSS

1 Town at the eighth mile of the Boston Marathon
7 1971 Tom Jones hit
16 Dict. fill
19 Charlie Chan player J. ___ Naish
20 Acted briefly
21 Online activity
22 V.I.P. in a limo?
24 Penn Station inits.
25 Sycophant's reply
26 Articles by nonstaffers
27 Singer Winehouse
28 Glass-enclosed porches
30 1999 film with the tagline "Fame. Be careful. It's out there"
32 Way of the East
33 Open
35 Dirty
36 Stories about halting horses?
39 Kisses, on paper
41 Team building?
42 1954 event code-named Castle Bravo
43 Swedish Chemistry Nobelist Tiselius
45 Detailed, old-style
47 Produce for show
51 Roundabout
53 Corduroy feature
56 Certain guy, in personals shorthand
58 Causes of meteorological phenomena?
60 "Q: Are We Not Men? A: We Are ___!" (hit 1978 album)
61 Eponymous German brewer Eberhard
63 Says, in teenspeak
64 Stir
66 They're in control of their faculties
67 Etc. and ibid., e.g.
69 Unequaled
70 Missile's course
72 Trudge (through)
73 Baton wavers
76 Miffs
77 Iceland?
81 Fully or partially: Abbr.
82 French-Belgian border river
83 Start of a sign on a gate
84 Scatterbrain
86 National League East player
88 Kind of atty.
90 Explorer ___ da Gama
94 MDX and RDX maker
96 National League East player
98 Barrier Ahab stands behind?
102 Literally, "back to back"
104 Lure
106 60-Across producer
107 Long-distance swimmer Diana
108 Something little girls may play
110 Fifth pillar of Islam
111 Body layer
113 Internet address letters
114 "What are you, some kind of ___?"
115 Cry after writing a particularly fun column?
119 Office note
120 Settle
121 Arab League V.I.P.'s
122 Eur. carrier
123 Small plane, perhaps
124 Common town sign

DOWN

1 "Treasure Island" illustrator, 1911
2 Showed delight over
3 River crosser
4 Eng. neighbor
5 U.S.A.F. Academy site
6 One who lifts a lot
7 Little stubble
8 Residence on the Rhein
9 Summer setting in MA and PA
10 Extremely arid
11 In ___ (really out of it)
12 Pitch maker?
13 "___ losing it, or . . . ?"
14 Investigators: Abbr.
15 Goes up and down
16 45, e.g.?
17 Connecticut town where "The Stepford Wives" was filmed
18 Italian road
21 Sen. McCaskill of Missouri
23 "Are you ___?!"
29 Like some good soil
31 Clergy attire
33 Out into view
34 Rock's Richards and Moon
37 Orchestra sect.
38 High, in the Alps
40 Legal suspension
44 Overthrowing, e.g.
46 Lead-in to while
48 Cutting remarks?
49 Slogan holder, often
50 It has a blade
52 Is shy
54 1887 Chekhov play
55 Tomb raider's find
56 Derisive
57 Where ax murderers' weapons are on display?
59 Lines on a musical staff
60 1973 Helen Reddy #1 hit
61 Tylenol rival
62 Troupe org.
65 Calls one's own
67 Ray, e.g., in brief
68 Like the bad guy
71 Phnom Penh money
72 Shaved, in a way
73 Bygone station
74 Part of N.C.A.A.: Abbr.
75 Indication of big shoes to fill?
78 Dip
79 Wishy-___
80 Words with snag or home run
83 Carpenter's supply
85 Dow Jones fig.
87 Blue blood, informally
89 "Flags of Our Fathers" setting
91 Pourer's comment
92 Catfight participants
93 Boot Hill setting
94 Title family name on TV
95 Eye part
97 Tiny laughs
99 One with bad looks?
100 Letters on a cross
101 Polite turndown
103 Best
105 Training staff
109 Fen-___ (banned diet aid)

by Brendan Emmett Quigley

ACROSS

1 Having chutzpah
6 Home of the Braves: Abbr.
9 Hale-___ (comet seen in 1997)
13 Take a chance
19 Page facing a verso
20 Arthur Miller play about the Salem witch trials, with "The"
22 Enigmas
23 Take heat from?
24 Downhill racer
25 Poet John who wrote "Lives of X," an autobiography in verse
26 Last request, part 1
29 Rains in Spain
30 Twigs, perhaps
31 Animal more closely related to the mongoose than the dog
32 Inhuman
35 Groundbreaking inventions?
36 Cabinet inits. since 1979
38 Part of a range: Abbr.
39 Records
40 Not maj.
41 Endorsers, typically
44 Election ending?
45 Request, part 2
52 Barney's buddy, in cartoondom
54 Veiled comment?
55 "Sense and Sensibility" author
56 "Thumbs way up!" review
57 Unlike drive, reverse has just one

59 Lord's land
61 With 95-Across, chef whose recipes are used on the International Space Station
63 National Institutes of Health location
65 Request, part 3
66 How good investors invest
68 Profitless
69 Bill
71 On Soc. Sec., typically
72 "The King and I" setting
73 Park ___
76 Disfigure
77 God, in Granada
79 Request, part 4
84 ___ culpa
85 Actress Mimieux of "Where the Boys Are"
86 Supply in a loft
87 Alludes (to)
89 Lambert airport's home: Abbr.
92 "___ pig's eye!"
93 Created
95 See 61-Across
96 ___ ballerina
98 Salma Hayek, for one
101 1970s Renault
102 End of the request
108 European carrier
109 Part of many an autobiography's author credit
110 Morticia, to Fester, on TV's "The Addams Family"
111 Gander : goose :: tercel : ___
112 More chic
113 Clothing retailer Bauer
114 Erica Jong's phobia, ostensibly

115 "Yonder window," according to Romeo
116 Uno + due
117 Actions

DOWN

1 Very dry
2 Only female attorney general
3 Sch. known for its discipline
4 Having grooves
5 'Hood inhabitant
6 Existing
7 Crowd in Calais?
8 Grease up
9 Propaganda technique introduced by Hitler in "Mein Kampf"
10 M.D.'s who deliver
11 What dead men don't wear, per a 1982 film title
12 Tasty tubes
13 Suggestive
14 W.W. I's so-called "U-Boat Alley"
15 Reptilian, in a way
16 ___ Abdul-Jabbar
17 Tab, e.g.
18 "Shogun" sequel
21 Soft
27 Not exactly
28 One of two title roles (in the same film) for Spencer Tracy
32 Bellyache
33 Peppy
34 Desire, for one
35 Sign in the stands
37 Noted bunny lover
40 Jason's jiltee
41 Matador's move
42 Social worker
43 Scattered (about)

46 Pirate whose treasure is recovered in Poe's "The Gold-Bug"
47 Keeper of a flame?
48 Total
49 Dickens's shortest novel
50 Bad guys
51 Count (on)
53 Benin, until 1975
58 Matter of law
60 Lassitude
62 Deep bleu sea
63 Bigmouth, for one
64 Pollen producer
66 Hair-raising
67 Ein Berliner, often
69 "Picnic" playwright
70 Clarifying words
74 ESPN sportscaster Dick
75 Treebeard, e.g.
78 Manuscript encl.
80 Ace's specialty
81 Slaves
82 Spinachlike plant
83 Won back
88 Unseen part of the moon
89 Marijuana cigarette, slangily
90 Like some Afghan leaders
91 In the cards
93 Ecological groupings
94 Not AWOL
95 Poe poem that ends "From grief and groan to a golden throne beside the King of Heaven"
97 Word of thanks
99 Quickly
100 Edison rival
101 Cubic decimeter

by Matt Ginsberg

103 Spend time
(with)
104 Cut, say
105 Give up
106 Aspirin, e.g.
107 Roger who won
the Best Actor
Tony for "Nicholas
Nickleby"

ACROSS

1 Demanded without reason
7 Leader of Lesbos?
13 Unlikely attenders of R-rated films
19 Honor
20 Injustice
21 Feel remorse for
22 November 5, in Britain
24 Not remote
25 Thin as ___
26 Depression
28 Humans last lived there in 2000
29 Wild sheep of the western United States
36 Mocks
37 "La Gioconda" mezzo-soprano
38 Flies over the Equator
39 Salt Lake City player
40 Annual Sunday event, with "the"
43 Breezes (through)
44 Best Actor of 1991
49 Treat like a hero, maybe
52 In direct opposition
53 Gaudy jewelry, in slang
54 Broad
55 Alphabet quartet
56 Trail to follow
58 Ring figure
59 It's quite different from the high-school variety
66 Transfix
67 Eurasian ducks
68 Climactic scene in "Hamlet"
69 Parrying weapon
70 Blackmore's Lorna
72 City 70 miles SSW of Toledo
76 ___ state

77 Viking, for one
81 La Scala cheer
82 Events registered by seismometers, in brief
83 Resident: Suffix
84 Foamcore component
87 "Doctor Zhivago" role
89 Deserving a lower insurance premium
91 Army supply officer
96 Spigoted vessel
97 Italie et Allemagne
98 Single-handedly
99 Equitable way to return a favor
102 Egg roll topping, perhaps
109 Thatched
110 Perfume ingredient
111 Mrs. Woody Allen
112 It may be bilateral
113 Belgian city with an 1854 manifesto
114 Like shorelines, often

DOWN

1 Lose strength
2 Prefix with pressure
3 Standoffish
4 Give bad marks
5 Signs of a bad outlet
6 "Venice Preserved" dramatist Thomas
7 Part of U.N.L.V.
8 Natural bristle
9 Year that Michelangelo began work on "David"
10 One desiring change
11 National flower of Mexico

12 Illinois city, site of the last Lincoln-Douglas debate
13 Favorable
14 TV pooch
15 FedEx rival
16 Moon of Mars
17 Unabridged
18 Rudder locations
20 Move, to a real-estate broker
23 Kipling novel
27 Procure
29 Batting average, e.g.
30 ___ citato
31 ___ Bator
32 Quaint "not"
33 Caboose
34 Some deodorants
35 Abbr. after Cleveland or Brooklyn
36 Fair
40 Four Holy Roman emperors
41 Bazaar units
42 Iowa college
43 Go rapidly
45 Charge for cash
46 Large chamber group
47 Ancient Greek coins
48 Pickup attachment
49 Start of something big?
50 Shooting star, maybe
51 Mad magazine cartoonist Dave
54 Spoonful, say
56 Bygone blades
57 Kitten "mitten"
58 Second string
59 Bossman or bosswoman
60 Stinky, as gym clothes
61 Pizza place

62 Capri, e.g., to a Capriote
63 Magazine founded by Bob Guccione
64 ___ of Nantes, 1598
65 "Super Duper ___" (anime series)
70 "Forty Miles of Bad Road" guitarist
71 Flip over
72 Some offensive linemen: Abbr.
73 Port near Nazareth
74 Purveyor of chips
75 Open court hearing
77 ___-à-porter
78 "And ___ thou slain the Jabberwock?": Carroll
79 Spillane's "___ Jury"
80 Within striking distance
81 "It's c-c-c-cold!"
84 Pipsqueak
85 Word with page or wood
86 ___ Stadium, opened in 1923
87 Feeling evoked in drama
88 Basketball datum
89 Security system component
90 Playground retort
92 Prefix with economics
93 Celtic speaker
94 ___ beetle
95 "Don't even bother"
100 Sun Valley locale: Abbr.

by Barry C. Silk

ACROSS

1 2003 Stanley Cup champions
7 Portrays
12 It's found in many pockets nowadays
16 Command to an overfriendly canine
20 Genus of poisonous mushrooms
22 Brewing
23 Pasta used in soups
24 Actress Polo
25 Nickname for a bodybuilder
26 Flip
27 Junior in the N.F.L.
28 Bunch
29 Popular 1970s British TV series
32 Bug
34 Fraternity letters
35 Dungeon items
37 "Now you're talking!"
38 Took the risk
45 From __ Z
47 Radiate
51 When a second-shift employee may get home
52 City that overlooks a bay of the same name
53 Opening screen option on many an A.T.M.
56 "Think big" sloganeer
57 One inside another
59 Spot alternative
61 Fine-tunes
62 Split
63 Abbr. in a real-estate listing
64 Creator of the Tammany Hall tiger
66 Tic-tac-toe plays
68 Warner Brothers shotgun toter
69 "Whose woods these __ think I know": Frost
71 Liberals
73 Actor Brynner
74 __ rut
75 Keats, e.g.
76 Ilk
77 It may have two doors
79 Ralph who co-wrote "Have Yourself a Merry Little Christmas"
81 Cartoonist Keane
82 "The Praise of Folly" writer
84 Cause of unemployment
86 It might follow a slash mark
90 "Amen!"
91 Club alternative
92 Slangy street greeting
94 Ball with a yellow stripe
95 Arrangements
98 Four-star hotel amenity
99 J.F.K. info: Abbr.
101 Football defensive line position
102 Old musical high notes
103 Deuce beaters
104 Where to pick up pick-up sticks
106 Viking Ericson
108 Summer Mass. setting
109 Bug
110 "We __ please"
111 Nativity scene figures
114 __ Mae
116 Stead
117 Like most apartments
119 A hyperbola has two
121 Having stars, say
122 Deliver, as a harsh criticism
124 "Star Trek" TV series, to fans
125 Exasperated teacher's cry
128 Shade of blue
130 Kids drink from them
132 Comedian Margaret
133 Part of a shark's respiratory system
137 Missing glasses' location, usually
145 Genesis son
146 Issue
148 The second "R" in J. R. R. Tolkien
149 Wrinkles
150 Fan mag
151 Pixar fish
152 Africa's __ Mountains
153 A super's may be supersized
154 Result of pulling the plug?
155 Overflow
156 Unesco World Heritage Site in Jordan
157 Gives in return

DOWN

1 Block
2 Birds that can sprint at 30 m.p.h.
3 Extensive
4 One of a people conquered in 1533
5 French orphan of film
6 Camper's aid
7 Miss
8 "__ first . . ."
9 Arrangement of 40-Downs
10 "Ain't gonna happen"
11 Commercial prefix with foam
12 Cyclades island
13 Before: Abbr.
14 Longtime Boston Symphony conductor
15 Hollow center?
16 Barely fair, maybe
17 Sugar source
18 Read aloud
19 Exclamation of surprise
21 In itself
30 Went from second to first, say
31 Fasten with a pop
33 Will Ferrell title role
36 Erect
38 Not brought home
39 Off
40 See 9-Down
41 Awake by
42 Bootleggers' bane
43 Son-in-law of Muhammad
44 Go-ahead
46 Common hockey score
48 Proposed "fifth taste," which means "savory" in Japanese
49 Keeps
50 Put forth
54 "Do you want me to?"
55 Tasmania's highest peak
58 Z-car brand
60 International oil and gas giant, informally
62 Benedict III's predecessor
65 Misses, e.g.
67 Negative
70 Sentiment suggesting "Try this!"
72 Secured, in a way, with "on"
78 Cipher org.
80 T or F, e.g.: Abbr.
81 Construction project that gave rise to the Ted Williams Tunnel
83 Sphagnous
85 Some taters
86 Over
87 Building component?
88 Shrinking, perhaps
89 Took it easy
91 Gone bad
93 Frog legs, to some
95 Hold off
96 TV puppet
97 Precept
98 Pal of Kenny and Kyle
100 Tach reading

by Mike Nothnagel and David Quarfoot

105 Common entry point
107 Alpine sights
112 Behind
113 Happen, slangily
115 "I'll pass"
117 Plush
118 Connoisseur
120 Pawned
123 Head counts?
126 Tristram's love

127 More gloomy
129 Singer Mann
131 "That's ___!"
133 Look
134 Footnote abbr.
135 Impart
136 Player's call
138 Behind
139 "Bridal Chorus" bride

140 Bazooka Joe's working peeper
141 Ground cover
142 Early Chinese dynasty
143 Choice word
144 E-mail, e.g.: Abbr.
147 Cartoon feline

75 OFF WITH THEIR HEADS!

ACROSS

1 Swarm
5 Lots
10 11th-century year
14 Audibly shocked
19 Hot rod rod
20 One of the 4 Seasons
21 German article
22 Glow
23 "Will the long-winded ___ ___ his sermon?"
26 Philosopher Kierkegaard
27 Puts on
28 Power brokers
29 "Let me tell you . . ."
30 Mark, Anthony and others: Abbr.
31 "Tasty!"
32 "The majority of British ___ ___ policy coming to fruition"
34 Left over
36 Shoot out
37 Took care of
40 Washington State airport
43 Amaze
44 One of five Norwegian kings
48 "I noticed you use the ___ ___ often than the tarnished one"
51 Promised
52 Ties a second knot
53 Habit
54 Human ___ Project
55 Alphabet quartet
57 "The driver's crew decided to make the ___ ___ priority"
60 "Life ___ beach"
63 Welcome at the door

65 Crossed one's i's and dotted one's t's?
66 Promgoers: Abbr.
67 "The parishioners ignored the ___ ___ meat on Friday"
71 Understands
74 Train head
75 Work hard
76 Ultimatum's end
80 It might lead to a cloud formation, for short
81 "The judges put the names of each ___ ___ for the M.C. to read"
86 Pusher catcher, for short
87 Shoe letters
88 Retinue of Pan
89 YouTube offering
90 Baloney
92 Teacher: Var.
94 "As one member of the crew ___ ___ co-worker leaned on his shovel"
101 Nigerian export
102 Any ship
105 Company bought by Chevron in 2005
106 Dig
107 Box-and-one alternative
109 Mushroom variety
110 "You won't find any ___ ___ Turner album"
112 Wilder and Hackman
113 Wash. neighbor
114 Potato pancake
115 Race pace
116 Daisy type

117 It's frequently stolen
118 Calm
119 Tom Joad, e.g.

DOWN

1 Bad-weather gear
2 Apply
3 Dwellers in Middle-earth
4 Cross
5 Park in New York, say
6 Australia, e.g.
7 Automotive pioneer
8 It may come from a barrel
9 Take up wholeheartedly
10 Deserve
11 Deceive
12 Central
13 Like some boxes on ballots
14 Franciscan home
15 Relics of the Wild West
16 ___-ground missile
17 Derisive look
18 Copper
24 English portraitist Sir Joshua
25 1994 and 1997 U.S. Open winner
29 Green shade
32 Bucket of bolts
33 Grove in many an English churchyard
34 Pure
35 Your: Fr.
37 Lat. or Lith., once
38 Ursine : bear :: pithecan : ___
39 Amaze
41 Al's is almost 27
42 Place to hang your hat
43 Lady ___, first woman to sit in British Parliament

45 Sacks
46 Mail for a knight
47 Johnson and Johnson, e.g.
49 Kind of sale
50 "___ Nous" (1983 film)
51 Having all the money one needs
54 Bible distributor
56 Milk
57 Attach, as to a lapel
58 Cuisine choice
59 Many a pirate's appendage
60 "That is to say . . ."
61 Receiver of lists
62 Tick off
64 Actress Holmes
68 Record holder
69 About which the Bible says "Consider her ways, and be wise"
70 Confederate
72 "Hairspray" actor
73 Baseball bigwig Bud
77 Top
78 Beijing-to-Shanghai dir.
79 Ike's W.W. II domain
81 Broadcast signal
82 Compromises
83 Tore
84 Minister's deg.
85 Japanese-born Hall of Fame golfer
87 Daredevil Knievel
91 Poker call
93 Deseeded, as cotton
94 "Hasta ___"
95 Incorporate into a city
96 Fess Parker TV role

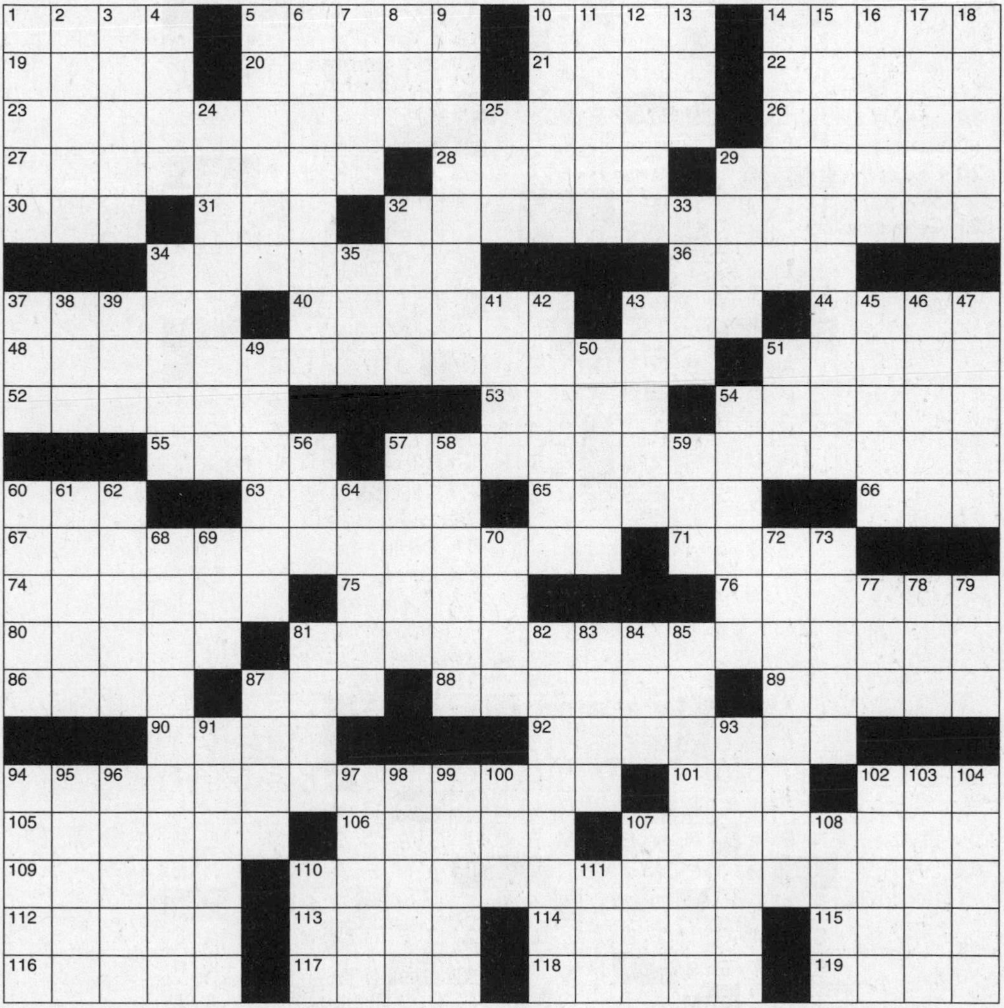

by Peter A. Collins and Joe Krozel

97 Greek marketplace
98 Folk percussion instruments
99 Old enough
100 Break down
102 Smarmy smile
103 Red River city
104 Related on the mother's side
107 ___ Hari
108 Football Hall-of-Famer Graham
110 Melodramatic response in comics
111 Jazz cornetist Adderley

ANSWERS

1

G	A	S	B	A	G		A	M	P	S	U	P		G	O	U	A	C	H	E
O	S	C	A	R	S		C	Y	R	A	N	O		E	N	L	A	C	E	D
S	P	E	L	L	T	H	E	R	O	S	E	S		R	O	A	R	I	N	G
H	I	N	D	I		A	R	A	M		A	I	D	A		O	N	C	E	
	C	A	E	S	A	R	S		P	O	R	T	A	L	D	A	N	G	E	R
		A	S	T	I		S	T	A	T		P	D	A	S					
C	L	O	G		A	N	A	T		T	H	E	P	O	D	S	Q	U	A	D
B	O	I	L	I	N	G	P	A	D		S	T	L			T	U	R	B	O
E	L	L	E	N		E	N	I	D		C	E	O	S		I	S	I	T	
R	A	Y		F	L	E	E	C	E	R			R	A	N	L	A	T	E	
			F	U	L	L	P	E	T	A	L	J	A	C	K	E	T			
E	L	M	U	N	D	O			G	O	U	L	A	S	H		I	O	S	
R	Y	E	S		S	I	C	S		S	I	N	E			R	O	N	D	O
I	L	O	S	T		A	W	E		S	T	U	D	P	U	F	F	I	N	
N	E	W	Y	O	R	K	P	E	T	S		A	T	O	I		F	O	E	S
			M	I	L	O		I	S	I	S		R	N	A	S				
P	A	N	A	B	O	U	T	T	O	W	N		D	E	A	L	E	R	S	
A	P	E	R		T	E	A	L		A	A	R	E		L	A	H	T	I	
B	E	R	L	I	O	Z		P	A	S	S	C	O	N	F	U	S	I	O	N
L	A	V	E	R	N	E		E	T	H	E	R	S		I	R	O	N	I	C
O	R	E	S	T	E	S		D	E	U	C	E	S		S	E	N	E	C	A

2

L	A	M	A		V	I	R	G	O		L	I	M	O		A	S	P	C	A
E	L	E	C		U	L	E	E	S		A	R	A	L		P	H	I	L	S
M	I	D	D	L	E	O	F	N	O	W	H	E	R	E		P	E	R	O	T
O	N	I	C	E		V	I	O	L	E	T			O	N	L	E	A	V	E
N	E	A		N	N	E		M	E	D	I	C	A	L	C	E	N	T	E	R
		B	I	O	T	Y	P	E				O	N	E	A	T		E	R	N
P	A	L	M		W	O	E		A	R	L	E	N		R	A	P	S		
S	P	I	R	I	T	U	A	L	L	E	A	D	E	R		R	A	H	A	L
S	I	T	E	S			H	E	I	D	I		A	C	T	L	I	K	E	
T	A	Z		M	A	T	E	O		U	N	C	O	I	L		M	P	A	A
			B	E	G	I	N	N	I	N	G	O	F	T	I	M	E			
A	L	F	A		R	E	S	E	N	D		A	F	T	O	N		A	M	P
B	E	A	N	B	A	G			B	A	S	T	E			E	S	T	E	E
S	E	R	G	E		S	E	C	O	N	D	I	N	C	O	M	M	A	N	D
		A	S	E	A		T	E	X	T	S		S	R	S		O	N	U	S
C	A	N		R	I	G	I	D				G	E	O	L	O	G	Y		
E	N	D	O	F	D	E	C	E	M	B	E	R		S	O	L		P	R	E
L	O	W	G	E	A	R			C	A	R	E	S	S		E	A	R	E	D
E	M	I	L	S		B	R	O	A	D	W	A	Y	C	L	O	S	I	N	G
B	I	D	E	T		I	B	E	T		I	S	S	U	E		A	C	T	E
S	E	E	D	S		L	I	D	S		N	E	T	T	Y		P	E	A	R

3

D	E	C	K			U	S	D	A		G	I	B	E		E	S	S	A	Y
I	V	A	N	A		S	T	E	M	C	E	L	L	S		C	O	U	P	E
M	A	N	O	R		B	U	R	Y	A	L	L	A	C	C	O	U	N	T	S
	C	A	R	T	S		P	E	L	T	S		S	A	I	N	T			
F	U	R	R	Y	C	O	O	K			D	E	P	T		H	T	T	P	
R	A	Y			O	R	R		A	C	M	E		E	Y	E	S	O	R	E
A	T	I	S	S	U	E		I	G	U	A	N	A	S		R	E	W	E	D
M	E	N	T	O	R	S		P	A	R	L	O	R		I	N	A	N	E	R
E	S	T	R	U	S		C	U	R	R	A	T	I	O	N	S		W	B	O
	H	E	P		P	O	T		I	D	E	A	L	S		T	I	O	S	
	V	E	E		D	E	L		K	E	Y		D	D	T		I	T	A	
L	I	M	P		V	A	L	U	E	D		E	N	S		N	T	H		
I	C	U		U	R	S	I	N	E	W	A	V	E		W	A	H	O	O	S
M	E	R	I	T	S		D	I	P	O	L	E		D	E	N	E	U	V	E
P	R	I	N	E		R	E	V	E	L	E	R		I	N	A	S	T	E	W
I	O	N	E	S	C	O		A	R	F	S		T	E	D		P	R	E	
D	Y	E	S		C	A	L	C			O	H	M	Y	G	O	U	R	D	
		C	A	N	D	O		B	O	O	Z	E		S	U	P	R	A		
H	O	U	R	L	Y	M	A	T	R	I	M	O	N	Y		T	R	I	T	E
A	E	S	O	P		A	M	B	U	L	A	N	C	E		S	A	T	E	S
G	R	O	W	S		P	S	A	T		N	E	E	T		H	Y	D	E	

4

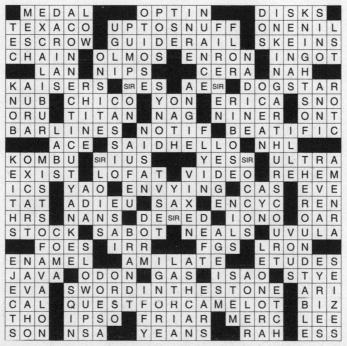

	M	E	D	A	L			O	P	T	I	N			D	I	S	K	S	
T	E	X	A	C	O		U	P	T	O	S	N	U	F	F		O	N	E	N	I	L
E	S	C	R	O	W		G	U	I	D	E	R	A	I	L		S	K	E	I	N	S
C	H	A	I	N		O	L	M	O	S		E	N	R	O	N		I	N	G	O	T
	L	A	N		N	I	P	S				C	E	R	A		N	A	H	
K	A	I	S	E	R	S		ES		A	E		D	O	G	S	T	A	R
N	U	B		C	H	I	C	O		Y	O	N		E	R	I	C	A		S	N	O
O	R	U		T	I	T	A	N		N	A	G		N	I	N	E	R		O	N	T
B	A	R	L	I	N	E	S		N	O	T	I	F		B	E	A	T	I	F	I	C
	A	C	E		S	A	I	D	H	E	L	L	O		N	H	L	
K	O	M	B	U		I	U	S			Y	E	S		U	L	T	R	A
E	X	I	S	T		L	O	F	A	T		V	I	D	E	O		R	E	H	E	M
I	C	S		Y	A	O		E	N	V	Y	I	N	G		C	A	S		E	V	E
T	A	T		A	D	I	E	U		S	A	X		E	N	C	Y	C		R	E	N
H	R	S		N	A	N	S		D	E	ED		I	O	N	O		O	A	R
S	T	O	C	K		S	A	B	O	T		N	E	A	L	S		U	V	U	L	A
	F	O	E	S		I	R	R			F	G	S		L	R	O	N	
E	N	A	M	E	L		A	M	I	L	A	T	E		E	T	U	D	E	S
J	A	V	A		O	D	O	N		G	A	S		I	S	A	O		S	T	Y	E
E	V	A		S	W	O	R	D	I	N	T	H	E	S	T	O	N	E		A	R	I
C	A	L		Q	U	E	S	T	F	O	R	C	A	M	E	L	O	T		B	I	Z
T	H	O		I	P	S	O		F	R	I	A	R		M	E	R	C		L	E	E
S	O	N		N	S	A		Y	E	A	N	S			R	A	H		E	S	S

5

```
M O U T H   S T R I P E   A L G A   A M Y
S U S H I   H A I K U S   S O R T   V I A
G R E E K L E T T E R S   K N E E S O C K
  F R E E B E E   P E R S I A   O N E S
E L O I S E     I O N I A   TAU (5) PHI
M I R V   T I (2) N S   P R I N C E D O M
M A C E D   O N (3) K E   P O R T O   R U E
A M E R I C A N PIE   B L U E   P I T T
  V A S E   D R A I N S   C E S A R
  R E G I S T R Y   I C E D   C O S T C O
M O M O N E Y   O I N K S   T O M C A T S
A M I N E S   B U N S   T R A D E I N S
L U N G S   W A R D E D   O L E O
A L E S   H I H O   R (4) B E R N A T H Y
W A N   P A O L O   D U CHI E S   S P R E E
I N T H E M A I N   A I RHO S E   P E E N
(1) PSI PHI W O R L D   J U L E P S
F O A M   B E I R U T   E M P A N E L
A M N E S I A C   F R A T E R N I T I E S
C A D   M A S K   F E D O R A   T O N T O
T R Y   U N E S   S Y D N E Y   S N E A D
```

(1) OMEGA (2) BETA (3) THETA (4) ALPHA (5) DELTA

6

```
B A L B O A   T W A N G S   M A S S E S
A N T E U P   G O I R I S H   E Q U I N E
G O S S I P G I R L I N T E R R U P T E D
  E S T I V A L   L O C A   O R E
P E L E   S T E   P I L A F S   M A N O R
F L E C K   I M O N I T   E D A M
F A T H E R K N O W S B E S T I N S H O W
T N T   N I A   R E P R I S E D   A R A
  H O A R S E R   A N N A   I L I A D
A P S O   T E E   I R T   C A R T E
G R E Y S A N A T O M Y O F A M U R D E R
H E L L O   H R S   O B I   G O D S
A L L E Y   S H E A   S A R A L E E
S A T   C H A R C O A L   C A B   M A O
T W O A N D A H A L F M E N I N B L A C K
  P E E L   M E N A C E   S A N E R
P E T R A   L E S S O R   W D S   Y O D A
O L E   T O O T   I N T E N S E
S E X A N D T H E C I T Y O F A N G E L S
I N A L I E   O S S U A R Y   R E G R E T
T A N A K A   S A I D N O   L E S S O N
```

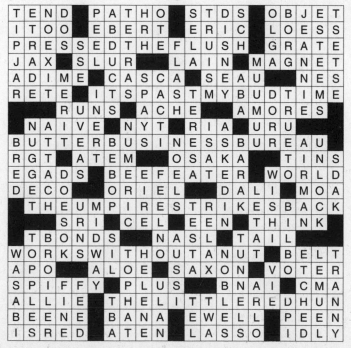

7

Puzzle 7

T	A	C	K	E	D	■	R	I	F	T	S	■	B	I	D	S	■	F	D	R
H	E	A	R	T	S	■	U	N	D	U	E	■	U	T	A	H	■	R	E	E
E	R	R	O	R	M	E	S	S	A	G	E	■	R	A	D	I	O	E	R	A
B	O	O	N	E	■	T	H	I	■	■	M	A	S	S	A	P	P	E	A	L
U	S	T	A	■	I	T	I	S	S	O	■	W	A	C	S	■	T	R	I	M
R	T	E	■	C	O	U	N	T	E	R	P	L	E	A	■	N	I	E	L	S
B	A	N	G	O	N	■	S	A	G	A	S	■	I	N	N	S	■			
S	T	E	E	R	I	N	G	■	B	A	N	■	V	I	S	E	■	P	U	B
■	R	E	C	E	I	V	I	N	G	L	I	N	E	■	B	O	N	O		
T	U	B	A	L	■	U	S	E	R	S	■	E	A	S	E	S	I	N	T	O
A	T	O	L	L	S	■	E	N	D	■	W	A	D	■	A	C	E	S	I	T
R	I	O	D	I	A	B	L	O	■	H	A	S	U	P	■	O	N	E	L	S
E	L	K	O	■	F	I	L	M	D	I	R	E	C	T	I	O	N	■		
S	E	P	■	R	E	N	E	■	E	T	H	■	T	A	S	T	I	E	S	T
■	R	A	M	S	■	O	A	T	E	N	■	L	E	A	N	T	O			
U	C	O	N	N	■	T	E	N	D	E	R	O	F	F	E	R	■	G	A	M
N	A	P	E	■	B	O	A	C	■	R	O	N	E	L	Y	■	F	I	R	M
C	R	O	S	S	W	O	R	D	S	■	U	T	A	■	C	A	R	L	Y	
L	A	S	T	C	A	L	L	■	P	E	C	K	I	N	G	O	R	D	E	R
O	F	A	■	O	N	E	A	■	A	L	P	E	S	■	R	I	A	L	T	O
G	E	L	■	T	A	R	P	■	S	M	A	S	H	■	E	L	D	E	S	T

Puzzle 8

T	E	N	D	■	P	A	T	H	O	■	S	T	D	S	■	O	B	J	E	T
I	T	O	O	■	E	B	E	R	T	■	E	R	I	C	■	L	O	E	S	S
P	R	E	S	S	E	D	T	H	E	F	L	U	S	H	■	G	R	A	T	E
J	A	X	■	S	L	U	R	■	L	A	I	N	■	M	A	G	N	E	T	
A	D	I	M	E	■	C	A	S	C	A	■	S	E	A	U	■	N	E	S	
R	E	T	E	■	I	T	S	P	A	S	T	M	Y	B	U	D	T	I	M	E
■	R	U	N	S	■	A	C	H	E	■	A	M	O	R	E	S	■			
N	A	I	V	E	■	N	Y	T	■	R	I	A	■	U	R	U	■			
B	U	T	T	E	R	B	U	S	I	N	E	S	S	B	U	R	E	A	U	
R	G	T	■	A	T	E	M	■	O	S	A	K	A	■	T	I	N	S		
E	G	A	D	S	■	B	E	E	F	E	A	T	E	R	■	W	O	R	L	D
D	E	C	O	■	O	R	I	E	L	■	D	A	L	I	■	M	O	A		
■	T	H	E	U	M	P	I	R	E	S	T	R	I	K	E	S	B	A	C	K
S	R	I	■	C	E	L	■	E	E	N	■	T	H	I	N	K	■			
T	B	O	N	D	S	■	N	A	S	L	■	T	A	I	L	■				
W	O	R	K	S	W	I	T	H	O	U	T	A	N	U	T	■	B	E	L	T
A	P	O	■	A	L	O	E	■	S	A	X	O	N	■	V	O	T	E	R	
S	P	I	F	F	Y	■	P	L	U	S	■	B	N	A	I	■	C	M	A	
A	L	L	I	E	■	T	H	E	L	I	T	T	L	E	R	E	D	H	U	N
B	E	E	N	E	■	B	A	N	A	■	E	W	E	L	L	■	P	E	E	N
I	S	R	E	D	■	A	T	E	N	■	L	A	S	S	O	■	I	D	L	Y

Puzzle 9:

```
A D A M   Y A P A T   R H O M B   E G G S
F I N E   O R A M A   A S P C A   L E A K
T A K E O U T O F C O N T E X T   L A Z E
A G A T H A S   M O N K   D I E S I R A E
      S N A P   O L A   A S S
  B L O O D L E S S R E V O L U T I O N
G O A D   M E R C K   I D A   S T O A
E N C O R E   T H E M I S S I N G L I N K
L I T R E       D E M   I N A S E C
I T I   R O O T S   T H O M M C A N
D O C T O R S W I T H O U T B O R D E R S
    E U R O A R E A   I N A L L   N E A
S T R A T I   R N A   E A G A N
S P A R E N O E X P E N S E   A D V I C E
E K G S   O T B   T O N A L   I N T R
  E A T S S H O O T S A N D L E A V E S
    A N T   X O O   S P A R
L O M I L O M I   N L E R   A T L A N T A
I R A N   L E M O N D R O P C O O K I E S
D A Z E   E R A S E   O S C A R   I N R E
S L E D   N E X U S   S A S S Y   N A N A
```

10

Puzzle 10:

```
H I N T   N A S H U A   T W I T S   F A Y
A L O U   B I C A R B   R E C A P   A V E
P I N T   C R O S S C O U N T R Y A C E S
  A S O B   E T T A   H I T U P   P E R M
    P R E   S T E   I S M S   R O U S E
  P E A C E   I N A C O M A   P I G P E N
S E A G O D   S T L O   D I R G E
M A K E M E   H O L M E S   C O H E R E D
U R I   I R A E   I M N O   E S T   O V O
    N I N   S E C   A U F   D E F A M E D
M A G O G   P L A I N F A C T   U S U R Y
A P O S T L E   B A D   R A E   L I L
P O L   H A R   A T O M   R A I L   U S A
S P E W E R S   L E A D T O   L U G S I N
    H A V E S   I C E L   K D L A N G
A U R I G A   H O U D I N I   A D A N O
D R A P E   C O T S   T N T   E D D
E C R U   H O W I E   C H A R   R I E L
S H I P T O S H O R E A D I O S   O M A N
T I N   M E M O S   B R A C T S   L U N A
E N G   C R O W E   W R Y E S T   A S A P
```

11

```
B S E V E N   M S S   P A I D   A W O R D
T O R I N O   O W N   A U R A   N O S E E
W H A L E R   H E E   G F O R T Y N I N E
E A S E   A G R E E T O   N E R O   X E R
L V I   V H F   T R A D E   M A N A T E E
V E N T I   I D E A M A P   E N E M Y
E I G E N   F A N T A S I A   B O A T
    N E T T V  [BINGO]  C O M E I N T O
D Y A D   W Y O   I S I X T E E N
D E P O S I T S  15 20 35 60 72  D E N T
T A R N I S H   8 21 44 50 65   V E R M O N T
    E T R E   12 17 FREE 49 71  D E R A I L E D
B F I F T E E N  11 16 31 48 68  R N A   S E W S
A S N E E D E D  7 19 40 53 61  A T L A S
S U I T   O H M E O H M Y   P E P S I
    N E A L E   R E T R E A T   I S L E T
N E E D L E D   S L O B S   W I E   U A W
A L T   L A I D   A N I S T O N   O N M E
I S E V E N T E E N   T I E   C A R D I N
L I E I N   O M N I   E A R   A T T E S T
S E N D S   R O A N   D N A   N F O R T Y
```

12

```
D I M   W I S P   C B S T V   A G E O L D
A N A   R O U E   A U D I O   V E N D O R
R A I S I N B R A N D I N G   E N G I N E
E N D A T   P E L T   S T A R T A N E W
D E S K   O S I E R S   U S E R
    S H O E   G R E E N S F E E D I N G
G A S   A R N E   N E A L   L E N Y A
O F M I C E A N D M E N D I N G   E S L
I R A N I S   V O A   A M O R T I Z E S
N O L T E   O O Z E D   D A R N
    L O N G T I M E N O S E E D I N G
    I D I O   S C R U M   B E A D S
B R I T A N N I A   A M I   H U E V O S
R U N   A I N T W E G O T F U N D I N G
I B O O K   G O A D   S E G A   N E T
G E N T L E B E N D I N G   L O L L
    R I L E   S T A R E D   O A H U
C O L A N D E R S   R I G S   O R S E R
A V E N G E   D R A W I N G P E N D I N G
T E E T E R   A T B A T   E A R L   A C E
E R R O R S   S A C H A   D R A Y   N E D
```

13

```
A P P A L   · P A C K   · I M A C   · [CU] D G E L
S H I N E   · A L A I   · M A M A   · L E O N E
C O S T A B R A V A   · P H A R M A C I S T
O T T   · T E R R I   · O R E   · P A T I N E S
T O O T H [DK] · M A R K E R G E N E   · G A B
· [SA] L I E N T   · R I I S   · A [DM] I R A B L E
· P R O U D   · T E S T S   · D Y S
R [ED] S   · B L I T Z   · R U B I K S
A G T S   · S I N O   · T O P E K A   · [KT] E L
F O R M A   · P A L A T A L   · F O R E S E E
A R O U N D T H E W O R L D I N [AT] D A Y S
E M P T I E R   · R E [XS] T O U T   · S A G O S
L E S   · T E E P A D   · P A T E   · M A R E
· C A M E A T   · B E N I N   · L E E
· A T O   · R E S T [EZ] · E N T E R
C R A N [KC] A S E   · P O E M   · G R A H A M
A M T   · J O H N [QP] U B L I C   · A T O N I C
P O I S O N [IV] · D R Y   · D O R I A   · I S A
L I A M N E E S O N   G R E E N W I T H [NV]
E R N I E   · R O L E   · A I D A   · A T R I A
T E A T S   · S O L D   · T B S P   · Y E A T S
```

14

```
M O R T S A H L   · E G G C U P S   · P S S T
T R E A T I E S   · L A R U S S A   · E L E V
S A M U E L A D A M S E S S A Y   · P A R T
· T E E D   · H O T W A R S   · N E V E R
A N T   · D E C C A   · R O C   · M O L I N A
P O E M   · N O H   · D O N K I N G D E C A Y
I K N O W   · L I A O   · D A M U P   ·
N I A V A R D A L O S E N V Y   · H E A T H
G A M E R A   · P A R O L E E   · W I R Y
· I M B U E   · D O W   · D J S   · N O D
Q U E N T I N T A R A N T I N O C U T I E
U R L   · O D E   · L O P   · R A Y O N
A D E N   · G O T O S E A   · C O V E R T
D U M A S   · T I T O P U E N T E T E P E E
· M O T I F   · E L I A   · S I E G E
M A X E R N S T E M M Y   · A K A   · L E A N
O U T S E T   · L A A   · A N I M E   · S L Y
S P E A R   · P E A R L E R   · N O N A
D A R K   · K U R T V O N N E G U T C A V Y
E I R E   · A N T E I N G   · P I N E T R E E
F R A S   · S T E R N E R   · A T T R A C T S
```

15

```
A N G L E ■ W I N ■ H O N U S ■ A D A M
C O O E D ■ J A N E ■ O M A N I ■ G A M E
H A R T E B U R N S ■ W E S T L O N D O N
T H E O R E M ■ O C A N A D A ■ P E A K S
■ F L A P ■ T A B O R ■ C R E W
G A F F E ■ S W I F T W A L K E R ■ W H A
I S O ■ S U E M E ■ A S T A I R E S
S N O W W H I T E ■ E T A T ■ I S T I N K
M E T E O U T ■ B E A D E A R ■ O G R E
O R E G O N ■ C A R R P A R K E R ■ H I D
■ B O D ■ P O L E ■ T R O U ■ A I T
E M U ■ S T E E L E M A N N ■ D I M P L E
L E N D ■ W I R E D U P ■ M O T O R E D
S A Y I D O ■ C E S S ■ S T O U T K I N G
A R A P A H O E ■ S I O U X ■ C I E
S A N ■ W I L D E S I N G E R ■ G L E N S
■ E S T D ■ A T M A N ■ N E R O ■
C A R L O ■ S C R I P P S ■ I N A S P O T
B R O W N W O O L F ■ P O U N D S T O N E
E L B A ■ T U B A L ■ L U N G ■ P I C K S
R O S Y ■ S L O P E ■ E T C ■ S T O P S
```

16

```
M A N E T ■ A L I E N A T E D ■ N O I R E
O C E A N ■ P A T R O N A G E ■ O S K A R
T H E S O L O M O N R G U G G E N H E I M
H E R E T I C ■ S A N T A A N A
■ S E T ■ M U S E U M ■ S T R
H I F I S ■ S O P R A N O S ■ R A F F L E
O N I N ■ P I A N O T U N E R ■ D A R T S
T E N ■ P O S T ■ M D V I ■ I B A R S
T V A ■ I T S ■ A B A ■ R I G ■ T E N S E
A I L ■ C A Y ■ B E G U I L E ■ I R K
M T M ■ A T S ■ C H A G A L L ■ O G L E S
A A A ■ S I P ■ D A P H N E ■ O N E L A P
L B J ■ S O A S ■ R E S ■ G M A ■ O R R
E L O ■ O N C U E ■ V I R A L ■ Y E A
S E R B ■ S E M I T R A I L E R ■ E D D Y
■ W A N ■ K A N D I N S K Y ■ T R W
S P O U S E ■ C E S S N A S ■ S E U R A T
E A R H A R T ■ D E E D I D O
A S K A ■ N A T A L I E W O O D ■ I G O R
T H O U ■ S P I R A L S H A P E ■ T H R U
O A F S ■ T A X P R E P A R E R ■ E T E S
```

17

```
A B B A E B A N ■ S D A K ■ ■ C E D R I C
R O I D R A G E ■ A E T N A ■ A Q U I N O
M Y G O A L I N L I F E I S ■ D U N L O P
E L M ■ ■ N A L D I ■ T O B E A C L U E
Y E O M E N ■ ■ D I N A ■ F A T T E S T
■ ■ U P T I M E ■ D E S I ■ U T E S ■
I N T H E N E W Y O R K T I M E S ■ G A G
A S H ■ ■ A L E E ■ E O N ■ ■ A I D E
S A S H A ■ C R O S S W O R D P U Z Z L E
■ ■ O R T ■ S H O E ■ ■ E P I T O M E S
T O O L B O X ■ ■ I V E ■ ■ I S I D O R E
O X Y M O R O N ■ ■ E L S E ■ A L Y ■
N E V E R T O L D A N Y O N E ■ S E G U E
A Y E S ■ ■ E A R ■ I D L E ■ ■ E S T
L E Y ■ S P O R T S I L L U S T R A T E D
■ ■ S C U M ■ S O L O ■ P A C I N O ■
■ S A V A N N A ■ N O V A ■ H O O V E S
P E T E R K I N G ■ S A P O R ■ ■ E T H
A D E L I E ■ T H A T B U T I T S T R U E
V A S T E R ■ S I G I L ■ T E S T R I D E
E N T E R S ■ ■ J E T E ■ O N E L I T E R
```

18

```
C A P S ■ B A T T ■ A B H O R ■ ■ C D S
A P O C R Y P H A ■ P I A N O ■ T W E E T
R E T R O S P E C T A C L E S ■ V I L L E
■ ■ B A T E ■ S K A T ■ F L E W A K I T E
E L E P H A N T O M ■ S P O R A D I C A L
A I L S ■ ■ Y A N ■ C O R T E S ■ P A S
R E L ■ C R A G ■ W A D I ■ D O T E ■
P S Y C H E D E L I C A C Y ■ N O D I C E
■ ■ A A H ■ A L A ■ E A T ■ M I S O S
C O N T R A B A N D O N ■ L I P B A L M S
U T A H ■ S E D G E ■ E F I L E ■ T A M E
O H F A T H E R ■ R O U L E T T E R M A N
M E T R O ■ R A J ■ A M O ■ I C I ■
O R A T O R ■ G U I T A R I S T O C R A T
■ ■ I L A Y ■ S V E N ■ N O E L ■ E G O
■ R E C ■ L E C T E R ■ S T L ■ A F E W
P E R H A P S O D Y ■ F O R E V E R I E S
H I R O S H I M A ■ Z O L A ■ A S A N ■
O S A K A ■ C E N T I P E D E S T R I A N
T E T E S ■ A R D E N ■ M A K E H A S T E
O R A ■ ■ N S Y N C ■ N Y E S ■ T H A W
```

```
A L E R . A D A G E . Z A P S . S U P R A
B E N E . C A M E L . E L A N . U S H E R
A N T H E M L I N E . B A S E T E N A N T
F O R E S E E . E C R U . S E A T . S T E
T R E A T S . S R T A . E A R N . F E A R
. E E R O . B E A R D I N G . C A R L Y .
. . P L A N T A I N D E A L E R . . . .
. C A S S E T T E . O O P . D I S . L P S
A R I E . D E I . L E N A . I N U T I L E
L O R C A . S N O O D . P A N T R Y B A R
I N F O R . E I N . A E C . A R E T E
G I A N T B I L L . A W R A P . S A L T S
N E R D I E R . S A P S . D I G . N E E T
S S E . S A M . H I P . R E L I S T E D .
. . M A D A M I M A D A M A N T . . .
G R A I N . A P E R I T I F . R A S P
R O N A . A N D S . E S T A . C O N T R A
A M O . O P I E . E L O I . L O N G R U N
P E D A N T X I N G . W E B P A G E A N T
E R A S E . O R E O . N S Y N C . L I E S
S O L E S . N A B S . S T A S H . A N D Y
```

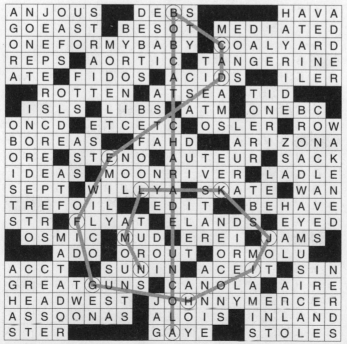

```
A N J O U S . D E B S . . H A V A
G O E A S T . B E S O T . M E D I A T E D
O N E F O R M Y B A B Y . C O A L Y A R D
R E P S . A O R T I C . T A N G E R I N E
A T E . F I D O S . A C I D S . I L E R
. R O T T E N . A T S E A . T I D .
. I S L S . L I B S . A T M . O N E B C
O N C D . E T C E T C . O S L E R . R O W
B O R E A S . F A H D . A R I Z O N A
O R E . S T E N O . A U T E U R . S A C K
I D E A S . M O O N R I V E R . L A D L E
S E P T . W I L L Y A . S K A T E . W A N
T R E F O I L . E D I T . B E H A V E
S T R . F L Y A T . E L A N D S . E Y E D
. O S M I C . M U D . E R E I . J A M S
. A D O . O R O U T . O R M O L U
A C C T . S U N I N . A C E I T . S I N
G R E A T G U N S . C A N O L A . A I R E
H E A D W E S T . J O H N N Y M E R C E R
A S S O O N A S . A L O I S . I N L A N D
S T E R . . G A Y E . S T O L E S
```

21

B	A	M	B	I		S	M	O	K	E		I	R	E	S	T		L	G	A
I	L	I	A	D		E	S	S	E	X		N	E	C	C	O		O	R	S
T	I	C	K	E	T	A	G	E	N	T		S	M	O	O	T	H	O	U	T
		L	A	U	D		S	O	C	I	A	L	W	O	R	K	E	R		
E	T	T	A		R	O	L	O		R	I	T	T			S	I	L	O	
D	R	I	V	I	N	G	I	N	S	T	R	U	C	T	O	R		E	S	S
S	E	D	A	N	S		M	E	E	S	E		H	E	R	E	S			
E	V	A		A	R	A	B	L	E					A	G	I	T	A	T	E
L	I	L		I	E	S		B	R	A	N	C	H	M	A	N	A	G	E	R
	B	A	R	D	O	T		R	H	E	A		N	A	C	R	E	S		
I	R	A	N		F	I	L	E	C	L	E	R	K		K	E	N	T		
S	Y	S	T	E	M		F	I	S	H		M	I	S	U	S	E			
U	N	I	O	N	O	F	F	I	C	I	A	L		L	A	T		S	H	E
P	E	N	N	A	M	E				K	E	N	O	B	I		W	A	Y	
	E	R	M	A	S		A	S	I	D	E		E	L	A	I	N	E		
G	A	T		M	A	R	K	E	T	I	N	G	D	I	R	E	C	T	O	R
E	V	A	N			E	G	O	S		E	S	T	S		T	H	I	S	
R	E	C	O	R	D	K	E	E	P	E	R		L	A	F	F				
B	R	O	W	B	E	A	T	S		N	O	V	E	L	W	R	I	T	E	R
I	S	M		I	N	L	E	T		O	N	E	N	D		A	V	I	A	N
L	E	A		S	T	E	R	S		R	A	T	S	O		Y	E	A	R	S

22

D	O	C	S		S	P	O	O	L		Z	I	N	E		V	I	S	E
O	P	A	H		P	L	A	N	A		T	O	N	A	L		I	N	C	A
S	Q	U	E	A	L	O	F	A	P	P	R	O	V	A	L		S	M	O	G
	S	P	R	I	T		I	D	E	A	M	A	N		S	H	A	W	L
O	N	E	H	I	T	T	E	R		T	I	E	D		G	E	N	T	L	E
R	O	W	E		S	E	X		W	I	L	D	E	B	E	Q	U	E	S	T
G	U	A	R	D		D	E	B	I	T			E	M	U				
S	N	Y	D	E	R		C	O	D		O	M	A	N		E	V	I	A	N
	S	N	I	P		B	E	A	V	I	S		F	L	A	N	G	E
S	K	I	P		S	I	P	S		B	E	N	I	C	E		N	C	A	A
L	O	C	I		Q	U	E	A	S	Y	R	I	D	E	R		Q	U	I	P
I	R	A	Q		U	S	A	G	E	S		G	E	R	M		U	R	N	S
D	A	N	U	B	E		L	E	T	S	G	O		T	A	T	I		
E	N	T	E	R		B	E	T	H		A	L	I		T	A	S	M	A	N
		E	A	U			I	N	F	R	A		C	H	I	C	A		
Q	U	A	L	M	S	G	I	V	I	N	G		O	U	T		I	S	M	S
U	N	D	I	E	S		M	E	R	E		I	N	D	I	A	N	T	E	A
A	S	H	E	N		A	P	R	O	P	O	S		I	M	A	G	O	
F	E	E	L		Q	U	A	I	N	T	M	I	S	B	E	H	A	V	I	N
F	A	R	O		B	E	L	L	Y		A	T	O	L	L		C	E	D	E
S	T	E	W		S	L	A	Y		R	I	L	E	Y		T	R	O	D

```
WAKED  SCRAP  OTTER  ARS
APERY  ARENA  BRINE  PET
BOLLA  SOPOR  SEAOFLOVE
ALLEN  HOODS  CARL   ISEE
SLY    SANSEI UTA    TATAR
HOMEBOYS      FORESTHILLS
    CLOPS  SOARED  EASES
ALGAL   WORLD    DARE
TOILET  EVA    RUER   MIA
LOL    RETAILS UNLIT  INT
ATL    OLIVEBRANCHES  NPR
SEI    SLEET  ABOLISH TUE
TDS    SIRS   AVE   TINCTS
   BRAN    KITES   ROOST
  ARAIL  SPACER  GOTIN
EMERALDCITY    FIRSTDAY
LUSTS  ROC  SALAMI    IVE
OSHA   MYRA  TRILL  SATES
PEABRAINS  ARETE  HEIRS
EMP   DICES  ROGET  AROSE
DEE   ALERO  EWERS  HONES
```

```
LAVA   MASSE  PENCE  NCAA
ASIS   ELTON  OCEAN  AHAB
BACKGROUND    SHORTSTORY
SPEARGUN  EATON  RATIOS
    FEED  BARB   TAVERNS
FOSTER  MORTAL  ACER
ASHEN  HOUSEGUEST   BAR
ITOR  POUR    CAKE  RUSE
TIP  CHARGECARD   CACHE
HAWTHORN  ERLES  GAWKED
   IRONY   RIO   GRILL
CANAPE  AVISO  TRANSEPT
AUDIS   DEEPFREEZE  DIE
ATON  GOON    URGE  RONA
NOW   UPSTANDING  VOWEL
    ETTU  SCORNS  SOUNDS
ZEALOTS    CUES   LULL
INSITU  AMENS  LARGESSE
LETTERHEAD   STEPFATHER
CREE  AERIE  ERASE  TONI
HOPS  LYONS  RAKED  ETTE
```

```
D C C A B ■ D O L L S ■ P O L E M I C S
A H O R A ■ R E X A L L ■ A N A L O G U E
V A L I D ■ A M A N D A ■ T E N S P O T S
I S L A M ■ C O L D S T O R A G E ■ T O A
D E E ■ A S I T I S ■ H I C ■ ■ S T U M
■ ■ G E N E S E S ■ C O Y O T E S T A T E
■ J E N N E T S ■ M O N E T ■ T H O ■
■ A S T E R S ■ B A L L S ■ T R A M C A R
A L T E R S ■ F U L L Y ■ B E A N P O L E
S O U R S ■ M A R L A ■ S L A D E ■ M A L
C U D S ■ C O R N E R S T O R E ■ A F R O
E S E ■ G O N G S ■ S T A C Y ■ S T O M A
N I N T E N D O ■ S T O R K ■ F L O R I D
D E T E N T E ■ F O U N T ■ B R A N T S ■
■ ■ P I E ■ C R U D E ■ B R A V E S T
C O M I C S T R I P S ■ K E E N E S T ■
A R I D ■ O U T ■ S N E A K S ■ A P E
N I L ■ C O M M O N S T O C K ■ H O T E L
T A K E A N A P ■ T E E T H E ■ I S I T I
E N E R V A T E ■ W A L T E R ■ P L O T Z
D A R E S N O T ■ T R E Y S ■ S O N Y A
```

```
C O S T A R ■ C A B S ■ B R A Y ■ A M B S
A R C A N E ■ A L O E ■ L A V A ■ N E L L
M I A M I A D V I C E ■ A K I N ■ T R U E
P O L ■ S L E I G H ■ S N E A K ■ I C E D
E L I T E ■ R A N C H A D D R E S S I N G
R E A R ■ B A R ■ O I L ■ Y E A ■ F O E
■ I G O T ■ F E U D ■ T A U S
■ A D M I S S I O N I M P O S S I B L E
S P I L L S ■ R I O ■ C A P O N E ■
P R A Y ■ C O N M E N ■ R H O D I U M
E I N ■ S T O C K A D O P T I O N ■ R N A
C L A M O R S ■ R A T O U T ■ R A C K
■ A L I E N S ■ C P R ■ U N I Q U E
■ A D J U S T F O R T H E F U N O F I T
■ C R A B ■ L U A U ■ N I N E ■
R A E ■ L O X ■ N B C ■ C I T ■ S T A G
A D A G E O F A Q U A R I U S ■ S T O R E
D E M O ■ L I T U P ■ E A T O U T ■ O R R
I M I N ■ A L L A ■ W O M E N S A D L I B
S I N G ■ L E A R ■ A L B S ■ S L E E V E
H A G S ■ A S S T ■ R E S T ■ R E N D E R
```

```
P A R E █ A T T I C █ L A R D S █ V A S E
A M E N █ R O O N E █ A T B A T █ O R Y X
R I N D █ P E A R L S S W I N E █ L A N E
I C E A G E █ D E T E C T █ I V T U B E S
S A W L O G S █ M I R A █ A S I A N █
█ L O G I C █ C A L M T H E S T O R M
O L D █ F I N A L █ A P E █ S E G U E
L O O K Y O U L E A P █ H U M P █ E L B A
M A N N █ S I G N U P █ P E A G R E E N
O T H E R S █ C A T N A P █ S B A █
S H O W S P H O T O G R A P H S S H O W S
█ V I E █ O N E I D A █ T H E N H L
S K I N P E E L █ S N A R L S █ I L I E
W I N O █ S L O P █ T H E O T H E R O N E
A W A S H █ F A S █ S M E A R █ W E T
N I N E A Q U A R T E R █ A A R O N █
█ B L U R T █ A X E R █ M A D E O F F
P U L L T A B █ A N C H O R █ N E W C A R
S H U E █ C A R S C H A S I N G █ A E R O
S O L E █ K N U T E █ B I J O U █ R A G S
T H U D █ S E M I S █ S N O R E █ K N O T
```

```
C L O G S █ A H E M █ T H A W █ R A P T
R A V E L █ S E T A E █ H U L A █ O L I O
T B O N E S T E A K S █ E D B R A D L E Y
█ T E P I D █ E S M E █ A S S I S T S
O R B I T E R █ G M A T █ A N T O N █
M A U L E D █ X R A Y V I S I O N █ C O S
E B B E D █ L E E D S █ S T A R E D O W N
N I B S █ G O N G █ L O O N Y █ O F N O
S N L █ M O N O █ L I M N █ S A F E R
█ E R O S E █ U S E M E █ H U B E R T
A R B I T E R █ N A D E R █ T O P L E S S
B E R A T E █ C R O S S █ A P E E K █
R E A L S █ P L A N █ B R E R █ L A P
A L I T █ D A Y A N █ C U T S █ W A D E
D I N O S A U R S █ T S A R S █ P A T E R
E N S █ H Y D E P A R K N Y █ M U S C L E
█ T A T A S █ M A Y S █ T E E T H E S
O C E A N I C █ E P I C █ N O T B E █
R I G H T M I N D █ N A T U R A L F O O D
C I A O █ E T R E █ S P E N T █ O U T T O
A I D E █ R Y A N █ S A N E █ S L O B S
```

```
C A S H I N S   C H I R A C   W A G N E R
O N E O C A T   H E L E N A   A R R I V E
R O C K Y M U S I C I A N S   R E A G A N
E S T E   E M T   K A P U T   D A P H N E
    A S P I E   S I L A S   E T S
A C T O N   E N E M Y   T E L   I V Y
T R I C K O R T R E A T Y   L A T I S H
M O R T A R   S Y N C H   P I R A N H A S
S W E A R A T   S H E B A   G L E A N S
    V A L E   W A T E R Y L O O   D E T
B A B E   M I A   I S A   M E S S
A G E   S C A R Y F A C E   D E C O
B A L B O A   I S O L A   S T A P L E S
A T L A N T I S   A T B A T   C H E E T A
  E Y R I E S   B L O O D Y T H I R S T Y
C C C   E L I   S T O R E   E S S E S
C U E   B E E P S   S O N A R
P A R L O R   A L I A S   N A G   A D U E
I N V O K E   P A N C A K E B A T T E R Y
K E E N A N   E N C I N O   L I N E A G E
E S S A Y S   D E E D E D   E N T E R E D
```

```
B U S C H   M A R I   J O V E   D O N A
I G L O O   C A D I Z   A X E D   E R A S
T H U M B S A R I D E   V E R O B E A C H
    R E B E L L E D   H A Y S   A P P L E
L A S S I E   B U L G E   E A S I E R
I L O   E S P O   E R I C   A N N O Y
L O V E S T O R Y   A S H C A N   E N O S
A H E M   R O O M S T O L E T   D O D O
C A R O   U N S N A P   K O R A N   B E T
    T O P O   M A D E D O   A T I L T
E L M E R S   G A I T E R S   G R O S S O
Q U E S T   S U R E S T   C O A T
U N D   S E P I A   T A R P O N   I R A S
A G I O   V U L G A R T E R M   N E I L
L E A N   E N D O R A   L O T T O G A M E
  S P O O R   N E W T   J E E R   P E W
    E N D S U P   A S O N E   S L O P E S
G A R D E   S I T S   M U C I L A G E
I T S A S H A M E   W A R T S A N D A L L
F L O G   E G A N   A T S E A   D E L E S
T I N A   P E S T   H O E D   O N S E T
```

31

```
A P T L Y ■ W E N T ■ T R U R O ■ S T A G
P A S E O ■ I D E A ■ W E B E R ■ H E L L
B R E A K I N G I N T O S O N G ■ O N T O
■ ■ F O R G I N G A H E A D ■ B O D E S
L I P ■ H E M E ■ S N O R T ■ C A T E R S
O N E ■ A L A R M ■ G U V ■ C H A I R ■
B A T S M A N ■ A M O R E T T O ■ N A B S
B H U T A N ■ E X E S ■ A R P E G G I O
I O N E ■ D A V I T ■ J O N ■ I N T E N D
E L I A ■ M I L ■ D O U G ■ N T H ■ ■
D E A L ■ K I L L I N G T I M E ■ E F T S
■ ■ I C I ■ N A N A ■ T E A ■ M A I L
W A L N U T ■ E E K ■ H O R E B ■ O L L A
E X E G E S E S ■ D O S S ■ R O O S T S
B E S T ■ C O S T F R E E ■ V A R N I S H
■ S H A H S ■ R A J ■ A M A N A ■ T A E
S H E E D Y ■ F E T O R ■ A L A N ■ Y T D
M O R S E ■ P O A C H I N G E G G S ■ ■
U T A H ■ H O L D I N G U P T H E L I N E
R E P O ■ E L I O T ■ O D I E ■ R U R A L
F L E W ■ P E O N Y ■ R E E D ■ Y E A T S
```

32

```
B U T I D ■ L O O K F ■ C R A G ■ S T I R
O M A N I ■ I T A L O ■ P O C O ■ H O L E
A P I N G ■ E S K E R ■ A U T O ■ E R L E
S I P ■ R E D ■ L I A R ■ S U N G ■ P U N
T R A ■ E S O ■ E N N E ■ S P A R S E S T
S E N D S A W A Y ■ A P S E ■ B E N D E R
■ U S I N G ■ U N S E A T ■ W O O D Y
B O E R ■ ■ T O N G ■ M U U M U U ■ ■
O F F O N A T ■ P A L S ■ R A P T U R E
N L F ■ E V A D E ■ E M B A N K ■ S P A N
G A O ■ D I N E R S ■ U L S T E R ■ H I C
O T R A ■ A G L A R E ■ A P H I D ■ I S A
S E T R A T E ■ O X E N ■ E T A B L E S
■ C L E N C H ■ I N K Y ■ E L S E
S T O A T ■ T R A I T S ■ E L I D E ■
C O R N E R ■ O R B S ■ S T O V E P I P E
R E V E R S E S ■ E T A T ■ V A T ■ M A V
A N I ■ S T A S ■ T A T A ■ E N O ■ B Y E
W A L L ■ O V I D ■ G A L A S ■ U N I O N
L I L A ■ R E N O ■ E R A S E ■ R O B L E
S L E D ■ E D G E ■ R I G H T ■ A H E A D
```

33

```
J A M S   T A M I L   S H A D S   P A L E
A S A P   E R I C A   H A Z E L   I B E X
Y O G I   S A L E M   A D O L E S C E N T
  F I N D S B A D I N D I V I D U A L S  
    D E E S     N E E     S P Y    
S T A L E R   T H A W   R M S   R U S S A
N A M E D A S H U T T L E A T L A N T I S
A X E     T E T E   O N C U E   E R R S
P I N E T R E E S   L A O   B O A   I R E
    L O B E D   R A D I I     S O N A R
I N C O M I N G R E T U R N S S O U G H T
M O A N S     E A T U P   S T I N T  
A M S   K O S   S R S   S T A T E S M A N
G E T S   R I C K I   C O E N     E C O
E A R T H S P R I M A R Y A D V O C A T E
S T O R E   S Y N   L E A D   A L A N I S
    E R A     A P E     E L A L    
  U S U A L L Y S T O P S A L L F O E S  
P R E S S T I M E S   S A T I E   R A K E
O G L E   E M C E E   U N I T Y   I R I S
W E L L   R E A D A   P E T E S   E N D S
```

34

```
  A R R   C A R O M   I M A M S   U T A H
A L A E   A L E U T   N O R M A   N O R A
S I N G I N I N T H E G R A I N   K E E N
C E L I B A T E   O D O R   D A N A N G
E N A M E L   G O U T O F A F R I C A
N O T E   A P O D   L I L I T H
T R E N T   N A T   S A L A R Y   H O N
  T H E G L O V E D O N E   D R I V E
E R G   E L E A   A M A S   D R E I S E R
V A R   M O L D   T I M E S   E M I G R E
I S O N   P A I R   R U B S   S O L I
C H O I C E   N E P A L   B R A D   W A D
T E M P U R A   A U T O   D A L I   N Y S
E R A S E   G A L L A B O U T E V E
E S T   F A R M E D   M E T   A S T R O
  T H A L I A   I N D Y   C R I B
  T H E K I N G A N D G I   E M A I L S
T O E C A P   R E I N   S C R A P P L E
E S T A   P L A N E T O F T H E G A P E S
S C O T   E E L E D   R E L I C   D E T S
T A P E   R A L L Y   E B O A T   E D S
```

```
T A S K   O T I C     M O V I E     C F C
G E T A   T E S L A   A P A C E   A U R A
I S A Y   E N A I T C H E L A L L S T A R
F O L G E R S   C A I R N   R E I S S U E
  P E E A I T C H D E E S T U D E N T
  M E R   O R E     E I S       H O L
A B A B   O N E   N A S A L   S E C E D E
E M T E E V E E H O S T   L O R E L E I
S T E E L E   S O T T O   C A N O E I S T
  A I R S   B A R C L A Y   S E N S E
T R I G   A L L B R O K E N U P   N E A R
H O N E S   Y E S I D I D   P Y L E
E M A N A T E D   Z O N E D   G U N F O R
G E N T L E R   E M G E E E M G R A N D
A R I S T A   H O S E S   N A Y   E V A S
P O M     T E L     S T R   I P O
  A I T C H E M E S S P I N A F O R E
N O T S U R E   S A R A I   I N A R A G E
C E E P E E E A R T R A I N I N G   T B A R
O N L Y   S P I E L   D A N G S   E L L A
S O Y   T E D D Y   L E S T   R Y E S
```

```
L A H R   E T H I C   M I D A S   C U S S
E L E E   R A I S E   A L A S T   A T I T
C U R T J E S T E R   T O N G A   T A T A
A L T R U I S M   T W I S T A N D S H U T
R A Z E D   E E G   I N T E R C O M
    A A S   R U S E     D E L E T E D
F U N D I N G F A T H E R S   S L O W E R
U L E   C O A R S E     O O M   W Y L E
G A S H   W R A P   B A L L A S T   L E A
U N T I M E L Y   B U L L E T I N B A R D
  D A D A   O R R I S   A D U E
F R E E Z I N G P I N T   R H E T O R I C
R I D   E N D U R E S   L O A D   N A N A
O P I E   S S A   M A O R I S   V C R
D E N I M S   T H E C A S T I S C L E A R
O N A T E A R   N O P E   H O E
  H E R E W E G O   R E O   T A L E S
Q U I E T A S A M U S E   A N E C D O T E
T S A R   N A G E L   M I S S T H E B A T
I N S O   A L O A F   T R E E D   R O T H
P A I R   C E N T S   S A L T S   S S S S
```

37

```
C A B A N A █ C A N N E S █ █ M A F I A S
A L A M O S █ O R I O L E █ W O M A N L Y
R O B O T S █ L A N D E R █ H O I S T E D
I H A V E N O O B J E C T I O N S T O █
B A S E L █ T R Y A █ █ T Y E S █ █ █
█ █ L I R A █ █ P A S T O R █ B I T E
S P E D █ L O N G T E D I O U S P L A Y S
T O L I F E █ T E H R A N █ █ L U M P S
A R I E L █ A S T R O █ K I L L E R B E E
Y E S M A A M █ I O N █ R A I D S █ █
S S E █ █ J O H N B █ K E A N E █ E S E
█ █ S P A C E █ S N L █ C D R A C K S
T H E N I X O N S █ H O D G E █ O B O E S
H E R O S █ █ L E A P E R █ N E L L I E
I A L W A Y S F E E L F R E S H █ E I N S
S T E S █ A L L W E T █ A W L S █ █ █
█ █ T R U E █ S E T A █ A S S A I
█ W H E N I W A K E U P A T T H E E N D
A S I A T I C █ M I L I E U █ R A V I N E
N O T D O N E █ B E A T E N █ A R E N A S
I C H I N G █ I L L E S T █ P A R E N T
```

38

```
F R A U █ A S M A D █ P E C S █ B E S T
E A R P █ L E A V E N █ S T L O █ A L P O
T H E B I G C H I L I █ T H E F A R M E R
E S S E N █ A L E C S █ N A I L D O W N
█ █ A T T I L A T H E H O N E Y █ █
N E C T A R Y █ E E R O █ █ C L I P
E C O █ C I A O █ V J S █ S E A M A N
S H O R T O R D E R C O O K I E █ N E V A
T O T O █ O L E O S █ O D D B A L L S
█ P S I S █ I N N █ R A G A █ D O T
H A V E O N E F O O T I N T H E G R A V Y
A B E █ O V E R █ A G O █ O S S A █
M A R I N A T E █ S C O T T █ G A E L
A T O M █ D O E S N T R I N G A B E L L Y
S E N A T E █ D U O █ T A R A █ T K O
█ D A N E █ L O S T █ L A M P O O N
█ P I C K U P T H E T A B B Y █
M A I D E N L Y █ S I E V E █ O T H E R
I N T H E D E L I █ C H I C A G O H O P I
S O T O █ I W I N █ K A T H I E █ O L I N
S N O W █ A S E A █ T A S T E █ N E C K
```

39

N I P S	S C A L E	B O S C	C O O E D
A S I A	H A P A X	U N T O	H U R R Y

F A N T A I L E D P I G E O N — A T A L E

T A K E S I T — Y E L L O W W A R B L E R

A C C E P T E D — N E E — A L T O

O N S E C O N D — B A Y S — A B L E

A B C — H O I — H A I L — D R O O L

N U K I N G — R A Z O R B I L L E D A U K

G R A N N Y — G O U P — I O N S

E S T E E M — T A O S — F I L E S — R O C

L A O S — S C A R L E T I B I S — B E B E

S R O — S H U L A — M E A N — S H A D E S

A T O R — M A N N — E E L E R S

D O U B L E B A R F I N C H — R E L Y O N

D A V A O — L A R D — E I S — E N A

S T A N — E S P Y — L E F T H A N D

D A L Y — A H A — I R A L E V I N

W H O O P I N G C R A N E — A S T A I R E

H A D N T — C H I P P I N G S P A R R O W

A R I E L — H I T E — N O I S E — B E N T

M I N D Y — S A I L — A W N E D — Y O Y O

40

P I T A S — T E A C H — P A T A C A K E

I R I S H — A T S E A — M A R I N A T E D

N O T T I N G H I L L — A B B E Y R O A D

A N T O N I A — S T S — L A S — T I N Y

T I L — S A L — I T A L — A W E

A C E S — C O P — C O V E N T G A R D E N

O P I N E D — N A T U R E S — A G O

P A D D I N G T O N — S I A M — L Y O N

I L I A C — A N O N — V A M O O S E

K I O S K S — R H E I N — P E T I T

E A R — L O N D O N L O C A L E S — L O S

M E N U S — D E V I L — S H T E T L

G A P E D A T — S A G A — A U D I O

R U E D — T M E N — E A T O N P L A C E

A D E — D I E S E L S — R E M I S S

B I L L I N G S G A T E — S E X — A R C H

I D A — A V I V — L O W — E L O

S W A N — R U T — F O B — E N A B L E S

L I M E H O U S E — F L E E T S T R E E T

O P E N E N D E D — E V E N T — T E N S E

T E N S P E E D — D E F O E — S A T E D

41

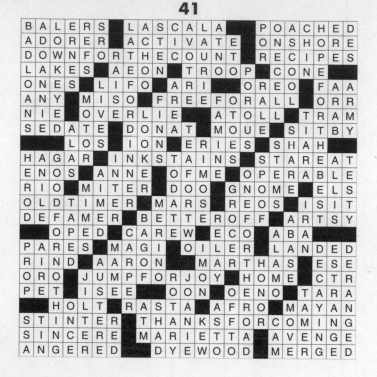

```
B A L E R S   L A S C A L A     P O A C H E D
A D O R E R   A C T I V A T E   O N S H O R E
D O W N F O R T H E C O U N T   R E C I P E S
L A K E S   A E O N   T R O O P   C O N E
O N E S   L I F O   A R I   O R E O   F A A
A N Y   M I S O   F R E E F O R A L L   O R R
N I E   O V E R L I E   A T O L L   T R A M
S E D A T E   D O N A T   M O U E   S I T B Y
      L O S   I O N   E R I E S   S H A H
H A G A R   I N K S T A I N S   S T A R E A T
E N O S   A N N E   O F M E   O P E R A B L E
R I O   M I T E R   D O O   G N O M E   E L S
O L D T I M E R   M A R S   R E O S   I S I T
D E F A M E R   B E T T E R O F F   A R T S Y
      O P E D   C A R E W   E C O   A B A
P A R E S   M A G I   O I L E R   L A N D E D
R I N D   A A R O N   M A R T H A S   E S E
O R O   J U M P F O R J O Y   H O M E   C T R
P E T   I S E E   O O N   O E N O   T A R A
      H O L T   R A S T A   A F R O   M A Y A N
S T I N T E R   T H A N K S F O R C O M I N G
S I N C E R E   M A R I E T T A   A V E N G E
A N G E R E D   D Y E W O O D   M E R G E D
```

42

```
D A H S   B A R E S   A C T S   P O S E R
E B A N   E C O N O   T R E K   I L E N E
T I M O N A H A L F   R I S E   E A R T H
E D U C A T E D   A R I E L W A R F A R E
R E P O T   S M U   H A R A S S   P E A
      N A H   A P R I L S   K O S H E R
O P H E L I A P A I N   C R E P T
V I I   I R R   P O R T I A D E A L E R
E N S   E A T   M E S H I N G   N I E C E
R E P S   B E G U N   O E D   B E N T O N
      A P O L L O S   D E L U D E S
T E N A C E   R T E   F O R U M   D D A Y
S A I N T   N I E L S E N   I S R   O R A
P U C K I N G O R D E R   G O O   W O W
      E L I O T   C A S S I U S I N O N
T E R R E T   F A T L I P   T E D
A L E   R O C O C O   E L K   T O B I T
B A N Q U O S H O U R S   O N E T O O N E
L I E U T   C O L A   T I T U S A D R U M
A N G I E   A S I T   A C C T S   I N S P
S E E D S   R E N E   T E H E E   T E E S
```

43

```
A S L E E P ■ H A L L O ■ ■ ■ S T A C K ■
L O U V E R ■ A R M E N I A ■ O R I O N S
B O N A C O N T E N T I O N ■ B I R D I E
S T A N ■ T A C T ■ T O T A L ■ A B A C I
■ ■ ■ T O T H E T U N A T E N B U C K S ■
C O C A I N E ■ A C S ■ ■ W A L D O ■ ■
A B A C K ■ E S T E ■ S P I N E ■ N E O
H O W C I L I A M E ■ T O R S O ■ E D N A
N E S T ■ I N R E ■ D I N O ■ B L U E S
■ ■ M A N N A W A R ■ W I S E A C R E
O S B O R N E ■ R I V E T ■ L E A N T O S
T H E B E A S T ■ P I S A M I N D ■ ■ ■
R U L E D ■ R E E D ■ M O A N ■ B E A U
O L A Y ■ S N E R D ■ D E C C A C A R D S
S A T ■ G L U E S ■ P O R K ■ A L G A E
■ H I L U M ■ B O P ■ S A V I O R S
T H E B A R B A R A S E V I L L E ■ ■ ■
R O B E D ■ S C O O T ■ I D I O ■ B U S H
A W A R D S ■ T U B A T O O T H P A S T E
M I L I E U ■ S E A G U L L ■ A S I D E S
■ E L A N D ■ ■ B E T A S ■ S I T A R S
```

44

```
C A M U S ■ M U S T A C H E ■ S P A R S ■ S H O E
A W A S H ■ I M P E R I A L ■ U R I A H ■ H U N S
B A D N E W S B E A M E R S ■ N E R V E G A M E S
A R M ■ E E L E R Y ■ I D O S ■ I R A ■ A G A
L E A H ■ I R E D ■ T H E I C E ■ S P R I N G Y
■ G A R R Y ■ S O F I A ■ M O N ■ H A R N E S S
G R A V I D ■ W I G W A M ■ T I E S O N
O O Z E S ■ G A M E T E K E E P E R S ■ T O S C A
O B I T S ■ A L A N ■ R E G R A D E ■ L E C T O R
D O N H O ■ R O A S T S ■ I S R ■ L O A ■ E O N S
S T E E L D R U M ■ W E B S ■ K M A R T ■ M O M E
■ L E O ■ H I Y O ■ S W A N E E ■ E G A N
C O M A ■ M E T H A N E O F C A W D O R ■ N E N E
A H A S ■ I M E A S Y ■ S L A Y ■ O A T
S O R T ■ N I N J A ■ E T A L ■ M O O N R A K E R
T H A W ■ G R F ■ C E L ■ G A P E A T ■ A S I D E
R O C O C O ■ E B O N I C S ■ L I S I ■ P A N D A
O H A R A ■ M E O W T H A T H U R T S ■ A L G I D
■ M R M O T O ■ R U N O U T ■ P H A S E S
T Y P E D I N ■ T O A ■ O N T O P ■ P R O M O ■
H E A D I N G ■ L E N D E E ■ R O R Y ■ B L T S
A M P ■ F E E ■ A N T E ■ S T E R E O ■ O R Y
M E A L F R E S C O ■ B A T M A S T E R S O M E N
E N Y A ■ A S P E N ■ U N B U T T O N ■ P R O N G
S I A M ■ L E A S E ■ S T A T I O N S ■ Y E N T E
```

```
R A P I D   H O P E   N E R D   D U S K S
O M A N I   A M E N   O B I E   O N T O P
B U C K E T S E A T   T O M F O O L E R Y
E L I   C A E N   R E I N S   F R O N D S
D E N M A R K   P A R T Y   M I M O S A
  T O A S T   A R I A   I O T A S
  S T A G N A N T P O N D   T E P E E
R P M   R E E D S   U R G E D   S L I M
E R A T O   T W O   A T L A S E S   A G T
P E L I C A N   S H O O T   L A U G H S
  H A R T F O R D C O N N E C T I C U T
R E P E A T   U R A L S   R A L L I E D
H A R   L E O N A R D   W E E   S A N E R
E T O N   R H Y M E   T I G E R   G N U
A S P I C   B O A R D I N G P A S S
  L I M O N   E N D S   D U E T S
  T H E T O Y   T A N K S   L I N E O U T
A R U B A N   T E N S E   E A S T   O B I
B U L L D O Z I N G   R A M S H A C K L E
R E C U E   I D O L   E D I T   N O T E R
A R E E L   P E R E   D O T S   S P O T S
```

```
W E S T   I C I   H A R A R E   T E A M
O N E R   N O S E   I R A N I S   R A J A
R O T E   S Q U E A L O F A P P R O V A L
S C A M P I   Z E L D A   E V E R T
T H E B A S Q U E S A R E L O A D E D
  L U T E   L A M P S
A N G E L   D U H S   A I M A T   Z E B U
S C A R A B   M A O   N O A H S Q U A R K
H A W S   A L E V E   I T S A   U N T I E
Y A K   B R O K E U P   D E I S T S
  P A Q U I N R E L I E V E R S
R A Z O R S   Z O M B I F Y   T A N
A B O M B   P T A S   C A S I O   H O P I
F I N E Q U A R T S   A G E   G A E L I C
T E E S   C R A S S   L E N T   B A D G E
  S L I C E   A B E D
  Q U E A S Y A S O N E T W O T H R E E
A M U S E   A P I S H   U S U A L S
Q U A L M S F O R T H E P O O R   N O E S
U N I T   H A W A I I   N U N N   T U N A
A I D A   E A S T E R   S T E   S L A Y
```

47

```
A C R O S S   C H A F F     D I P P I E R
C L A R K E   R E S U L T   U T R I L L O
H E N R Y W R I N K L E R   D O O N E I N
T W I   B E A M     N O S E O U T
    J O D I E F R O S T E R   D O J O S
C O D E X   A I R E   N A M E S A K E
O R E S   S H A R O N S T O N E R   C A N
N I B S   W A R M T O   O R C S   S K Y S
M O R E   E I N     R A H   L A P S E
A L A S   D R E S S L E R   C O P A
N E W   W E S L E Y S N I P E R S   R A M
    R A I N   A N T E D A T E   A L L A
S K I R T   M O L     G U M   M A Y S
E E N Y   C O R A   S E C E D E   U N D O
T A G   P H O E B E C R A T E S   S C A N
U N E R R I N G   L A I R     P E E R S
P U R E E   S O N D R A L O C K E R
    P A R T N E R     W R E N   P G A
C O L O M B O   V I R G I N I A M A Y O R
C R I S P I N   A C C U S E   T A B L E T
I D L E S S E   H A V E R   S N E E R S
```

48

```
D I A L E R   S A T   A L L     M O P U P
A S L O P E   H O R A T I O   S A L I N A
M A D C A P   A N I M A T E   A L I E N S
  D O H     C H E X A N D B A L A N C E S
B O R A   S A D   I N A   T O Y   E R A
I R A N   P R O S E A N D C O N S   A V G
D A Y D R E A M T   G O O P   K N E E
    K E N T   E M B L E M   A M I D
L A T E N T   P R O L E   P A L E N Q U E
A S H Y   G E N O A   S O N A R   U M A
I C Y   F A R E A N D S Q U A R E   I B M
R A M   A G I R L   D A U N T   H E R O
S P E C T A T E   R E D I D   B H U T A N
    A P E R   D O U R E R   H A I G
Z E N O   F I R N   E L I A S H O W E
I N D   W H I N E A N D D I N E   A V O N
P C S   H E N   R O E   P E D   N E R D
C O P S E A N D R O B B E R S   D R S
O R A T E D   R O U L A D F   U N C L E S
D E C A L S   A M N E S I A   S H R I N E
E D E N S   W E D   E T D   S L Y E S T
```

49

```
A B A T E S   ■   C L A R E T   ■ S C A M P
S E V I L L A ■ T R I R E M E   ■ P A N E L
T H E M O U S E H A S M I C E ■ A R E N A
O E R ■ N E S T E D ■ ■ M E T S ■ O M A N
R A S P ■ ■ T H E L O U S E H A S L I C E
■ D E A L S ■ ■ E M P ■ E N T I C E D
■ ■ S U R E S T ■ A D D A ■ D E N
■ W H Y C A N T A G R O U S E ■ M A R L
M A Y S ■ S A U R ■ M I L ■ ■ A U G
C H U T E D ■ B R E E D B A B Y G R I C E
K I N E T I C ■ G L O ■ A R O U S E S
A N D M O T H E R G O O S E ■ S O B E R S
Y E A ■ U V A ■ M A L E ■ B R N O
■ S I A M ■ B E G E T S H E R G E E S E
■ N A T ■ N U D E ■ L E G E N D
S T E E L I E ■ G A R ■ M O I R A
W H Y C A N T T H E M O O S E ■ N A B S
I R E D ■ A C R O ■ B R I E F S ■ C U E
P I L O T ■ H A V E L I T T L E M E E S E
E V I T A ■ E L E V E N S ■ S T O R M E D
S E D E R ■ S A L A D S ■ E G R E S S
```

50

```
■ T H I R D R A T E ■ R E B U S ■ E C U A
O R A T O R I C A L ■ U T O P I A N I S M
T O P S B O T T O M ■ F A T S S K I N N Y
T D S ■ B O A S ■ P U S H Y ■ I D E A L
■ ■ R E P ■ S K I S ■ D D S
M A J O R S M I N O R ■ B E A R S B U L L
A V O W ■ A M A N A ■ A L I E ■ E S A U
L I N D A ■ S A R A N ■ H E S S ■ D A T S
P L A Y S W O R K ■ H E A V Y S L I G H T
H A S ■ H O N E ■ B A R I ■ A M E S S
■ C O S T C O ■ A S S E N T
A S P C A ■ R I G S ■ M A N E ■ F W D
S P R I N G S F A L L ■ H I R E S F I R E
B I O G ■ O T A Y ■ A B O R T ■ T O X I N
I R M A ■ T R I O ■ N O T C H ■ R E N T
G O S R E T U R N ■ C A S H S C H A R G E
■ R A M ■ V E R Y ■ H E Y
A G A I N ■ M I S E R ■ W E A L ■ Z A G
L E F T S R I G H T ■ P A R K S D R I V E
F L A T T E N O U T ■ S W E E T I E P I E
A T R Y ■ A G R E E ■ T E N S E N E S S
```

51

```
E A T M E   E R A   C I T E   A R A R A T
S C R A M B L E D   O N E M O R E T I M E
S A Y H E Y K I D   H U S B A N D T O B E
E S T E R S   N E V E R S   T A H I T I
S T O R Y   V E N I R E   B E Z E L
        B A D D I E   K O S   N A B O B
R A D   S E M I S   P E U   R O I
I R E   C A P N   R E T I N A E   S I Z E
D U M D U M S   D A M A S C U S S T E E L
O B I E S   H E L P   T E E T E R
F A T T E D C A L F   T E R R A C O T T A
    E M I L I A   A I R S   U K I A H
P R I C E E A R N I N G S   F O R E S E E
L U N T   U P C C O D E   M A M E   N B A
U S C   E E N   E A V E S   T O D
S T A B S   F L Y   B O U T O N
    R A H A L   T A R T A R   C O I G N
  C L O V E N   F O R K E D   G A U C H E
S L O W I N G D O W N   R O Y A L T I E S
R A I N O R S H I N E   P R E S I D E N T
O R N E R Y   L E S S   E S T   F O R T S
```

U.S. Presidents hidden in the answers: Monroe, Hayes, Bush, Adams, Taft, Carter, Pierce, Wilson, Taylor, Harrison

52

```
T H E O S C A R   S O N A T A   L I S P S
N O N O N O N O   S O O N E R   E N C R E
O N T H E W A T E R F R O N T   N I H I L
T E R S E   A W S   E R N   N O T I M E
E Y E   B I T E   P L A I C E   I N E S
S S E   P E T E R J A C K S O N   A D D
    S I T S   A N O   O N E A L L
L A W L E S S   B I C   E N C   S L E D S
E T H I C   O M A   H A N   A S S Y R I A
S L I M E D   U N F O R G I V E N   S N L
O A T   A M I G O   A U D E N   L E T
T S E   C L A R K G A B L E   T A H I T I
H E C K L E R   O Y L   F A D   G E S T E
O S H E A   I L K   L E S   R O A S T E R
    R E N A T O   O I L   I B I S
  H I P   M A R L E E M A T L I N   C O D
M E S H   A L D O U S   B E L T   A P U
A C T O U T   S U V   R O E   A B N E R
H U M U S   S H I R L E Y M A C L A I N E
A B A S E   R I S E U P   E X A M I N E S
L A S E R   S P A S M S   D E B A T E R S
```

53

```
K O O L B I D  ■ R E G S  ■ ■ C E C I L I A
O N L E A V E  ■ A R O O M ■ U N I T I N G
I C E T R A Y  ■ I N T R A ■ P R U S S I A
■ E S S E N  ■ E L E C T S  ■ S I D E A ■
■ ■ D A D D Y S H A C K  ■ C A L M S ■ ■
I O C  ■ M I A T A  ■ G O O D F A T S
S T A R H A Z E R  ■ W E B B  ■ R I A
O H D E A R  ■ D E N I M  ■ J V D R I P S
L E G P A R T Y  ■ S E G E R  ■ E S T E E S
D R E S S  ■ H A S T E  ■ R E S E T S  ■
E S S  ■ N I X E D D R I N K S  ■ A D O
■ S E E S I N  ■ S O L T I  ■ A S L A N
S N A T C H  ■ S A U T E  ■ S P Y B E A N S
P O P R U I Z  ■ T H O S E  ■ O M E N I I
A L P  ■ E Y E S  ■ S W I S S M I S T
M I L K D V D S  ■ O P T I C  ■ S H E
■ E E N I E  ■ L O X P R O F I L E
■ G O N N A  ■ S H R I N E  ■ A S W A N
G O A T E E S  ■ S O A M I  ■ P U T I T O N
N U T T R E E  ■ O S H E A  ■ I R O N A G E
P R E S O R T  ■ ■ A S S N  ■ C O P Y B O Z
```

54

```
H I G H C  ■ B I O  ■ F O R  ■ D I O C E S E
O N E A L  ■ A S C R I B E  ■ E N R O L L S
I N N I E  ■ N O T I F I C A N H E L P I T
■ T R A N S L A T E  ■ T I A  ■ T A P E
U K E  ■ I H A V E  ■ S I M B A  ■ S I R
T I E D  ■ M E T E  ■ I M P O S I T I O N S
E L L E R B E E  ■ A M A I N  ■ T O V
■ B O Y S  ■ S T A R K  ■ N E S T S
T A B O O  ■ B O O G I E  ■ H O E  ■ T I P
E V E N T H O R I Z O N  ■ D I A S P O R A
M A L E  ■ A U E L  ■ M O T T  ■ E G A D
P L U S S I G N  ■ D I S A C C H A R I D E
T O G  ■ U G H  ■ B O R E R S  ■ F L E E S
S N A R E  ■ O N I C E  ■ S P A M  ■
■ I D A  ■ F E A S T  ■ C A R R A D I O
D R Y V E R M O U T H  ■ L O N I  ■ N I N A
E A U  ■ S M U R F  ■ J I N G O  ■ N E T
O M N I  ■ R T E  ■ H U N G A R I A N
D O N T B E A S T R A N G E R  ■ G R E T A
A N A L Y S T  ■ I N H O U S E  ■ H E R O N
R A N L A T E  ■ M A N  ■ A T E  ■ T A S T Y
```

55

```
MEADOW   SMASH   GOODTIME
OPTIMA   LECHE   ACCREDIT
PORKERFARCES   LATINATE
ESA  LCDTV   ASEA  OPART
   AERIE   ATIT   SPINES
PRETTYCRASHACCOUNT
LEWIS    LIEN  COST   SAS
ONEL   OGLES   ASTEROIDS
TORTEBRAG   COB   SOFTON
   NOAH  BAABAA   NAPS
  IGAVEITMYBRESTSHORT
TNUT   LIBELS   THAI
ATCAMP   ASE  CROWCHIRP
PECTORALS   GLOSS   OTOE
ELI  ROBT  TRUE   CHELA
  HOMERAWAYFROMHOMER
  ALANIS   TENS  ALOES
  ROMPS   SELF  ONAIR  CUT
MOTLIEST   FRISTFRIGHTS
ESTEEMED   TERSE  ESPANA
TEATREES   HEROD  SHAPER
```

56

```
TIPSTER   EATS   TOWROPE
UNITERS   SCOUR  UNAIRED
TELAVIV   CURRENTEVENTS
EXOTICPORTS   MAT  ELATE
LITES   TOE  RABID   TEL
ALER  BLOW  HERO  OGLED
REDSHOES   ROCKBANDS
   ORT  SINUS   BASALTS
SPRINGBREAKS   MET   TARP
HOOKE  EAR  SEDATED   VIA
RISERS  CUR  DID  DESIST
USC  SCHEMES  NRA  BASTE
NOON  RAD  STAGECOACHES
KNEEPAD   TEARY   HIT
  HIPJOINTS   TELECAST
  MAINE  CRTS  FEDS  ASHE
JAM  DOTES  BAN   ALTER
ENORM  OED  GOLDRECORDS
STRAIGHTLINES  OUTHIDE
TRAINEE   YOURE  DREIDEL
SALLIED   USSR   SORCERY
```

```
A N I M ■ B A S I C ■ N E M O ■ B I P E D
T O N I ■ A L I A S ■ A D A M ■ E L A N D
T O E N A I L C L I P P E R S ■ D I D O S
I N S U L T S ■ ■ H O N K ■ F R E D ■
C A S E Y S T E N G E L ■ S T R O D E I N
■ N E T S ■ A V I O N I C ■ R I O ■ D O O
■ ■ S T R E T T O ■ A K E E M ■ E N D
A T P L A Y ■ T E L E P H O N E ■ N I A
A R I A ■ P U R I M ■ R I A ■ D Y E V A T
B O N A ■ E S E ■ P I T Y ■ S E R E
A I S L E ■ S L U T S K A Y A ■ S A L A D
■ T A M A ■ E N R Y ■ A R T ■ S O L O
E N R A P T ■ A A A ■ G A M M A ■ E P I C
M I I ■ T H I R D G E A R ■ B E R E T S
M V P ■ Y E S N O ■ A M A D E U S ■
Y E E ■ H I E ■ N A T U R A L ■ H I S T
S A D C A S E S ■ P O T A T O M A S H E R
■ S E N T ■ O G P U ■ C O R O L L A
S Q U A D ■ S P O R T S E Q U I P M E N T
G U I S E ■ E U R O ■ P O T T S ■ E P E E
T O T E D ■ A P E X ■ A S S E T ■ R P T S
```

```
R I C S ■ S L A V S ■ S E P A L ■ R D S
E L L A ■ P E R O T ■ U S O N E ■ E R I S
C L A Y M A N E X E M P T I O N ■ J A M A
A S S H E ■ T A P P E T S ■ D I S O W N S
P E S E T A ■ O U I ■ P A N P I P E S
S E A L O V E A P P R O V A L ■ I C I L Y
■ L O A T H ■ A I L ■ W R E N ■
L I M O ■ T H E B E A S T ■ A A A ■ C B S
E L Y ■ M A Y D O U B T A W I L L ■ E A T
A L L G I R L ■ S R S ■ O R T ■ E N T R
K E A T S ■ C H O C T A W ■ L A T H E
A G U E ■ H O O ■ O O P ■ S P A R E M E
G I G ■ K E Y P A W N M O V I N G ■ R A T
E T H ■ U R L ■ N O D E S I R E ■ L S T S
■ T A W S ■ G O V ■ S O U S A ■
A D E L A ■ M I N E D O V E R M A T T E R
B U R L I V E S ■ O N E ■ O L E O L E
A M M E T E R ■ D E S T I J L ■ I S L E D
S P I N ■ G R A Y T O I L E O F C H I N A
H O L D ■ A I D E D ■ M E T A L ■ O F A N
■ N E E ■ N E E D S ■ E D E M A ■ W E S T
```

59

```
W A L E S A   A R C     G E R   S K I T S
A B O R T S   L O O   R E N O   T E N E T
D I S G U S T I N G W I N D S   J E A N E
S E E   A A H E D   E G R E T   A P R O N
  S E R M O N O N T H E D I S M O U N T
I C A N T       O T T     G E N T S
G O D I S F I G U R E   A B E T S
G L A D   A R M S   R I G O R S   D O D O
Y A Y S   B E A D S   N E H I   S U P E R
    D I S C O U N T E R C U L T U R E
A N G O R A     S I R     S A Y S N O
F O O D A N D D I S L O D G I N G
R E A D Y   R O D E   S O U S A   M S E C
O L D S   P A G O D A   C M L V   O T R O
    N I G E L   D I S M A Y Q U E E N
  P A T E N     O O N     U N P I N
C A B B A G E D I S P A T C H K I D S
A L L O R   D O N A T   A M A I N   A L E
P L A N E   D U C K A N D D I S C O V E R
R I T E S   A G U A   E A R   S E R E N A
I D E S T   S S R   E S S   A S T R O S
```

60

```
  R E S   Y A Z   L A S T     S P C A   A S P
  O C T   U R E   U S U A L   A L A N   M P H
  T H E A M E R I C A N C E N T U R Y   O R O
S H O L O M   O R R     A M I N O   A N I T
R K E L L Y   E V E R Y T H I N G M U S T G O
S O D A     I D S   E A R     E S S A I
      Z E N       F R U S T A     A F L O W
T H E C A T C H E R I N T H E R Y E   A L S O
E U R O P E   E L O   H E N M A N   V A I L
A G O G     A X I O M S   B O A S T   O D E D
R O S S I N I   S M O K E A N D M I R R O R S
      D O R M   L I V     A I R E
J U M P I N T O T H E F I R E   N E C K T I E
E R O O   E A T I T   F L U T I E   E A S T
T I T S   O X I D E S   E R R   P O R T I A
E C H T   F I V E S T A R R E S T A U R A N T
S H E D S   E S T A T E     R P I
  R O A S T   R A N   S P Y   H E E L
V A N C O U V E R C A N U C K S   P A I R U P
I B I S   M I N E O     Y A Y   L Y R I C S
J A G   I N D E P E N D E N T C O U N S E L
A S H   G E O M   N A O M I   H U T   C P I
Y E T   O R L Y   B M O C   S R O   H A D
```

61

```
C P U S ■ G R O ■ E L D E R S ■ L E V I S
L U T H E R A N ■ M E R L O T ■ E X I S T
A L I E N A T E ■ T O O T S Y ■ W H O L E
M I L L E N I U M ■ S P O I L S ■ A L E R
■ ■ ■ D O P Y ■ I N N O C U L A T E
E M B A R A S S M E N T ■ A N E
I N A J A M ■ A L A ■ H A R R A S S E S
N O R A H ■ M I N I S C U L E ■ I L L
S P E X ■ D O H ■ O G L E ■ G I Z M O
■ S E N O R ■ I Z E ■ M E E K E S T
■ I M P R O P E R L Y S P E L L E D
A C C O U N T ■ B O K ■ T E R M S
S H E E N ■ O M A N ■ E G O ■ T H A I
I O U ■ N O T I C A B L E ■ O R A L S
S U P E R C E D E ■ E P A ■ P E E W E E
■ X E R ■ P E R S E V E R E N C E
A C C O M O D A T E ■ S T I R
B O U T ■ W A V E R S ■ O C C U R E N C E
O R R I S ■ M A R K E T ■ H A S A G O A T
V N E C K ■ E N S U E S ■ E R A S A B L E
E S S A Y ■ S T E P P E ■ D S L ■ D U C S
```

62

```
J O N E S ■ M A G I ■ S H E E T ■ A L A R
E M O T E ■ C R U D ■ C O R D I L L E R A
S A N T A ■ H E R E Y O U G U M A G A I N
T R O U S S E A U ■ I N S O ■ B R E V E T
■ ■ H O N ■ E P E E ■ C A D R E S
F I R Y O U R L O V E ■ S A L
A R O A R ■ Y O G I ■ S U C R E ■ I C A L
Z O O M E D ■ G R E A T B A L S A F I R E
E N D S ■ R I S E ■ T O O T S ■ B A S R A
■ P I C O ■ T E L L ■ F A L C O N
C E D A R F U N N Y L I T T L E C L O W N
O C E L O T ■ A R I D ■ R I S K
L O B E S ■ C A N O E ■ S I L T ■ E G A D
O L I V E R O C K N R O L L ■ S I M O N E
R I T E ■ E R N I E ■ G A L E ■ N I G E R
■ V E E ■ E L M O S T G R O W N
■ A R A B I A ■ P A N E ■ T A R
S T A P L E ■ L U L U ■ K E E P O R D E R
P A W P A W P I T I F U L M E ■ U V U L A
A L L I T E R A T E ■ M A I M ■ P E E L E
M E S A ■ D E M O N ■ A N T S ■ S R T A S
```

63

```
JETSFAN  ANGULAR  KALEL
ACETONE  REPLETE  AMINO
NOWEANSITUATION  ZELIG
ONEPM  TNUT    PEROXIDE
SOSO  GLAREDAT  WOO
   NEHI  ORIGINALSCENE
ARP  MANN  ERROLL  OMAN
FEELINGSTATION  ERSATZ
LUELLA  YALE  LEADA  GOO
ANKA  INDIRA  CINQ
TEAMDUNCAN  SHEENGUARD
  AUST  EMBEDS  AZUR
SKA  DELON  AARE  EASTLA
UNICEF  ABANDONEDSHEEP
MEWS  OCTANE  SLUE  CDE
PEATORCHESTRA  OCTA
  HCL  RESONANT  MISS
JUMPSEAT  BING  SODOI
ONYOU  MINNESOTATWEENS
TIMOR  PREYSON  TEABAGS
STYLE  SEASONS  EMBASSY
```

64

```
PCLAB  ANASAZI  ABRAM
ERATO  INUNISON  ARROWS
WYMAN  TILTATWINDMILLS
  RUSSO  BNAI  ARIEL
INSISTENCE  ERNIEFORD
TOP  QUA  RADS  ACES  VEE
AMENU  SBARRO  MEN  FEDS
LACIE  YUK  APOP  JARRE
  DIPSY  MEDI  RUT  ARBOR
  ASTOOP  INCAPS  CREST
ESL  ISLE  ABO  SACK  EES
NARCO  IRONON  ARMPIT
CLEAN  OCT  ANIL  DONHO
LALAS  ROAR  WED  TROVE
AZAN  SFO  ADVISE  JIVES
SAT  EARP  ASIS  SOU  ERS
PRICELIST  CHECKSINTO
  VOLTA  EAVE  BESTS
FLIPPERANDERSON  ILLGO
LETSON  GOAROUND  CAVER
ASYET  ARRAYED  EMILY
```

65

```
T O S C A L E     M A M B O     A G H A S
A R E A R U G     A D A P T E R     D R A F T
S C A R I N G     G E O R G E L A Z E N B Y
S A N G     A S S I S I     B O B     C A S E
    S C O W     I T I S S O     N O H O
    O P E C     M A R T I N I     A O R T A L
S O N A R S     I T E     R O G E R M O O R E
T U N N E L S     E S L     O N D E M A N D
A S E T     E W E S     A P A R T     S A D E
M E R S     W I G     A D A M     I T I N
P L Y     T I M O T H Y D A L T O N     D J S
    G U S T     B O D S     S L Y     B A A L
    H M O S     E A S Y A     D U E L     I N M E
F E E L S B A D     Y A O     S A L L I E D
I A N F L E M I N G     U M S     N O L E S S
E D U C E S     A S P I R I N     D A H L
    O S S O     C O R O N A     M U C H
O A H U     I M F     E R A G O N     D R E I
P I E R C E B R O S N A N     P A S S A I C
E R A S E     R A S H E S T     A N T O I N E
R E P E L     E T T A S     L O U N G E S
```

66

```
L A D D     A L B U M     J A I     S A W S
A G R I     L E O N E S     O W N     R A B A T
B U Y A B L E B E L T     H O T P O T A T O
S E C R E T S     M O R A L L Y S A F E R
    L I T E     C O L O N     G E N T R Y
T H E S A L I V A T I O N A R M Y
H E A T S     N A S H     D E Y     A D A M
U R N S     A I L S     H A Z E     O C A L A
D O S     M E G A     G R A S     S A R O N G S
    C O R O N E R O N T H E M A R K E T
    P A O L O     C L A U D I A     I N N E R
H U M M A B L E B E G I N N I N G S
E R I T R E A     O M E N     S M E E     B M W
A S S E S     R O W E     G A P S     B R I O
L E S S     P G A     M A R E     E L I T E
    R I O T I N G I M P L E M E N T S
C H O S E N     M E E S E     L A N G
R E N T A S E N A T O R     S L I D I N G
A T T A C K D O G     R E D S K E L E T O N
S T A R T     I R E     G A I T E R     R O N A
H Y P E     T A D     D O P E Y     S N O W
```

67

```
URSA  DEADCALM   IPANEMA
NOES  UNLOADED   RAVAGED
QUAKINGASPENS   ALAMODE
UNROBE  BARNS  STE   YIP
ODIUM  SAGA   QUEBECACT
TENT  APSE  SOUP  LLANOS
ERG  BLOT  SKUA  OUST
    QUATERNARYAGE   CHAS
 STURM  RIOT  SIR  SHORT
STOOGES  GOES  RISE  SRA
QUAILINGAT  QUESTAFTER
UPS  ENOL  SLUG  HEWLETT
IOTAS  CEE  YELP  WAULS
BRYN  QANTASAIRWAYS
   GLUT  AMOK  OARS  FOE
STRIPE  OPAL  EXIT  MANX
QUEENANNE   TAIL  HASAT
URN   SEE  SWARM  GENTLE
ANTONIA  QUIETAMERICAN
STAINER  VERBATIM  LARD
HOLLERS  CRYOGENS  ARKS
```

68

```
TOPSOFF  CANDID   GROPE
EVENPAR  ADORNED  HOHOS
REPOSSESSEDAUTO  ISHOT
SNUB   EAT  CRANE  SELA
ESP  RELYINGONINSTINCT
   BOXY  RAI  SLASH  RUE
TRUANT  CONGA   AHYES
REPAIRMANUAL  METRO
IFS  AOL  MEALS  TEST
NUTCASE  REPORTFORDUTY
ATALL  JEERSAT  CORER
RETAILOUTLETS  NIAGARA
YSER  BLADE  TAD  SEN
   ESSEN  RECONMISSION
PINTA  SLANT  GOEASY
GNU  LLAMA  HRS  MINX
REMOTEPOSSIBILITY  SRO
AXED  BEDEW  LEG  AMEN
TIRED  REVERSEENGINEER
ELITE  SLEEPIN  OLDNAVY
DECOY  ARTIST  NOSIREE
```

69

```
A C R E . P L E B E . S A M O A . A C T S
R O O M . O A R E D . A F O U L . C O H O
C A S E C L O S E D . F O O T L O C K E R
S T E R E O . T R A D E R . S U P R E M E
. . . G A S . . A R E . C R E A S E S
T I M E S . A P R E S . C O E D . .
I N A N E . R O A D H A Z A R D . D O T
P S S T . S A R G E . M O R E . S N O R E
O U T . S C R E E N D O O R . O C E L O T
F R E E L O A D . E L M . C U R L .
F E R V E N T . S A L E S . S E L V A G E
. C E D E . E F T . C H A P E R O N
O R A N G S . S P R A Y P A I N T . S A T
P U R S E . C I A O . A E G I S . M I T E
T E D . W A L L S T R E E T . S A G E R
. . T H R O . E N T R E . L I N E S
C A L I B E R . C C X . . J U N .
O D Y S S E Y . L A T H E D . O R M O N D
P O O L P L A Y E R . G R A P H P A P E R
A R N E . I L E F T . T I T A N . S E M I
Y E S T . E L A T E . V E E P S . T R O P
```

70

```
L A P L A T A . A P E S U I T . P E N S
E C L A I R S . R O M A N C E . P E R O T
S H O W M E T H E M O N K E Y . E D I N A
T E T R . E R A S E . G N U . N E A T E R
. . E P S O N . T R I P L E K L U T Z
P O R N O . S T R A I T . O W I E .
D R A C U L A . R I C A . U G A N D A N S
A F T E R A S K O R T . A M O R . R E O
S E E . S N I D E . P L A N K A H E A D
. M A I E R . M O I . V O I L A
. W I N K W I N K S I T U A T I O N .
E N O L A . Y I N . S H O A T
B A R K T E N D E R . E S S E N . C T R
A T M . D I R T . A V E R A G E J O K E
N O S E D I V E . B R E R . P A L M T O P
. L E S E . C O I N E D . A B Y S S
G U N K C O N T R O L . U V U L A
U T A H A N . E A T . A C M E S . R B I S
I T M A Y . I N F L A T A B L E K R A F T
L E E R S . D E T E N T E . M I N I B A R
E R S T . S T Y G I A N . A T T E S T S
```

71

```
N A T I C K ■ S H E S A L A D Y ■ ■ W D S
C A R R O L ■ H A D A C A M E O ■ C H A T
W H E E L E D A U T H O R I T Y ■ L I R R
Y E S ■ O P E D S ■ A M Y ■ S O L A R I A
E D T V ■ T A O ■ F R A N K ■ S O I L E D
T A L E S O F W H O A ■ X E S ■ A R E N A
H T E S T ■ ■ A R N E ■ I T E M E D ■
■ ■ T R O T O U T ■ R O T A R Y ■ R I B
■ S W M ■ W E A T H E R W H Y S ■ D E V O
A N H E U S E R ■ G O E S ■ T H E C A N
D E A N S ■ A B B R S ■ A L O N E
V E C T O R ■ P L O D ■ M A E S T R O S
I R K S ■ I S L E O F W H I T E ■ A D V
L Y S ■ B E W A R E ■ A I R H E A D ■
■ M A R L I N ■ D I S T ■ V A S C O
A C U R A ■ M E T ■ W H A L I N G W A L L
D O S I D O ■ D E C O Y ■ E N O ■ N Y A D
D R E S S U P ■ H A J ■ D E R M A ■ W W W
A N U T ■ T H E E D I T O R I A L W H E E
M E M O ■ D E T E R M I N E ■ A M E E R S
S A S ■ O N E S E A T E R ■ M A I N S T
```

72

```
B R A S H ■ A T L ■ B O P P ■ R I S K I T
R E C T O ■ C R U C I B L E ■ A R C A N A
U N A R M ■ T O B O G G A N ■ C I A R D I
T O D I E Q U I E T L Y I N M Y S L E E P
■ A G U A S ■ T I N D E R ■ H Y E N A
B E S T I A L ■ H O E S ■ H H S ■ M T N
E N T E R S ■ M I N ■ P A Y E E S ■
E E R ■ L I K E M Y G R A N D F A T H E R
F R E D ■ I D O ■ A U S T E N ■ R A V E
■ G E A R ■ D E M E S N E ■ E M E R I L
B E T H E S D A ■ N O T ■ S H R E W D L Y
A T C O S T ■ I N V O I C E ■ R E T D
S I A M ■ A V E N U E ■ M A R ■ D I O S
S C R E A M I N G I N T E R R O R ■ M E A
■ Y V E T T E ■ H A Y ■ R E F E R S
S T L ■ I N A ■ B O R N ■ L A G A S S E
P R I M A ■ L A T I N A ■ L E C A R
L I K E T H E P E O P L E I N H I S C A R
I B E R I A ■ A S T O L D T O ■ N I E C E
F A L C O N ■ C L A S S I E R ■ E D D I E
F L Y I N G ■ E A S T ■ T R E ■ D E E D S
```

73

```
S A I D S O  ▮  L A M B D A  ▮  P R U D E S
A C C E P T  R A W D E A L  R E P E N T
G U Y F A W K E S N I G H T  O N S I T E
▮  A R A I L  ▮  G L O O M  ▮  M I R
▮  R O C K Y M O U N T A I N B I G H O R N
J A P E S  L A U R A  T S E T S E S
U T E  O S C A R S  S A I L S
S I R A N T H O N Y H O P K I N S  M O B
T O E T O T O E  B L I N G  D A M E
▮  M N O P  S P O O R  B O X E R
P R O F E S S I O N A L W R E S T L I N G
R I V E T  S M E W S  D U E L
E P E E  D O O N E  L I M A O H I O
Z E N  P U B L I S H I N G C O M P A N Y
B R A V A  A T E S T S  I T E
S T Y R E N E  P A S H A  S A F E R
Q U A R T E R M A S T E R G E N E R A L
U R N  E T A T S  A L O N E
I N K I N D  C H I N E S E M U S T A R D
R E E D E D  R O S E O I L  S O O N Y I
T R E A T Y  O S T E N D  E R O D E D
```

74

```
D E V I L S  ▮  L I M N S  I P O D  ↓B O Y
A M A N I T A  A F O O T  O R Z O  T E R I
M U S C L E S  S A S S Y  S E A U  H E A P
↑S T A I R S↓S T A I R S  V W B E E T L E
N U S  I R O N S  A L L→
←I T↑T O C H A N C E  A T O  E F F U S E
O N E A M  H I L O  E S P A N O L  I M A X
N E S T E D  F I D O  H O N E S  L E A V E
B R S  N A S T  X S A N D O S  E L M E R
A R E I  T H E←  Y U L  I N A  O D I S T
S O R T  S E D A N  B L A N E  B I L
E R A S M U S  ↓S I Z I N G  D I V I S O R
→O N  S P A D E  S↑D O G  N I N E
S E T↑S  S P A  A R R  →E N D  E L A S
T R E Y S  T O Y S H O P  L E I F  E D T
A N N O Y  A I M T O  M A G I  G I N N I E
L I E U  O N L E A S E  F O C I  R A T E D
L E T R I P  T N G  S I T↓A N D S H U T↑
A Q U A  T E A T S  C H O
G I L L S L I T  →W H E R E Y O U←T H E M
A B E L  E M I T  R E U E L  C R E A S E S
Z I N E  N E M O  A T L A S  K E Y R I N G
E D D Y  T E E M  P E T R A  R E P A Y S
```

```
T E E M █ A L O A D █ M L I X █ A G A S P
A X L E █ V A L L I █ E I N E █ S H I N E
R E V E R E N D E V E R E N D █ S O R E N
P R E T E N D S █ E L I T E █ L I S T E N
S T S █ Y U M █ H I S T O R Y I S T O R Y
█ █ U N E A T E N █ █ █ E M I T █
S A W T O █ S E A T A C █ A W E █ O L A V
S P O T L E S S P O T L E S S █ S W O R E
R E W E D S █ █ W O N T █ G E N O M E
█ █ R S T U █ P I T S T O P I T S T O P
I S A █ A S K I N █ E R R E D █ S R S
M A N D A T E A N D A T E █ G E T S █
E N G I N E █ T O I L █ █ O R E L S E
A T E S T █ F I N A L I S T I N A L I S T
N A R C █ E E E █ N Y M P H S █ V I D E O
█ J I V E █ █ P E D A G O G █
L A B O R E D A B O R E D █ O I L █ S H E
U N O C A L █ G O F O R █ M A N T O M A N
E N O K I █ S O N A T I N A O N A T I N A
G E N E S █ O R E G █ L A T K E █ T R O T
O X E Y E █ B A S E █ S T A I D █ O K I E
```

The New York Times

Crossword Puzzles

The #1 Name in Crosswords

Available at your local bookstore or online at nytimes.com/nytstore

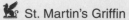 St. Martin's Griffin